DONALD BARTHELME

Not-Knowing

The late Donald Barthelme was a longtime contributor to *The New Yorker*, winner of a National Book Award, a director of PEN and the Authors Guild, and a member of the American Academy and Institute of Arts and Letters. His sixteen books—including *Snow White*, *The Dead Father*, and *City Life*—substantially redefined American short fiction for our time.

About the Editor

Kim Herzinger teaches at the University of Southern Mississippi. He is the author of books and articles on D. H. Lawrence, modern and contemporary literature, Sherlock Holmes, and baseball, and is now at work on a cultural biography of Donald Barthelme.

Books by DONALD BARTHELME

Come Back, Dr. Caligari
Snow White
Unspeakable Practices, Unnatural Acts
City Life
Sadness
Guilty Pleasures
The Dead Father
Amateurs
Great Days
Sixty Stories
Overnight to Many Distant Cities
Paradise
Forty Stories
The King
The Teachings of Don B.
Not-Knowing

For Children

The Slightly Irregular Fire Engine

Not-Knowing

The Essays and Interviews of DONALD BARTHELME

Edited by
KIM HERZINGER

With an Introduction by
JOHN BARTH

Vintage International
Vintage Books / A Division of Random House, Inc. / New York

FIRST VINTAGE INTERNATIONAL EDITION, FEBRUARY 1999

Published in the United States by Vintage Books, a division of Random House, Inc., New York, and simultaneously in Canada by Random House of Canada Limited, Toronto. Originally published in hardcover in the United States by Random House, Inc., New York, in 1997.

Original publication information for the essays and interviews contained within may be found in the "Notes" section beginning on p. 321.

The Library of Congress has catalogued the Random House edition as follows:

Barthelme, Donald.
Not-knowing : the essays and interviews of Donald Barthelme /
edited by Kim Herzinger ; with a foreword by John Barth.—1st ed.
p. cm.
ISBN 0-679-40983-1
I. Herzinger, Kim A., 1946- . II. Title.
PS3552.A76A6 1997
814'.54—dc21 97-9170

Vintage ISBN: 0-679-74120-8

www.randomhouse.com

Printed in the United States of America
10 9 8 7 6 5 4 3 2 1

PREFACE

This book, like *The Teachings of Don B.*, provides readers with a number of Donald Barthelme's shorter works, which until now have been almost impossible to come by. Gathered from the sometimes elusive magazines and journals that offered their first publication, only the most dedicated enthusiast of *Barthelmismo,* to use Thomas Pynchon's useful word, will have had the opportunity to read these pieces before now.

Toward the end of his life Barthelme was considering putting together a new book, comprised mainly of the pieces that are now collected here for the first time. His working title was *Pleasantries,* and it was to include "Being Bad," "On the Level of Desire," "Nudes" (his introduction to *Exquisite Creatures*), and "Worrying about women . . ." (from *Here in the Village*) from among his writings on art; the six movie reviews he did for *The New Yorker,* as well as "Earth Angel," his review of *Superman III;* "After Joyce" and "Not-Knowing"; and, finally, four pieces that appeared in *The Teachings of Don B.:* "Return," "The Art of Baseball," "Challenge," and "More Zero."

Pleasantries, then, was going to contain parodies, satires, and fables, as well as essays. All were written with different motives and for different purposes than the fictions. Nonfiction, especially the essay, is usually generated by an idea that precedes the writing; fiction, especially Barthelme's fiction, often discovers the ideas it is interested in even as it is being written. As we might expect, however, the writing in these essays is as richly textured and brilliantly realized as that of the fiction. And, as always, any attempt by an editor to firmly and definitively categorize these slumgullions—as Barthelme once called them—runs directly into his refusal to play within the accepted boundaries of literary genres.

Despite Barthelme's characteristic unclassifiability, decisions about what to put in and what to leave out of this book were relatively simple. The essays, though they often contain features we frequently associate with fiction or parody or satire, are distinguishable from Barthelme's other work by the degree to which they put themselves in service to their subjects. They tend to be more topical, more insistent, more accessible, and their "subjects"—the generating ideas—have a greater and more obvious centrality.

Critic Jerome Klinkowitz has suggested that Barthelme's "Notes and Comment" pieces (there were thirty-one of them, and with this book we will have reprinted all but three) came as close as he ever would to "pure writing, a practice where discrimination between fact and fantasy was not an issue." Klinkowitz argues that Barthelme's fondness for these pieces, evidenced by his collecting eleven of them in *Here in the Village* (published in a limited edition in 1978 and reprinted in full here), was the result of a developing interest in the "location of himself as a writer in his world—not just among Barth, Vonnegut, and the others (although *Here in the Village* plays with that as well)—but on the street, in front of the store windows, and in the shops and service establishments themselves where life, in the form of readable texts and plottable narratives, is going on" ("Barthelme's Canonical Village," *The Review of Contemporary Fiction,* XI, 2, Summer 1991).

Klinkowitz's case for the importance of *Here in the Village* is an interesting one, and I think rightly made, but the suggestion that Barthelme was ever dislocated from "his world" is one that this collection of essays and interviews will go some distance in discouraging. Barthelme's "world" always included street and store window, art gallery and bar, daughters and banned books, embarrassing presidential behavior, hollow-core doors, baked clams, sweetly speaking architects, Nondiscernible Microbioinoculators, sunlight roaring through new green leaves, and all the rest of those things that populate *our* world, too. As William H. Gass says, "Barthelme has managed to place himself in the center of modern consciousness. Nothing surrealist about him, his dislocations are real, his material quite actual" ("The Leading Edge of the Trash Phenomenon," in *Fiction and the Figures of Life*). Or, as Barthelme himself says in "Not-Knowing," "Art thinks ever of the world, cannot not think of the world, could not turn its back on the world even if it wished to."

Barthelme was not one to habitually confuse realism with reality. As is usually the case with writers known for their fabulism, he was acutely aware that many people actually like reality, and very often choose to live in it. He was fond of saying, in fact, that however agitated its surface might be, his work was always a meditation on reality. The novels, stories, parodies, satires, and essays always situate themselves where life is "going on." Barthelme's meditations on the reality of city life in *Here in the Village* may be said to approach the subject somewhat more straightforwardly than the stories in, say, *City Life,* but in both we are witness on every page to people colliding with the reality of the city—its tensions, noise, jarring confusions, juxtapositions, adventures, sadnesses, and delights. He was able to give us his meditations on reality from different angles of vision and by doing so produce different species of insight and pleasure.

It is, of course, tempting to declare that with the publication of *Not-Knowing, The Teachings of Don B.,* and the next volume—which will contain all the Barthelme stories that were uncollected, all those not collected in *60 Stories* or *40 Stories,* and a few unpublished pieces—that we will have been busy establishing Barthelme's canon. But alas, not so. What we will have, in fact, established is the full range of his work. From this, finally, Barthelme's canon will eventually be configured.

We have chosen to publish the full range of Barthelme's work for rather simple reasons. As a character in one of his stories says, "Our reputation for excellence is unexcelled, in every part of the world. And will be maintained until the destruction of our art by some other art which is just as good but which, I am happy to say, has not yet been invented." These are Barthelme's words (from "Our Work and Why We Do It") although he, of course, would never have used them to describe himself and his work. But others would. He was one of the "great citizens of contemporary world letters" (Robert Coover); he was "one of our greatest of all comic writers" (John Hawkes); he was able to convey in his work something of "the clarity and sweep, the intensity of emotion, the transcendent *weirdness* of the primary experience" (Thomas Pynchon). Simply put, he was without question one of the most important and influential writers of his time. Any procedure that would leave significant portions of his work sequestered and out of print, the quarry of researchers and Barthelme specialists, would be a disservice not only to Barthelme, but to readers of contemporary literature, who ought to have the opportunity to poke and rummage through the whole of his work without having to spar with an unseen editor bent on scissoring whatever might be thought to be unworthy of them. Readers deserve to read the work, all of it, and the work deserves to be read.

The interviews, perhaps, require some special mention. In recent years, interviews have become a primary source of information about writers, a circumstance that is likely to continue as long as writers—like the rest of us—continue to conduct most of their correspondence by telephone and e-mail. The days of the great collections of letters are probably over, and although it is unlikely that the interview form will entirely replace the function once served by such collections, at least we no longer have to wait for decades to acquire the kind of understanding about a writer and a writer's work that, once, only letters provided.

Barthelme agreed to a number of interviews during his writing life, and although he was disinclined to talk about himself and even more disinclined to talk about other writers—except to praise what he thought praiseworthy in their work—the interviews included here offer something of what might reasonably be understood to be Barthelme's thoughts about writing as well as his thoughts about a great many other things having to do with "his world." The interviews range over the last eighteen years of Barthelme's life, and readers will have the opportunity to watch his notions as they expand, change, and settle. Two of the interviews have never been published, and I am particularly pleased to be able to provide the full text of the Pacifica Radio interview of 1975, which is, whatever its insufficiencies, the most sustained series of public statements Barthelme ever made.

Interviews, like letters, sometimes encourage readers and critics to invest them with an authority they do not rightly have. Although interviews promise an opportunity to get a glimpse of a writer's thoughts at something like ground level—seemingly intimate responses made more consequential by the false authority of apparent spontaneity—so also do they tend to force a writer into direct statements about matters that simply cannot be answered with direct statements. Barthelme spent a lifetime defamiliarizing the familiar, and sometimes the effect of an interview is to reverse that process. After reading the interviews, readers may well have the same feeling that Dr. Watson has after Sherlock Holmes takes him step by step through one of his astounding deductions. We are surprised at how easy it all seems, at least until we remember once again that he is Holmes, and we are only Watson.

This is not hard to remember once we return to Barthelme's more fully accomplished works—the novels, the short fiction, the satires, the parodies, the fables, and the essays—to which the interviews can, finally, only be useful adjuncts. The reader is asked always to return to them, for they are where the magic is.

In this book, as in *The Teachings of Don B.*, the editorial apparatus has been kept to a minimum, although certain crucial information—the likely dates of composition for unpublished work, the dates of publication for published work, and so forth—is included in the "Notes" at the back of the book. As before, in cases where a work originally appeared untitled, we have supplied a first-line short title as a convenient, but not definitive, way of identifying it.

—Kim Herzinger

INTRODUCTION

"How come you write the way you do?" an apprentice writer in my Johns Hopkins workshop once disingenuously asked Donald Barthelme, who was visiting. Without missing a beat, Donald replied, "Because Samuel Beckett was already writing the way *he* does."

Asked another, likewise disingenuously, "How can we become better writers than we are?"

"For starters," DB advised, "read through the whole history of philosophy, from the pre-Socratics up through last semester. That might help."

"But Coach Barth has already advised us to read all of *literature*, from Gilgamesh up through last semester. . . ."

"That, too," Donald affirmed, and turned on that shrewd Amish-farmer-from-West-Eleventh-Street twinkle of his. "You're probably wasting time on things like eating and sleeping. Cease that, and read all of philosophy and all of literature. Also art. Plus politics and a few other things. The history of everything."

Although I count myself among the ideal auditors of my late comrade—invariably delighted, over the too-few decades of his career, by his short stories, his novels, his infrequent but soundly argued essays into aesthetics, and his miscellaneous nonfiction pieces (not to mention his live conversation, as above)—I normally see *The New Yorker,* in which so much of his writing was first published, only in the waiting rooms of doctor and dentist. I have therefore grown used to DB-ing in happy binges once every few years, when a new collection of the wondrous stuff appears (originally from Farrar, Straus & Giroux; anon from Putnam; later from Harper & Row; finally from Random House) and I set other reading aside to go straight through it, savoring the wit, the bite, the exactitude and flair, inspired whimsy, aw-shucks urbanity, irreal realism and real irreality, wired tersitude, and suchlike Barthelmanic pleasures.

Finally, it says up in that parenthesis of his publishers. The adverb constricts my spirit; I feel again what I felt when word came of Donald's illness and death in 1989, at age merely fifty-eight, in the fullness of his life and happy artistry: my maiden experience of survivor-guilt, for we were virtual coevals often assigned to the same team or angel-choir or Hell-pit by critics friendly and not, who require such categories—Fabulist, Postmodernist, what have they. We ourselves, and the shifting roster of our team-/choir-/pit-mates, were perhaps more impressed by our *differences* than by any similarities, but there was most certainly fellow-feeling among us—and was I to go on breathing air, enjoying health and wine and food, work and play and love and language, and Donald not? Go on spinning out my sometimes hefty fabrications (which, alphabetically cheek by jowl to his on bookshelves, he professed to fear might topple onto and crush their stage-right neighbor), and Donald not his sparer ones, that we both knew to be in no such danger?

Well. One adds the next sentence to its predecessors, and over the ensuing years, as bound volumes of mine have continued to forthcome together with those of his other team-/choir-/pit-mates, it has been some balm to see (impossibly posthumous!) Donald's appearing as before, right along with them, as if by some benign necromancy: first his comic-elegaic Arthurian novel *The King* (1990); then *The Teachings of Don B.* (1992), a rich miscellany eloquently foreworded by TCP-mate Thomas Pynchon; now *Not-Knowing;* and still to come, a collection of hitherto unpublished and/or uncollected short stories.

Benign it is, but no necromancy. We owe these last fruits not only to Donald's far-ranging muse but to the dedication of his literary executors and the editorial enterprise of Professor Kim Herzinger of the University of Southern Mississippi. Thanks to that dedication and enterprise, we shall have the print-part of our fellow whole, or all but whole. Never enough, and too soon cut off—like Carver, like Calvino, all at their peak—but what a feast it is.

* * *

Its course in hand displays most directly the high intelligence behind the author's audacious, irrepressible fancy. The complementary opening essays, "After Joyce" and "Not-Knowing" (that title-piece was for years required reading in the aforementioned fiction-writing seminar at Johns Hopkins); the assorted reviews and pungent "comments" on literature, film, politics; the pieces "On Art," never far from the center of Donald's concerns; the seven flat-out interviews (meticulously edited after the fact by the interviewee)—again and again I find myself once again nodding yes, yes to their insights, obiter dicta, and mini-manifestos, delivered with unfailing tact and zing. See, e.g., "Not-Knowing" 's jim-dandy cadenza upon the rendering of "Melancholy Baby" on jazz banjolele: as astute (and hilarious) a statement as I know of about the place of "aboutness" in art. Bravo, maestro banjolelist: Encore!

Here is a booksworth of encores, to be followed by one more: the story-volume yet to come, a final serving of the high literary art for which that high intelligence existed.

And then?

Then there it is, alas, and for encores we will go back and back again to the feast whereof these are end-courses: back to *Come Back, Dr. Caligari,* to *Unspeakable Practices, Unnatural Acts,* to *Snow White* and *City Life* and the rest. Permanent pleasures of American "Postmodernist" writing, they are. Permanent literary pleasures, period.

—John Barth

ACKNOWLEDGMENTS

Thanks to Charles Ruas; Judith Sherman; The Wylie Agency; Susanna Porter; Julie Grau; Wayne Alpern; Rie Fortenberry; Derek Bridges for his skills and dedication as editor and transcriber; and Angela Ball—who waited this out.

And special thanks once again to Marion, Frederick, and Steven Barthelme for their help and patience.

CONTENTS

On Writing

AFTER JOYCE

Writing about revolutionary art in an early essay titled "The Calling of the Tune," Kenneth Burke says:

> For the greater the dissociation and discontinuity developed by the artist in an otherworldly art that leaves the things of Caesar to take care of themselves, the greater becomes the artist's dependence upon some ruler who will accept the responsibility for doing the world's "dirty work."

This description of the artist turning his back on the community to pursue his "otherworldly" projects (whereupon the community promptly falls apart) is a familiar one, accepted even by some artists. Joyce, Gertrude Stein, and the writers of the *transition* school (Burke mentions them specifically) are seen as deserters, creating their own worlds which are thought to have nothing to do with the larger world. The picture is, I think, entirely incorrect, but I want to talk not about Burke's alleged wrongness on this point but about something else.

Burke's strictures raise the sticky question of what art is "about" and the mysterious shift that takes place as soon as one says that art is not about something but *is* something. In saying that the writer creates "dissociation and discontinuity" rather than merely describing a previously existing dissociation and discontinuity (the key word is "developed"), Burke notices that with Stein and Joyce the literary work becomes an object in the world rather than a text or commentary upon the world—a crucial change in status which was also taking place in painting. With Joyce, and to a lesser degree Gertrude Stein, fiction altered its placement in the world in a movement so radical that its consequences have yet to be assimilated.

Satisfied with neither the existing world nor the existing literature, Joyce and Stein modify the world by adding to its store of objects the literary object—which is then encountered in the same way as other objects in the world. The question becomes: what is the nature of the new object? Here one can see an immediate result of the shift. Interrogating older works, the question is: what do they say about the world and being in the world? But the literary object is itself "world" and the theoretical advantage is that in asking it questions you are asking questions of the world directly. This sounds like a species of ventriloquism—the writer throwing his voice. But it is, rather, a stunning strategic gain for the writer. He has in fact removed himself from the work, just as Joyce instructed him to do. The reader is not listening to an authoritative account of the world delivered by an expert (Faulkner on Mississippi, Hemingway on the corrida) but bumping into something that is *there,* like a rock or a refrigerator. The question so often asked of modern painting, "What is it?," contains more than the dull skepticism of the man who is not going to have the wool pulled over his eyes. It speaks of a fundamental placement in relation to the work, that of a voyager in the world coming upon a strange object. The reader reconstitutes the work by his active participation, by approaching the object, tapping it, shaking it, holding it to his ear to hear the roaring within. It is characteristic of the object that it does not declare itself all at once, in a rush of pleasant naïveté. Joyce enforces the way in which *Finnegans Wake* is to be read. He conceived the reading to be a lifetime project, the book remaining always *there,* like the landscape surrounding the reader's home or the buildings bounding the reader's apartment. The book remains problematic, unexhausted.

Valéry once wrote: "Sometimes I think that there will be place in the future for a literature the nature of which will singularly resemble that of a sport. Let us subtract, from literary possibilities, everything which today, by the direct expression of things and the direct stimulation of the sensibility by new means—motion pictures, omnipresent music, etc.—is being rendered useless or ineffective for the art of language. Let us also subtract a whole category of subjects—psychological, sociological, etc.—which the growing precision of the sciences will render it difficult to treat freely. There will remain to letters a private domain: that of symbolic expression and of imaginative values due to the free combination of the elements of language."

Joyce's books present first of all a linguistically exciting surface, dense, glittering, here opaque, here transparent. "The grocer's bawd she slips her hand in the haricot bag, the lady in waiting sips her sup from the paraffin can, Mrs Wildhare Quickdoctor helts her skelts up the casuaway the flasht instinct she herds if a tinkle of tunder, the widow Megrievy she knits cats' cradles, this bountiful actress leashes a harrier under her tongue, and here's the girl who she's kneeled in coldfashion . . ." The Ellmann biography tells us that Joyce "defended his language . . . as a largely emotional medium built up by sifting and agglutination . . ." In fact he proceeds like a man weaving a blanket of what might be found in a hardware store. The strangeness of his project is an essential part of it, almost its point. The fabric falls apart, certainly, but where it hangs together we are privileged to encounter a world made new. Similarly, almost any brief quotation from Gertrude Stein discloses a willingness to follow language wherever it leads (and if it leads nowhere, to make capital of that): "I very recently met a man who said, how do you do. A splendid story." These perversities answer perfectly Valéry's specifications.

It has been argued that the ontological status of the literary work has always been just this, that *Pilgrim's Progress* is an "object" in this sense just as *Finnegans Wake* is. But such arguments ignore the changed situation that ensues when the writer is aware of and exploits the possibilities of this special placement. Joyce and Stein reap the benefits of a new strategy. Their creations modify the beholder. I do not think it fanciful, for instance, to say that Governor Rockefeller, standing among his Mirós and de Koonings, is worked upon by them, and if they do not make a Democrat or a Socialist of him they at least alter the character of his Republicanism. Considered in this light, Soviet hostility to "formalist" art becomes more intelligible, as does the antipathy of senators, mayors, and chairmen of building committees. In the same way, Joyce's book works its radicalizing will upon all men in all countries, even upon those who have not read it and will never read it.

As Marshall McLuhan has said in another connection, *the medium is the message.*

The artist's effort, always and everywhere, is to attain a fresh mode of cognition. At the same time he struggles to disembarrass himself of procedures which force him to say things that are either commonplace or false. What makes the literary object a work of art is the intention of the artist. When Roy Lichtenstein proposes as art a blown-up comic strip, a replica in every detail except in scale of an actual comic strip, we are presented with the artist's intention, his gesture, in its nakedness. (His "statement" might be, characteristically, a question: *What do you think of a society in which these things are seen as art?*) In this way social and historical concerns reenter the ambience of the work. Far from implying a literature that is its own subject matter, the work that is an object is rich in possibilities. The intention of the artist may range in any direction, including those directions which have the approval of socially minded critics. What is important is that he has placed himself in a position to gain access to a range of meanings previously inaccessible to his art.

The writers who have taken advantage of this particular strategy are few, and the reasons for this are obvious. Not only have there been highly visible failures, but even the successes have been intimidating. *Finnegans Wake* is not a work which encourages emulation. Ezra Pound announced early on that in those portions of it that he had read, the rewards were not worth the labor of decipherment, and this has remained the general (if covert) opinion. Writers borrow Joyce's myth-patterning or stream-of-consciousness and regard *Wake* as a monument or an obsession, in any case something that does not have to be repeated. Similarly, Gertrude Stein is seen as an interesting eccentric, slightly foolish, who had something to do with the career of Ernest Hemingway and bought a great many valuable pictures at extremely low prices. *Transition* becomes a neglected battlefield littered with the empty cartridge boxes and dead horses of the Revolution of the Word. Fiction after Joyce seems to have devoted itself to propaganda, to novels of social relationships, to short stories constructed mousetrap-like to supply, at the finish, a tiny insight typically having to do with innocence violated, or to works written as vehicles for saying no! in thunder. (The operator of the thundersheet is immediately under suspicion; we suspect him of being a happy man.)

Two essays by Mary McCarthy suggest the situation of fiction after Joyce, or at least of those writers who have chosen to consider his work a detour rather than the main road. In the first, "The Fact in Fiction," Miss McCarthy argues that the novel, conceived of as a collection of facts, cannot survive a confrontation with the contemporary world, conceived of as a texture of implausibilities. Faced with the Bomb, Buchenwald, and the population explosion, the novelist stutters: ". . . it would seem that the novel, with its common sense, is of all forms the least adapted to encompass the modern world, whose leading characteristic is irreality. And that, so far as I can understand, is why the novel is dying."

What is curious is the way Miss McCarthy would limit her medium. She begins by defining the novel in such a way as to include all the great works of the past and render the future doubtful, by defining the novel as a structure of fact and going on to declare the erection of such structures no longer possible because the facts have turned into "irreality." She is not much concerned with how these doomed towers are stuck together, only with the aggregate that forms their substance. In the second essay, "Characters in Fiction," she explicitly condemns monkeying around with new designs: "An impasse has been reached within the art of fiction as a result of progress and experiment." Formal innovation, she finds, has crowded out an interest in people, plot, character, the social. Throughout both essays she argues persuasively for a return to fiction's traditional virtues, to recipes for jam and recipes for Mrs. Micawber.

This sounds like a declaration of bankruptcy spiced with a denunciation of that guilty partner who has made off with the cash. The facts of contemporary life are not "real" facts, like the facts available to Tolstoi; therefore either my enterprise is impossible or I must return to the kind of material it can accommodate, that is, to the substance of the nineteenth-century novel. Strangely, one detects here a fear of science, the "language game" in which the concepts *progress and experiment* have their original home. Science has compromised forever a naïve optimism in regard to these ideas (and Miss McCarthy has said that *The Group* is about the idea of progress). Anxiety about the Bomb is translated into an abomination of literary innovation. In any case, Miss McCarthy's conservative manifesto adequately expresses a real dilemma—that of the writer betrayed by outmoded forms.

Let me note very briefly the work of certain writers who have chosen the opposite path, and speculate about the results, some fruitful, some not. The fiction of these writers seems to employ one of two modes: that of aggression and that of play.

The manufacturers of the Hostile Object are the more numerous.

The reader approaches the object, which is ticking like a bomb. Here is William Burroughs disclosing the method he uses to ensure the integrity, and thus the threatening quality, of his surface:

> Since work in progress tentatively titled *a distant hand lifted* consists of walky, talky messages between remote posts of interplanetary war the cut up and fold in method here used as a decoding operation. For example agent K9 types out a page of random impressions from whatever is presented to him at the moment::street sounds, phrases from newspapers or magazine, objects in the room Etc. He then folds this page down the middle and places on it another page of typewriter messages and where the shift from one text to another is made/marks the spot. The method can approximate walky talky immediacy so that the writer writes in present time. . . .

The form of the work, in other words, suggests that a chunk of a large building may fall on you at any moment. Burroughs' form is inspired, exactly appropriate to his terroristic purpose. He has approximated what might be heard tuning across the broadcast band of a radio built to receive all the asylums of the world. A high noise-to-signal ratio, randomness, and shouts of pain mingle to produce an unbearable tension. Burroughs cannot be read for very long at a sitting; like Joyce, he enforces contemplation, dictates the way in which his work must be approached.

Burroughs' Dr. Tetrazzini, dancing into the operating theater throwing rusty scalpels before him, takes his place among a whole crew of fictional murder-rapist-addict-criminal-saints. His fellow terrorist Norman Mailer, not nearly so adept at planting booby traps yet seriously attempting to construct a work of art on the terrain of murder, cancer and the big orgasm, has contributed in "The Time of Her Time" a basic text. Genet presents himself maneuvering in erotic reverie. James Purdy offers a fratricide (in "63: Dream Palace") and Terry Southern and Hubert Selby, Jr., create very different sorts of fictional prostitutes as occasions for sorties against the bourgeois consciousness. The safety of the bourgeois is everywhere menaced by the form. Selby in particular manages a prose as flat, anonymous and coldly accusing as a crusted bandage lying in the street. Reading one of his stories is a form of self-mutilation, akin to the disciplines of the flagellant. These artists respond to the world by adding to it constructs which are hostile to life, and Burroughs, most in debt to Joyce, makes the deepest wounds.

Beckett would seem to belong to this camp but is, on the contrary, almost pure comedian. His pessimism is the premise necessary to a marvelous pedantic high-wire performance, the wire itself, supporting a comic turn of endless virtuosity. No one who writes as well as Beckett can be said to be doing anything other than celebrating life. Commanded to swim or drown, he swims where Burroughs chooses to drown. Observe him in action:

> "But betray me," said Neary, "and you go the way of Hippasos."
> "The Akousmatic, I presume," said Wylie. "His retribution slips my mind."
> "Drowned in a puddle," said Neary, "for having divulged the incommensurability of side and diagonal."
> "So perish all babblers," said Wylie.

Like that Beckett character who had seen people smile and thought he knew how it was done, Beckett himself painstakingly and with the utmost scholarly rigor retraces the rationales of simple operations, achieving comic shocks along the way by allowing language to tell him what it knows. His art is reductionary in that, like a painter, he throws ideas away. The things he throws away are precisely those Miss McCarthy cherishes: character, social fact, plot, gossip. What is retained as the irreducible minimum is the intent of the artist, in Beckett's case a search for the meanings to be gleaned from all possible combinations of all words in all languages—a heroic lifework thoughtfully compromised in favor of, and adumbrated in, the researches of *Watt, Molloy, Murphy, Malone Dies.*

Among American writers, Kenneth Koch has chosen something of the same kind of problem, although he approaches it with different aims in view. In his novel *The Red Robins* (excerpts from which appeared in LOCATION #1) Koch's strategy is to re-enter the history of the novel and fix upon a particular kind of American subliterature, that of the Rover Boys, Tom Swift, *The Motion Picture Boys' First Venture,* and especially a certain kind of light novel popular around the first World War. These books, sentimental, ingenuous, and trivial, furnish a ground of positions, attitudes, and allusions against which to enact his search for poetry. He too dispenses with character, action, plot and fact, dispenses with them by permitting them to proliferate all over the landscape and by resolutely short-circuiting the expected order of things. There is a continual handling and mishandling of sentimental clichés. Ace, the mythic aviator, has "the rough tenderness of people who love the air. His face is lined with tiny blue dots, and through every line on his face you can see the sky." There is pure linguistic play with abrupt changes of mood and intentionality: "The baby native lambs were waiting for him at the shore, they took him into their little tuft houses, swept out especially for him (I mean for you!), gave him a glass of water in her waiting arms." Things lump themselves together in apparently random fashion with liberating effect: "Continuing our search for human beings, we rose into the sky."

J. P. Donleavy recreates in his novel *A Singular Man* the mind at play, not entirely successfully. One disapproving critic has noted that his paranoid hero, Smith, wealthy, irresponsible, and totally self-indulgent, is almost perfectly a man acting out the infant's dream of omnipotence, and this is the case. The difficulty here is not, as the critic implies, the writer's culpability in imagining such a man, but the slightly underinspired character of Donleavy's prose, which nevertheless affords some remarkable passages. Henry Green and Vladimir Nabokov similarly, in their elaborate mystifications, partake of this tendency, demonstrating a consciousness of the word as object, of the medium as message.

The new French novelists, Butor, Sarraute, Robbe-Grillet, Claude Simon, Philippe Sollers, have on the other hand succeeded in making objects of their books without reaping any of the strategic benefits of the maneuver—a triumph of misplaced intelligence. Their work seems leaden, self-conscious in the wrong way. Painfully slow-paced, with no leaps of the imagination, concentrating on the minutiae of consciousness, these novels scrupulously, in deadly earnest, parse out what can safely be said. In an effort to avoid psychologism and unwarranted assumptions they arrive at inconsequence, carrying on that traditional French war against the bourgeois which ends by flattering him: what a monster! Miss Sarraute, in her latest novel, *The Golden Fruits,* attempts a satirical version of the Paris literary scene which some people have found acute and funny. For others it is vitiated by the somber avant-gardism of the device which structures it, a chorus of unidentified voices. It is as if French novelists do not know how to play.

Play is one of the great possibilities of art; it is also, as Norman O. Brown makes clear in his *Life Against Death,* the Eros-principle whose repression means total calamity. The humorless practitioners of *le nouveau roman* produce such calamities regularly, as do our native worshippers of the sovereign Fact. It is the result of a lack of seriousness.

1964

NOT-KNOWING

Let us suppose that someone is writing a story. From the world of conventional signs he takes an azalea bush, plants it in a pleasant park. He takes a gold pocket watch from the world of conventional signs and places it under the azalea bush. He takes from the same rich source a handsome thief and a chastity belt, places the thief in the chastity belt and lays him tenderly under the azalea, not neglecting to wind the gold pocket watch so that its ticking will, at length, awaken the now-sleeping thief. From the Sarah Lawrence campus he borrows a pair of seniors, Jacqueline and Jemima, and sets them to walking in the vicinity of the azalea bush and the handsome, chaste thief. Jacqueline and Jemima have just failed the Graduate Record Examination and are cursing God in colorful Sarah Lawrence language. What happens next?

Of course, I don't know.

It's appropriate to pause and say that the writer is one who, embarking upon a task, does not know what to do. I cannot tell you, at this moment, whether Jacqueline and Jemima will succeed or fail in their effort to jimmy the chastity belt's lock, or whether the thief, whose name is Zeno and who has stolen the answer sheets for the next set of Graduate Record Examinations, will pocket the pocket watch or turn it over to the nearest park employee. The fate of the azalea bush, whether it will bloom or strangle in a killing frost, is unknown to me.

A very conscientious writer might purchase an azalea at the Downtown Nursery and a gold watch at Tiffany's, hire a handsome thief fresh from Riker's Island, obtain the loan of a chastity belt from the Metropolitan, inveigle Jacqueline and Jemima in from Bronxville, and arrange them all under glass for study, writing up the results in honest, even fastidious prose. But in so doing he places himself in the realm of journalism or sociology. The not-knowing is crucial to art, is what permits art to be made. Without the scanning process engendered by not-knowing, without the possibility of having the mind move in unanticipated directions, there would be no invention.

This is not to say that I don't know anything about Jacqueline or Jemima, but what I do know comes into being at the instant it's inscribed. Jacqueline, for example, loathes her mother, whereas Jemima dotes on hers—I discover this by writing the sentence that announces it. Zeno was fathered by a—what? Polar bear? Roller skate? Shower of gold? I opt for the shower of gold, for Zeno is a hero (although he's just become one by virtue of his golden parent). Inside the pocket watch there is engraved a legend. Can I make it out? I think so: *Drink me,* it says. No no, can't use it, that's Lewis Carroll's. But could Zeno be a watch swallower rather than a thief? No again, Zeno'd choke on it, and so would the reader. There are rules.

Writing is a process of dealing with not-knowing, a forcing of what and how. We have all heard novelists testify to the fact that, beginning a new book, they are utterly baffled as to how to proceed, what should be written and how it might be written, even though they've done a dozen. At best there's a slender intuition, not much greater than an itch. The anxiety attached to this situation is not inconsiderable. "Nothing to paint and nothing to paint with," as Beckett says of Bram van Velde. The not-knowing is not simple, because it's hedged about with prohibitions, roads that may not be taken. The more serious the artist, the more problems he takes into account and the more considerations limit his possible initiatives—a point to which I shall return.

What kind of a fellow is Zeno? How do I know until he's opened his mouth?

"Gently, ladies, gently," says Zeno, as Jacqueline and Jemima bash away at the belt with a spade borrowed from a friendly park employee. And to the park employee: "Somebody seems to have lost this-here watch."

Let us change the scene.

Alphonse, the park employee from the preceding episode, he who lent the spade, is alone in his dismal room on West Street (I could position him as well in a four-story townhouse on East Seventy-second, but you'd object, and rightly so; verisimilitude forbids it, nothing's calculated quicker than a salary). Alphonse, like so many toilers in the great city, is not as simple as he seems. Like those waiters who are really actors and those cab drivers who are really composers of electronic music, Alphonse is sunlighting as a Parks Department employee although he is, in reality, a literary critic. We find him writing a letter to his friend Gaston, also a literary critic although masquerading *pro tem* as a guard at the Whitney Museum. Alphonse poises paws over his Smith-Corona and writes:

Dear Gaston,

Yes, you are absolutely right—Postmodernism is dead. A stunning blow, but not entirely surprising. I am spreading the news as rapidly as possible, so that all of our friends who are in the Postmodernist "bag" can get out of it before their cars are repossessed and the insurance companies tear up their policies. Sad to see Postmodernism go (and so quickly!). I was fond of it. As fond, almost, as I was of its grave and noble predecessor, Modernism. But we cannot dwell in the done-for. The death of a movement is a natural part of life, as was understood so well by the partisans of Naturalism, which is dead.

I remember exactly where I was when I realized that Postmodernism had bought it. I was in my study with a cup of tequila and William Y's new book, *One-Half.* Y's work is, we agree, good—*very* good. But who can make the leap to greatness while dragging after him the burnt-out boxcars of a dead aesthetic? Perhaps we can find new employment for him. On the roads, for example. When the insight overtook me, I started to my feet, knocking over the tequila, and said aloud (although there was no one to hear), "What? Postmodernism, too?" So many, so many. I put Y's book away on a high shelf and turned to the contemplation of the death of Plainsong, A.D. 958.

By the way: Structuralism's tottering. I heard it from Gerald, who is at Johns Hopkins and thus in the thick of things. You don't have to tell everybody. Frequently, idle talk is enough to give a movement that last little "push" that topples it into its grave. I'm convinced that's what happened to the New Criticism. I'm persuaded that it was Gerald, whispering in the corridors.

On the bright side, one thing that is dead that I don't feel too bad about is Existentialism, which I never thought was anything more than Phenomenology's bathwater anyway. It had a good run, but how peeving it was to hear all those artists going around talking about "the existential moment" and similar claptrap. Luckily, they have stopped doing that now. Similarly, the Nouveau Roman's passing did not disturb me overmuch. "Made dreariness into a religion," you said, quite correctly. I know this was one of your pared-to-the-bone movements and all that, but I didn't even like what they left out. A neat omission usually raises the hairs on the back of my neck. Not here. Robbe-Grillet's only true success, for my money, was with *Jealousy,* which I'm told he wrote in a fit of.

Well, where are we? Surrealism gone, got a little sweet toward the end, you could watch the wine of life turning into Gatorade. Sticky. Altar Poems—those constructed in the shape of an altar for the greater honor and glory of God—have not been seen much lately: missing and presumed dead. The Anti-Novel is dead; I read it in the *Times.* The Anti-Hero and the Anti-Heroine had a thing going which resulted in three Anti-Children, all of them now at M.I.T. The Novel of the Soil is dead, as are Expressionism, Impressionism, Futurism, Imagism, Vorticism, Regionalism, Realism, the Kitchen Sink School of Drama, the Theatre of the Absurd, the Theatre of Cruelty, Black Humor, and Gongorism. You know all this; I'm just totting up. To be a Pre-Raphaelite in the present era is to be somewhat out of touch. And, of course, Concrete Poetry—sank like a stone.

So we have a difficulty. What shall we call the New Thing, which I haven't encountered yet but which is bound to be out there somewhere? Post-Postmodernism sounds, to me, a little lumpy. I've been toying with the Revolution of the Word, II, or the New Revolution of the Word, but I'm afraid the Jolas estate may hold a copyright. It should have the word *new* in it somewhere. The New Newness? Or maybe the Post-New? It's a problem. I await your comments and suggestions. If we're going to slap a saddle on this rough beast, we've got to get moving.

Yours,
Alphonse

If I am slightly more sanguine than Alphonse about Postmodernism, however dubious about the term itself and not altogether clear as to who is supposed to be on the bus and who is not, it's because I locate it in relation to a series of problems, and feel that the problems are durable ones. Problems are a comfort. Wittgenstein said, of philosophers, that some of them suffer from "loss of problems," a development in which everything seems quite simple to them and what they write becomes "immeasurably shallow and trivial." The same can be said of writers. Before I mention some of the specific difficulties I have in mind, I'd like to at least glance at some of the criticisms that have been leveled at the alleged Postmodernists—let's say John Barth, William Gass, John Hawkes, Robert Coover, William Gaddis, Thomas Pynchon, and myself in this country, Calvino in Italy, Peter Handke and Thomas Bernhard in Germany, although other names could be invoked. The criticisms run roughly as follows: that this kind of writing has turned its back on the world, is in some sense not about the world but about its own processes, that it is masturbatory, certainly chilly, that it excludes readers by design, speaks only to the already tenured, or that it does not speak at all, but instead, like Frost's Secret, sits in the center of a ring and Knows.

I would ardently contest each of these propositions, but it's rather easy to see what gives rise to them. The problems that seem to me to define the writer's task at this moment (to the extent that he has chosen them as his problems) are not of a kind that make for ease of communication, for work that rushes toward the reader with outflung arms—rather, they're the reverse. Let me cite three such difficulties that I take to be important, all having to do with language. First, there is art's own project, since Mallarmé, of restoring freshness to a much-handled language, essentially an effort toward finding a language in which making art is possible at all. This remains a ground theme, as potent, problematically, today as it was a century ago. Secondly, there is the political and social contamination of language by its use in manipulation of various kinds over time and the effort to find what might be called a "clean" language, problems associated with the Roland Barthes of *Writing Degree Zero* but also discussed by Lukács and others. Finally, there is the pressure on language from contemporary culture in the broadest sense—I mean our devouring commercial culture—which results in a double impoverishment: theft of complexity from the reader, theft of the reader from the writer.

These are by no means the only thorny matters with which the writer has to deal, nor (allowing for the very great differences among the practitioners under discussion) does every writer called Postmodern respond to them in the same way and to the same degree, nor is it the case that other writers of quite different tendencies are innocent of these concerns. If I call these matters "thorny," it's because any adequate attempt to deal with them automatically creates barriers to the ready assimilation of the work. Art is not difficult because it wishes to be difficult, but because it wishes to be art. However much the writer might long to be, in his work, simple, honest, and straightforward, these virtues are no longer available to him. He discovers that in being simple, honest, and straightforward, nothing much happens: he speaks the speakable, whereas what we are looking for is the as-yet unspeakable, the as-yet unspoken.

With Mallarmé the effort toward mimesis, the representation of the external world, becomes a much more complex thing than it had been previously. Mallarmé shakes words loose from their attachments and bestows new meanings upon them, meanings which point not toward the external world but toward the Absolute, acts of poetic intuition. This is a fateful step; not for nothing does Barthes call him the Hamlet of literature. It produces, for one thing, a poetry of unprecedented difficulty. You will find no Mallarmé in Bartlett's *Familiar Quotations.* Even so ardent an admirer as Charles Mauron speaks of the sense of alienation enforced by his work. Mauron writes: "All who remember the day when first they looked into the *Poems* or the *Divagations* will testify to that curious feeling of *exclusion* which put them, in the face of a text written with *their* words (and moreover, as they could somehow feel, magnificently written), suddenly outside their own language, deprived of their rights in a common speech, and, as it were, rejected by their oldest friends." Mallarmé's work is also, and perhaps most importantly, a step toward establishing a new ontological status for the poem, as an object in the world rather than a representation of the world. But the ground seized is dangerous ground. After Mallarmé the struggle to renew language becomes a given for the writer, his exemplary quest an imperative. Mallarmé's work, "this whisper that is so close to silence," as Marcel Raymond calls it, is at once a liberation and a loss to silence of a great deal of territory.

The silencing of an existing rhetoric (in Harold Rosenberg's phrase) is also what is at issue in Barthes's deliberations in *Writing Degree Zero* and after—in this case a variety of rhetorics seen as actively pernicious rather than passively inhibiting. The question is, what is the complicity of language in the massive crimes of Fascism, Stalinism, or (by implication) our own policies in Vietnam? In the control of societies by the powerful and their busy functionaries? If these abominations are all in some sense facilitated by, made possible by, language, to what degree is that language ruinously contaminated (considerations also raised by George Steiner in his well-known essay "The Hollow Miracle" and, much earlier, by George Orwell)? I am sketching here, inadequately, a fairly complex argument; I am not particularly taken with Barthes's tentative solutions but the problems command the greatest respect. Again, we have language deeply suspicious of its own behavior; although this suspicion is not different in kind from Hemingway's noticing, early in the century, that words like *honor, glory,* and *country* were perjured, bought, the skepticism is far deeper now, and informed as well by the investigations of linguistic philosophers, structuralists, semioticians. Even conjunctions must be inspected carefully. "I read each word with the feeling appropriate to it," says Wittgenstein. "The word 'but' for example with the but-feeling. . . ." He is not wrong. Isn't the but-feeling, as he calls it, already sending us headlong down a greased slide before we've had the time to contemplate the proposition it's abutting? Quickly now, quickly—when you hear the phrase "our vital interests" do you stop to wonder whether you were invited to the den, Zen, Klan, or coven meeting at which these were defined? Did you speak?

In turning to the action of contemporary culture on language, and thus on the writer, the first thing to be noticed is a loss of reference. If I want a world of reference to which all possible readers in this country can respond, there is only one universe of discourse available; that in which the Love Boat sails on seas of passion like a Flying Dutchman of passion and the dedicated men in white of *General Hospital* pursue, with evenhanded diligence, triple bypasses and the nursing staff. This limits things somewhat. The earlier newspaper culture, which once dealt in a certain amount of nuance and zestful, highly literate hurly-burly, has deteriorated shockingly. The newspaper I worked for as a raw youth, thirty years ago, is today a pallid imitation of its former self. Where once we could put spurious quotes in the paper and attribute them to Ambrose Bierce and be fairly sure that enough readers would get the joke to make the joke worthwhile, from the point of view of both reader and writer, no such common ground now exists. The situation is not peculiar to this country. Steiner remarks of the best current journalism in Germany that, read against an average number of the *Frankfurter Zeitung* of pre-Hitler days, it's difficult at times to believe that both are written in German. At the other end of the scale much of the most exquisite description of the world, discourse about the world, is now being carried on in mathematical languages obscure to most people—certainly to me—and the contributions the sciences once made to our common language in the form of coinages, new words and concepts, are now available only to specialists. When one adds the ferocious appropriation of high culture by commercial culture—it takes, by my estimate, about forty-five minutes for any given novelty in art to travel from the Mary Boone Gallery on West Broadway to the display windows of Henri Bendel on Fifty-seventh Street—one begins to appreciate the seductions of silence.

Problems in part define the kind of work the writer chooses to do, and are not to be avoided but embraced. A writer, says Karl Kraus, is a man who can make a riddle out of an answer.

Let me begin again.

Jacqueline and Jemima are instructing Zeno, who has returned the purloined GRE documents and is thus restored to dull respectability, in Postmodernism. Postmodernism, they tell him, has turned its back on the world, is not about the world but about its own processes, is masturbatory, certainly chilly, excludes readers by design, speaks only to the already tenured, or does not speak at all, but instead—

Zeno, to demonstrate that he too knows a thing or two, quotes the critic Perry Meisel on semiotics. "Semiotics," he says, "is in a position to claim that no phenomenon has any ontological status outside its place in the particular information system from which it draws its meaning"—he takes a large gulp of his Gibson—"and therefore, all language is finally groundless." I am eavesdropping and I am much reassured. This insight is one I can use. Gaston, the critic who is a guard at the Whitney Museum, is in love with an IRS agent named Madelaine, the very IRS agent, in fact, who is auditing my return for the year 1982. "Madelaine," I say kindly to her over lunch, "semiotics is in a position to claim that no phenomenon has any ontological status outside its place in the particular information system from which it draws its meaning, and therefore, all language is finally groundless, including that of those funny little notices you've been sending me." "Yes," says Madelaine kindly, pulling from her pocket a large gold pocket watch that Alphonse has sold Gaston for twenty dollars, her lovely violet eyes atwitter, "but some information systems are more enforceable than others." Alas, she's right.

If the writer is taken to be the work's way of getting itself written, a sort of lightning rod for an accumulation of atmospheric disturbances, a St. Sebastian absorbing in his tattered breast the arrows of the Zeitgeist, this changes not very much the traditional view of the artist. But it does license a very great deal of critical imperialism.

This is fun for everyone. A couple of years ago I received a letter from a critic requesting permission to reprint a story of mine as an addendum to the piece he had written about it. He attached the copy of my story he proposed to reproduce, and I was amazed to find that my poor story had sprouted a set of tiny numbers—one to eighty-eight, as I recall—an army of tiny numbers marching over the surface of my poor distracted text. Resisting the temptation to tell him that all the tiny numbers were in the wrong places, I gave him permission to do what he wished, but I did notice that by a species of literary judo the status of my text had been reduced to that of footnote.

There is, in this kind of criticism, an element of aggression that gives one pause. Deconstruction is an enterprise that announces its intentions with startling candor. Any work of art depends upon a complex series of interdependences. If I wrench the rubber tire from the belly of Rauschenberg's famous goat to determine, in the interest of a finer understanding of same, whether the tire is a B. F. Goodrich or a Uniroyal, the work collapses, more or less behind my back. I say this not because I find this kind of study valueless but because the mystery worthy of study, for me, is not the signification of parts but how they come together, the tire wrestled over the goat's hind legs. Calvin Tomkins tells us in *The Bride and the Bachelors* that Rauschenberg himself says that the tire seemed "something as unavoidable as the goat." To see both goat and tire as "unavoidable" choices, in the context of art-making, is to illuminate just how strange the combinatorial process can be. Nor was the choice a hasty one; Tomkins tells us that the goat had been in the studio for three years and had appeared in two previous versions (the final version is titled "Monogram") before it met the tire.

Modern-day critics speak of "recuperating" a text, suggesting an accelerated and possibly strenuous nursing back to health of a basically sickly text, very likely one that did not even know itself to be ill. I would argue that in the competing methodologies of contemporary criticism, many of them quite rich in implications, a sort of tyranny of great expectations obtains, a rage for final explanations, a refusal to allow a work that mystery which is essential to it. I hope I am not myself engaging in mystification if I say, not that the attempt should not be made, but that the mystery exists. I see no immediate way out of the paradox—tear a mystery to tatters and you have tatters, not mystery—I merely note it and pass on.

We can, however, wonder for a moment why the goat girdled with its tire is somehow a magical object, rather than, say, only a dumb idea. Harold Rosenberg speaks of the contemporary artwork as "anxious," as wondering: Am I a masterpiece or simply a pile of junk? (If I take many of my examples here from the art world rather than the world of literature it is because the issues are more quickly seen in terms of the first: "goat" and "tire" are standing in for pages of prose, pounds of poetry.) What precisely is it in the coming together of goat and tire that is magical? It's not the surprise of seeing the goat attired, although that's part of it. One might say, for example, that the tire *contests* the goat, *contradicts* the goat, as a mode of being, even that the tire *reproaches* the goat, in some sense. On the simplest punning level, the goat is *tired*. Or that the unfortunate tire has *been caught by* the goat, which has been fishing in the Hudson—goats eat anything, as everyone knows—or that the goat is being *consumed by* the tire; it's outside, after all, mechanization takes command. Or that the goateed goat is protesting the fatigue of its friend, the tire, by wearing it as a sort of STRIKE button. Or that two contrasting models of infinity are being presented, tires and goats both being infinitely reproducible, the first depending on the good fortunes of the B. F. Goodrich company and the second upon the copulatory enthusiasm of goats—parallel production lines suddenly met. And so on. What is magical about the object is that it at once invites and resists interpretation. Its artistic worth is measurable by the degree to which it remains, after interpretation, vital—no interpretation or cardiopulmonary push-pull can exhaust or empty it.

In what sense is the work "about" the world, the world that Jacqueline and Jemima have earnestly assured Zeno the work has turned its scarlet rump to? It is to this vexing question that we shall turn next.

Let us discuss the condition of my desk. It is messy, mildly messy. The messiness is both physical (coffee cups, cigarette ash) and spiritual (unpaid bills, unwritten novels). The emotional life of the man who sits at the desk is also messy—I am in love with a set of twins, Hilda and Heidi, and in a fit of enthusiasm I have joined the Bolivian army. The apartment in which the desk is located seems to have been sublet from Moonbeam McSwine. In the streets outside the apartment melting snow has revealed a choice assortment of decaying et cetera. Furthermore, the social organization of the country is untidy, the world situation in disarray. How do I render all this messiness, and if I succeed, what have I done?

In a commonsense way we agree that I attempt to find verbal equivalents for whatever it is I wish to render. The unpaid bills are easy enough. I need merely quote one: FINAL DISCONNECT NOTICE. Hilda and Heidi are somewhat more difficult. I can say that they are beautiful—why not?—and you will more or less agree, although the bald statement has hardly stirred your senses. I can describe them—Hilda has the map of Bolivia tattooed on her right cheek and Heidi habitually wears, on her left hand, a set of brass knuckles wrought of solid silver—and they move a step closer. Best of all, perhaps, I can permit them to speak, for they speak much as we do.

> "On Valentine's Day," says Hilda, "he sent me oysters, a dozen and a half."
> "He sent me oysters too," said Heidi, "two dozen."
> "Mine were long-stemmed oysters," says Hilda, "on a bed of the most wonderful spinach."
> "Oh yes, spinach," says Heidi, "he sent me spinach too, miles and miles of spinach, wrote every bit of it himself."

To render "messy" adequately, to the point that you are enabled to feel it—it should, ideally, frighten your shoes—I would have to be more graphic than the decorum of the occasion allows. What should be emphasized is that one proceeds by way of particulars. If I know how a set of brass knuckles feels on Heidi's left hand it's because I bought one once, in a pawnshop, not to smash up someone's face but to exhibit on a pedestal in a museum show devoted to cultural artifacts of ambivalent status. The world enters the work as it enters our ordinary lives, not as world-view or system but in sharp particularity: a tax notice from Madelaine, a snowball containing a résumé from Gaston.

The words with which I attempt to render "messy," like any other words, are not inert, rather they are furiously busy. We do not mistake the words *the taste of chocolate* for the taste of chocolate itself, but neither do we miss the tease in *taste,* the shock in *chocolate.* Words have halos, patinas, overhangs, echoes. The word *halo,* for instance, may invoke St. Hilarius, of whom we've seen too little lately. The word *patina* brings back the fine pewtery shine on the saint's halo. The word *overhang* reminds us that we have, hanging over us, a dinner date with St. Hilarius, that crashing bore. The word *echo* restores us to Echo herself, poised like the White Rock girl on the overhang of a patina of a halo—infirm ground, we don't want the poor spirit to pitch into the pond where Narcissus blooms eternally, they'll bump foreheads, or maybe other parts closer to the feet, a scandal. There's chocolate smeared all over Hilarius' halo—messy, messy. . . .

The combinatorial agility of words, the exponential generation of meaning once they're allowed to go to bed together, allows the writer to surprise himself, makes art possible, reveals how much of Being we haven't yet encountered. It could be argued that computers can do this sort of thing for us, with critic-computers monitoring their output. When computers learn how to make jokes, artists will be in serious trouble. But artists will respond in such a way as to make art impossible for the computer. They will redefine art to take into account (that is, to exclude) technology—photography's impact upon painting and painting's brilliant response being a clear and comparatively recent example.

The prior history of words is one of the aspects of language the world uses to smuggle itself into the work. If words can be contaminated by the world, they can also carry with them into the work trace elements of world which can be used in a positive sense. We must allow ourselves the advantages of our disadvantages.

A late bulletin: Hilda and Heidi have had a baby, with which they're thoroughly displeased, it's got no credit cards and can't speak French, they'll send it back. . . . Messy.

Style is not much a matter of choice. One does not sit down to write and think: Is this poem going to be a Queen Anne poem, a Biedermeier poem, a Vienna Secession poem, or a Chinese Chippendale poem? Rather it is both a response to constraint and a seizing of opportunity. Very often a constraint is an opportunity. It would seem impossible to write *Don Quixote* once again, yet Borges has done so with great style, improving on the original (as he is not slow to tell us) while remaining faithful to it, faithful as a tick on a dog's belly. I don't mean that whim does not intrude. Why do I avoid, as much as possible, using the semicolon? Let me be plain: the semicolon is ugly, ugly as a tick on a dog's belly. I pinch them out of my prose. The great German writer Arno Schmidt, punctuation-drunk, averages eleven to a page.

Style is of course *how.* And the degree to which *how* has become *what*—since, say, Flaubert—is a question that men of conscience wax wroth about, and should. If I say of my friend that on this issue his marbles are a little flat on one side, this does not mean that I do not love my friend. He, on the other hand, considers that I am ridden by strange imperatives, and that the little piece I gave to the world last week, while nice enough in its own way, would have been vastly better had not my deplorable aesthetics caused me to score it for banjulele, cross between a banjo and a uke. Bless Babel.

Let us suppose that I am the toughest banjulele player in town and that I have contracted to play "Melancholy Baby" for six hours before an audience that will include the four next-toughest banjulele players in town. We imagine the smoky basement club, the hustling waiters (themselves students of the jazz banjulele), Jacqueline, Jemima, Zeno, Alphonse, Gaston, Madelaine, Hilda, and Heidi forming a congenial group at the bar. There is one thing of which you may be sure: I am not going to play "Melancholy Baby" as written. Rather I will play something that is parallel, in some sense, to "Melancholy Baby," based upon the chords of "Melancholy Baby," made out of "Melancholy Baby," *having to do with* "Melancholy Baby"—commentary, exegesis, elaboration, contradiction. The interest of my construction, if any, is to be located in the space between the new entity I have constructed and the "real" "Melancholy Baby," which remains in the mind as the horizon which bounds my efforts.

This is, I think, the relation of art to world. I suggest that art is always a meditation upon external reality rather than a representation of external reality or a jackleg attempt to "be" external reality. If I perform even reasonably well, no one will accuse me of not providing a true, verifiable, note-for-note reproduction of "Melancholy Baby"—it will be recognized that this was not what I was after. Twenty years ago I was much more convinced of the autonomy of the literary object than I am now, and even wrote a rather persuasive defense of the proposition that I have just rejected: that the object is itself world. Beguiled by the rhetoric of the time—the sculptor Phillip Pavia was publishing a quite good magazine called *It Is,* and this was typical—I felt that the high ground had been claimed and wanted to place my scuffed cowboy boots right there. The proposition's still attractive. What's the right answer? Bless Babel.

A couple of years ago I visited Willem de Kooning's studio in East Hampton, and when the big doors are opened one can't help seeing—it's a shock—the relation between the rushing green world outside and the paintings. Precisely how de Kooning manages to distill nature into art is a mystery, but the explosive relation is there, I've seen it. Once when I was in Elaine de Kooning's studio on Broadway, at a time when the metal sculptor Herbert Ferber occupied the studio immediately above, there came through the floor a most horrible crashing and banging. "What in the world is that?" I asked, and Elaine said, "Oh, that's Herbert thinking."

Art is a true account of the activity of mind. Because consciousness, in Husserl's formulation, is always consciousness *of* something, art thinks ever of the world, cannot not think of the world, could not turn its back on the world even if it wished to. This does not mean that it's going to be honest as a mailman; it's more likely to appear as a drag queen. The problems I mentioned earlier, as well as others not taken up, enforce complexity. "We do not spend much time in front of a canvas whose intentions are plain," writes Cioran, "music of a specific character, unquestionable contours, exhausts our patience, the overexplicit poem seems . . . incomprehensible." Flannery O'Connor, an artist of the first rank, famously disliked anything that looked funny on the page, and her distaste has widely been taken as a tough-minded put-down of puerile experimentalism. But did she also dislike anything that looked funny on the wall? If so, a severe deprivation. Art cannot remain in one place. A certain amount of movement, up, down, across, even a gallop toward the past, is a necessary precondition.

Style enables us to speak, to imagine again. Beckett speaks of "the long sonata of the dead"—where on earth did the word *sonata* come from, imposing as it does an orderly, even exalted design upon the most disorderly, distressing phenomenon known to us? The fact is not challenged, but understood, momentarily, in a new way. It's our good fortune to be able to imagine alternative realities, other possibilities. We can quarrel with the world, constructively (no one alive has quarreled with the world more extensively or splendidly than Beckett). "Belief in progress," says Baudelaire, "is a doctrine of idlers and Belgians." Perhaps. But if I have anything unorthodox to offer here, it's that I think art's project is fundamentally meliorative. The aim of meditating about the world is finally to change the world. It is this meliorative aspect of literature that provides its ethical dimension. We are all Upton Sinclairs, even that Hamlet, Stéphane Mallarmé.

1987

Here in the Village

INTRODUCTION

The following pieces were mostly written for *The New Yorker*'s Notes and Comment section, where one can appear on Wednesday (when the magazine is generally available in New York) being mad about whatever one was overstimulated by on Tuesday of the previous week or whenever the piece was written. That is, there's a short lead time, almost as short as a daily newspaper's, but still long enough to allow one to be angry in tranquillity. Not that everything here is a product of outrage; I dearly love the West Village, where I live, and some of the following (I hope) reflects that, and I care for the marvelous dangerous Oz-like city as a whole, and maybe that comes through, too. It's also not a bad place from which to hurl great flaming buckets of Greek fire (rhetoric) at the Government—not thinking that the Government is paying the slightest attention, but merely for the splendid exercise given the Citizenship muscle, far superior to merely filling out the old 1040 and signing the non-yea-or-nay check.

These pieces, then, may be thought of as a series of Letters to the Editor, which the Editor, in his Infinite Wisdom (or suffering from a Lost Mind), decided to print.

Walking around the Village: The vaguely rectangular vacant lot where the Women's House of Detention used to be is being made into a little park, and the first bushes, shrubs—whatever—were put in last Monday, and you can now get a dim idea of what the place is going to look like. It's going to be pretty. I don't know who the genius responsible for getting this done is, but I take off my hat to her. The Women's House of Detention was the place where they used to store women arrested for prostitution, mostly. The thing I remember about it best, aside from its social inutility and hideousness, is that one time a pal of mine who was in the anti-war-activist business got situated there because she had sat down in front of an Armed Forces Day parade. And stopped it, for a while. Anyhow, she was put in a cell with a woman who was in that other business, and that woman asked her what she was in for, and my pal told her. And the other woman immediately rushed to the cell door and yelled at the turnkey, *"Get these fucking housewives outta here!"* Anyhow, the planting is going in, and it looks mighty good.

On Tuesday, I was standing in my local liquor store (Lamanna's, on Sixth) buying a bottle of vodka when the wife of the super of our building came in, on much the same errand. Dialogue as follows:

SHE: You don't really drink that stuff, do you? It's poison.

ME: No, of course I don't drink it. I use it as an antiseptic. You know, like if I cut myself, I pour a little of this on the cut.

SHE: You sure do cut yourself a lot.

Well, that was a joke on me that I greatly enjoyed. The next interesting thing that happened was on Wednesday. I was attending a dinner party on our block and, lacking cigarettes, had gone out to get some. And on my way back I ran into this woman I know and she looked funny. And I said, "Robin, what's the matter?" And she said, "Joan has just tried to kill herself—pills—and she's in the emergency room at St. Vincent's with Herman, and I'm going out to buy her a pair of slippers." Joan is Robin's daughter, who is twenty-four and has been an addict since she was around sixteen (although lately she's been in a Methadone program), and Herman is Robin's husband, an industrial designer. Now, St. Vincent's emergency room is one of my favorite emergency rooms in the whole world. I know it well, from the time I accidentally stabbed myself in the chest with an X-Acto knife (paltry two stitches), and the time our former babysitter got raped, and the time my daughter ate the roach poison and I went down there, carrying kid and can, and the Poison Control Center there said, "Mister, that stuff don't even bother the roaches—they just get high on it, is all." So I whip into the St. Vincent's emergency room, and there is Joan, in white hospital gown and wheelchair, tubes patched into her right and left wrists leading to plastic bags of glucose, or whatever, hung on the walls, and Herman dithering about. Joan is making sentences, but just barely. She asks if I have a cigarette on me, I give her one, and the black uniformed guard standing nearby doesn't say a damned thing; he just smiles. So then I got on to what Herman and his daughter were talking about, which was *whether the attempt had been serious or not.* He said no, she said yes. So I kicked Herman in the leg four or five times, meanwhile patting him calmingly on the shoulder, and he realized what he was doing and shut up. I don't blame him; he was scared to death and babbling. Joan's O.K. now. I mean, medically.

The next interesting thing that happened was on Friday. I was going to an event at Westbeth in the early afternoon and I was stopped by four kids. They were boys, between twelve and fourteen, I judged, white, middle class, I judged, and two of them were carrying pieces of pipe. Dialogue as follows:

KID: Hey, Mister.

ME: Yep?

KID: Are you straight?

ME: You mean straight as opposed to gay?

KID: Yeah.

ME: Straight.

KID: Good man.

And they moved on. And I was later told by my hosts that there are these bands of little kids wandering around that part of the West Village beating up gays. And that it's been going on for about two years. And that nobody seems to be able to do anything about it. I thought that was interesting. And I also thought, Why didn't I tarry and reason with them, point out the error of this way of thinking? I don't know. I didn't. And I concluded that it was the natural momentum of New Yorkers, who tend to move past obstacles such as panhandlers, freaks, crazies, and people with big, brutish dogs as fast as they comfortably can. I absolved myself.

And then on Saturday I went to the Jane Street street festival. And they had this terrific band there—the Grover Cleveland High School Stage Band. A big band: four trombones, five trumpets, guitar, piano (electric), bass, drums, and *eight* saxes. They were playing Glenn Miller and Tommy Dorsey and Bob Crosby arrangements, and they were good. Very good. And what was interesting was that these kids had, on the stand, exactly the same expressions, attitudes, and moves that professional musicians have. The way a sax man tends to lean to the left, thrusting out a shoulder, when he's playing, or fiddle around with his reed when he's not playing. The pianist was a young Chinese, and the rest of them were all mixed up, black and white and Puerto Rican. There was one ringer in the trombone section, though, whom I took to be a teacher—young, but not so young as the others. Anyhow, when they played "Yesterdays," tears came to my eyes, which I don't much like in public, so I asked this girl if she wanted to dance. She wasn't a girl, really, she was a woman, and all the time we were dancing she had this three-year-old child (wearing glasses) clinging to her right leg. I didn't get her name, but I sure did enjoy that dance.

I have lately noticed that Con Edison is being very nice to me. This is new. A couple of months ago I found, skittering in nervous computer printout across the bottom of my bill, the words THANK YOU VERY MUCH FOR YOUR PROMPT PAYMENT. This was new. Con Ed had never thanked me before—or, indeed, saluted me in any way save for the dull iteration of the bill. In truth, at an earlier point in our generally pleasant relationship Con Ed had demanded a deposit of $98.05 from me, the result of a month or two of woolgathering on my part, when I did not pay its bills but did study, with intense interest, the new views of Nietzsche offered by Haar, Lingis, Deleuze, Granier, Blondel, Derrida, and that crowd. *I was busy!* I paid the $98.05 deposit, after fifteen years of faithful consumption, having no alternative—not even a scream or a yell. Since then, all has been peaches and cream between us. I have never said a word to them about having to walk down twenty-six flights in an East Sixty-sixth Street apartment building in the blackout in my cowboy boots. (Cowboy boots in New York are an affectation, as Nietzsche, Derrida, and Charles Luce would be the first to point out.) But today! Today, I got a Con Ed bill with love note attached. Dancing across the bottom of my bill (in lettering similar to that green or red tattooing one finds in the window of a calculator) were the words YOU HAVE AN EXCELLENT PAYMENT RECORD WITH US. THANK YOU. What satisfaction! What gratification! And what a future for this new, gay science, teaching the machine not only how to be civil but how to pretend it knows us, one and all.

A fable. One Day a shrewd and learned Vizier of the Intelligence Community, who thought nobody could pull the Alpaca over his Eyes, was manning his Desk, waiting for some lowly Other Rank to come up with another Crackbrained Scheme he could Swat, thus saving the Public many Doubloons and enhancing his own Position with the Cost-Consciousness Boys. He was lighting his Fancy Imported Hand-Carved Danish Briar when Old Charlie shuffled in, bearing a load of Blueprints and Specifications.

The Sachem quickly reached for an Eyes-Only Report to fiddle with and sat the Dear Old Soul down most cordially, because in his extensive experience Charlie was the biggest Ninny in the West Annex when it came to Ideas, and his Shuffle wasn't so great, either.

"Well, Charlie My Man, what is it today?" he asked with a Pretty Good rendering of Upper-Level accessibility.

"It is the damnedest thing, Carlisle," said Charlie. "You won't believe it."

Carlisle was in Total Agreement with this Evaluation, but he merely scraped a Thumb thoughtfully upon his Brain Pan.

"It is," said Charlie, dumping the Paperwork on the Rosewood, "a Nondiscernible Microbioinoculator."

"A what?" said Carlisle, seized by a Throe in the vicinity of the Tympanic Membrane.

"A Nondiscernible Microbioinoculator," said Charlie, "and it is a Very Spiffy Article—you have my word for it."

"What does it do?" asked the Supervisor, fetched in Spite of Himself.

"It delivers the Cobra Venom," said Charlie, "nondiscernibly. It can hit a bee's knee at a hundred metres, and, discern as hard as they can, the Other Side hasn't a Glimmering where the hell the Deadly Blow comes from."

The Vizier then Messed About in the masses of Paper for a space, and after Some Moments of Struggle perceived the outlines of the System in question.

"It's a dart gun," he said.

"No no no," said Charlie. "A Microbioinoculator, Nondiscernible."

"You want to shoot at people with this thing and give them the fatal Pain in the Neck?"

"Not people, Carlisle. Enemies of Freedom. And lookie here. There's a Secret Decoder Ring Cum Dog Whistle Capability concealed in the butt plate. And think what the Black Hats may or very possibly do have in the same line. And all you have to do is slam the Old Initials on this Buckslip here."

"How much, Charlie?"

"The price is not even Worth Mentioning," said Charlie. "Three mil and ten box tops from any popular-brand Breakfast Cereal."

"O.K., Charlie. I'll take it Under Advisement."

The Shrewd and Learned Person approved the three million but Negatively Endorsed the box tops, and congratulated himself on having Nixed rampant Damned Foolishness once again. The next day, he discovered that the box tops had been merely a Bargaining Counter and that the Infernal Machine had gone immediately into production, causing a Glow of Good Feeling in many Snug Homes in the vicinity of Langley, Virginia.

Moral: *What is Nondiscernible today may be Painfully Obvious tomorrow.*

After spending an exciting eight or nine days at Forest Hills a few weeks ago, I was struck with a thought. Forest Hills was (let us say) amply provided with commercial messages in which the stars and superstars declared their affection for particular brands of racquets, balls, clothing, suntan oil, cameras, luggage, airlines, et al. (Rod Laver, for one, is said to have some fifty contracts cooking). My thought involved turning myself into an Authors' Representative—not the conventional sort of literary agent, who sees to the sale of an author's work, but, rather, one who handles his Endorsements. This area is, as I'm sure you know, badly neglected. Being modestly well acquainted within what is known as the literary establishment, I felt I would have no difficulty signing up a dozen or so biggies immediately—a number of them are friends of my Aunt Ada, who gives them cauliflower cookies and good advice. Acquiring a stable, then, would be the easy part; the hard part would be matching the particular author's name—and, where appropriate, person—to the exactly right good or service. Typewriters were too easy. I.B.M., Remington, Royal, Smith-Corona, Olivetti, and the like were sitting ducks—no creativity on my part required. But typewriter covers? I envisioned a large color photograph of Jack Barth, for instance, leaning on a typewriter tastefully shrouded in a dashing goat-gray cover with a large autograph, "John Barth," plainly in view. "The big book *demands* a clean machine," the copy will read. "The John Barth typewriter cover delivers. Dacron polyester and worsted-wool gabardine, treated to resist rain, stain, and those funny little inimical particles that fill the air nowadays." Dynamite, no?

I then quickly sketched out a proposal for a line of writing wear: turtlenecks, colored socks, long black capes lined with pencil sharpeners, hair shirts, and warmup suits—either McGregor or Gleneagles, either Phil Roth or Bern Malamud. The Bill Gass sweatband. The William Styron wristlet. (Should wristlet and elbow brace be marketed together or separately?) Typewriter paper with the exclusive Joyce Carol Oates watermark—a breaking heart? Breakfast foods, Kurt Vonnegut—neat double play. Authors, unlike athletes, have no problems plugging whiskey, cigarettes, possibly even barbiturates—investigate. "When I finish a tough day at the typewriter," says poet-novelist Erica Jong, "it's a shot of Johnnie Walker Black Label for me!" Call Erica and ask her what she drinks. Air travel a natural for our leading literary Seldom Seen Kid (the phrase is Damon Runyon's). Who could resist the Tom Pynchon Getaway Adventure: Fourteen days of absolute absence, and we promise that you meet nobody—repeat, nobody. And what about *literary-criticism camps,* where beginners and middle-level performers can perfect their style and attack in beautifully wooded surroundings? "Let Anatole Broyard show YOU his fabulous backhand!" Hobnailed boots for young critics, either Puma or Adidas? Well, obviously my doors were going to be broken down by crass entrepreneurial types, but as I picked up the phone to order my new steel doors I flashed on one more scene: *painters.* NBC color coast-to-coast of Big Bill de Kooning hurling his brush to the court in anger after missing an easy ground stroke?

I like to think of myself as one not easily dazzled, but the recently announced plans for the new Senate Office Building-Cum Hanging Gardens have sent the old Cognitive Faculty into ecstasies of awe. Two private baths per Senatorial office! Sixteen-foot ceilings! Private rooftop restaurant! $135 million, of $1.35 mil per people's choice! Mere naive splendor seems an insufficiently round explanation for the phenomenon, and I have been puzzling about it. Clearly, the Senators will be doubling up in their new cubbys (else why *two* baths per office?). Clearly, they intend to meet their awesome tasks of Farsight & Divagation by *standing on each other's shoulders* (else why sixteen-foot ceilings?). We payers can only applaud such daring. Assuming an average Senatorial height of six feet and an average Senatorial head-and-neck of eleven inches, we get a total average Magnitude of eleven feet one inch—enough to see all the way to the Promised Land, and then some. Imagine Senator Javits standing on the broad and eloquent shoulders of Senator Moynihan (seniority), or Senator Case perched atop Senator Williams, or Senator Ribicoff aboard Senator Weicker, or Senator Cranston supported by the subtle, red-hatted Senator Hayakawa, all peering, peering, peering into the future—*and not one brow bumped* (clearance of four feet something)! Imagine the Senators, at the end of a hard day of Leadership, doing their agile, elegant back flips—*hup!*—as they un-team and head for their separate solid-silver showers. I earnestly suggest that an additional $50 million be appropriated for the shoeshine stand.

I went last week to see Madam Cherokee, my Reader and Spiritual Advisor, who maintains premises on Orchard Street devoted, as it were, to pulling the teeth of the future. Madam Cherokee is one of the classiest mages in the business (bandannas by Hermès, interiors by Knoll International), and whenever I am sore troubled and pressed by many woes I seek out the solid silver of her sooth and the pure, sparkling Baccarat of her clear-seeing. When I entered, Madam Cherokee was shuffling a deck of punched cards (she is hooked into an I.B.M 950 on a time-sharing basis) and looking over the latest issue of *Barron's*. "Good day, Donald," she said. "There is something on your mind." She was right, as always, and I wasted no time laying the matter before her.

"Madam Cherokee," I said, "how do I get in on the questionable-payments bonanza? As you know, our great American corporations are just falling all over themselves to make questionable payments to people. Hardly a day goes by without new questionable-payments announcements of ever-escalating grandeur. Why, just a fortnight ago R. J. Reynolds, the old-line tobacco company, announced questionable payments of $25 million to various parties since 1968, thus topping the Lockheed Corporation's total, which is just under $25 million, but scarcely threatening Exxon's all-time record of $46 million. The energetic Gulf Oil Corporation has proclaimed questionable payments of some $12.3 million, and there are promising new entrants—like International Minerals & Chemical, with over $3 million in questionable payments just revealed.

The S.E.C. calculates that at least two hundred titans of American business are into questionable payments, in addition to the industry leaders cited. What I want to know, dear Madam Cherokee, is how do I position myself near to the wide end of this great cornucopia? For my rag-and-bone shop is faltering, and once again I have been nixed for membership in my local Macramé Collective."

Madam Cherokee rose and ripped a few yards of the latest from the A.P. machine chattering cozily to itself in the corner.

"First off," she said, "you got to be able to do one of these giant conglomerations a little service. Some little beneficence. For instance, you got any use for one hundred F-whatever-it-is fighter aircraft with auxiliary systems and the appropriate training and maintenance contracts?"

"Not this week," I said. "Were I to purchase same, would I then be in line for a questionable payment?"

"Not automatically," said Madam Cherokee, "but you'd be standin' on the right street corner. Well, let's see. There's Rebatin', Short-Weightin', Rate-Settin', and six different flavors of Fixin'. All with questionable payments attached." She paused. "And, of course, you could run for office."

"But if successful," I pointed out, "I would then be exposed to the city of Washington, D.C., and concomitant moral dangers so hideous as to make a mere little inconsequential questionable payment—"

"I know, I know," she said. "I didn't say it was going to be *easy.*" Then the seer abruptly closed her eyes and began a kind of chant. "With a few ragged men, Francisco Pizarro conquered Peru. With a few ragged men, Sam Houston whipped Santa Anna at San Jacinto. With a few ragged men, André Malraux cleaned up Paris. With a few ragged men, A. P. Giannini founded the Bank of America. With a few ragged men—"

"I understand!" I exclaimed. "You mean that I should incorporate. Then I myself, possibly with a few ragged vice-presidents, would be a corporation. Fit to deal in and to be dealt these wondrous subventions which today energize, activate, inspirit, spur, rouse, and rally our American system of enterprise."

"I suggested nothing," said Madam Cherokee. "You draw your own conclusions." She gazed for a long moment into a flask of L'Air du Temps, by Nina Ricci, Paris. "I see here early repeal of the 1971 Wild Free-Roaming Horse and Burro Act. You might look into horsemeat. That'll be two hundred, baby. And make the check out to my Guatemalan subsidiary."

In the morning post I received what I regard as a rather astonishing communication from the magazine *Writer's Digest.* The magazine, addressing me by name, disclosed that it was planning, for early publication, a cover story "on the link that some people see between writing and drinking" and that it would like to include me "in a roundup piece summarizing the drinking habits of the top writers in America today."

After noting that I had been promoted to Top Writer (gratifying indeed after so many years of corporalship), my second, scandalized reaction was, *"How did they find out?"* I mean, I do take a drink now and again. In fact my doctor, who is the soul of tact, once characterized my consumption as "slightly imprudent." But how the devil did *Writer's Digest* discover this? Does the *whole city* know?

Zizzled with horror, as you may well imagine, I turned next to the magazine's questions, my answers to which they proposed to print (along with a recent photo and a listing of my vodka-soaked work to date). Such is the power of the questionnaire *qua* mechanism that, helplessly, I began penciling in answers, as follows:

1. "How would you describe your own drinking habits? ——— Light ——— Medium ——— Heavy ——— Other?"

Medium. Light is sissy and Heavy doesn't go down so well with Deans, Loan Officers and Publishers, and who in the world would want to be Other?

2. "When you feel like having a few drinks, what do you usually have?"

Zip-Strip on the rocks. Too easy, let us proceed to—

3. "Any favorite hangouts for drinking?"

Yes, Godot's, but I can't give you the address because you know the place is and I mean we want to keep it that way even though the toppest writers in America "hang out" as you put it there and goodness gracious Elaine's is what we *don't*—Also, in bed, sobbing lightly.

4. "Favorite drinking companions?"

Joe Conrad, Steverino Crane, Pete Hamill and Tom Aquinas.

5. "Heaviest drinkers/writers that you know—or *have* known—of?"

Oh, this is a mean one, WD. I could do a lot of I-didn't-know-what-I-was-doing-my-God-I-didn't-think-they'd-actually-*print*-the-Goddamn-thing damage here, couldn't I? Because I know for a fact that ************ is even more slightly imprudent than I, and that ****** von ******, thought to be sober as white bread, takes a little bang at ten o'clock in the morning, to get himself started. Off the record, I'll tell you nothing.

6. "Do you see any affinity between hard drinking and the writing life? Explain."

Well, climb up on my knees here, WD. When you've been staring at this Billy-by-damn keyboard all your life, decade after decade, you get a little thirsty. The thing is, *the keys don't move.* The "e" is in the same place, every day. The "h" is in the same place, decade in, decade out. The "g" is fixed, eternally. It makes you, like, *thirsty.* Any piano tuner would understand, I think.

There is something President Carter can do that will enable him to go down in history as the greatest American President since Abraham Lincoln. He can free the banks. As everyone knows, banks have historically been second-class citizens in America. They are everywhere hated, despised, reviled. The ordinary citizen would no more say a kind word for a bank than he would bash his begonia plant over the head with a chair. As early as 1908, Woodrow Wilson noted, "The banks in this country are remote from the people and the people regard them as not belonging to them but to some power hostile to them." See? Hostility. Not-belongingness. It is time for a change.

Freeing the banks—"nationalizing" them, as it were—will have several important consequences. The interest rates will go down. I suggest 4 percent, coming and going. That is, I pay a bank 4 percent when I borrow from it, and it pays me 4 percent when it borrows from me. That seems fair. The huge excess of money now generated by the banks and placed by them in private hands (technically called "profit") will disappear. The important point here is that for the first time a bank will be on a footing of equality with any other citizen. That the equality involves an adjustment downward rather than upward on the financial scale is logically no bar to the taking of this crucial step. Equality is equality.

Now, I am not against "profit" (sometimes called "profits," meaning, I suppose, more than one). My old mother down in Texas told me two things; the first is unprintable and had to do with relations between the sexes, and the second was "Screw every dollar out of the bastards that you can." I believe in profit. Keeps the wheels whirling and all that. This is called "incentive." A good thing. My one quibble is that from what I hear around town the banks incentivize very few of their fellow-citizens. *Very* few relative to the size of the population. Only a handful, in fact. A bad thing. It is divisive, counterproductive, and not at all sacred. Doesn't have to be that way.

A bank is fundamentally a device for moving money around. Sort of a switchboard situation. Now, if you talk to a banker about this he'll say, No, no, you don't understand. And he's right, I don't understand. I don't understand nine hundred of the things banks do to earn their profits. If I mention this to the banker, he'll mumble something about "risk." And he's got a point. It is well known that banks are daredevil risk-takers, as brave as the famous diving horses of Atlantic City. It is true that they like some kinds of risk better than other kinds of risk. The banks have a peculiar tendency to jump for what is called a "good risk." This may seem like a contradiction in terms to a layman, but to a bank it does not. Poor people, slum clearance, low-cost housing, and the City of New York are examples of "bad risks." But consider what would happen if the banks were freed (nationalized). *They could take any kind of risk they wanted to take!* "Bad" as well as "good"! They could be just like the rest of us, and make mistakes. Instant self-respect!

Now, it may appear to some that my proposal has what might be called a "Communist" or "Socialist" tinge. Not right. In point of fact, I met a Communist once and didn't like him at all. He was wearing clothes I didn't like, he was rude, and he ate his peas by picking up each individual pea with two fingers of his right hand. Anyhow, there is nothing Communist or Socialist about this proposal. I think of it as "nationalist."

A more serious question is: If the banks are nationalized, can the government handle this additional burden? I mean, can the government do anything efficiently? The recently reported incident wherein a U.S. spy submarine attempted to surface under the hull of a U.S.S.R. naval vessel during Soviet fleet maneuvers does not inspire superconfidence. But in fairness it must be said that the government does *some things* well. The Library of Congress. The Coast Guard. Whatever the difficulties, the moral issue is clear. We can and must rescue these poor banks from the intolerable weight of shame, discrimination, and (let us be plain) prejudice under which they have labored for centuries. We must enable them, and other free Americans, to say "Bank is beautiful." I call upon the President to act, immediately.

Letter to a literary critic:

Yes, you are absolutely right—Post-Modernism is dead. A stunning blow, but not entirely unanticipated. I am spreading the news as rapidly as possible, so that all of our friends who are in the Post-Modernist "bag" can get out of it before their cars are repossessed and the insurance companies tear up their policies. Sad to see Post-Modernism go (and so quickly!). I was fond of it. As fond, almost, as I was of its grave and noble predecessor, Modernism. But we cannot dwell in the done-for. The death of a movement is a natural part of life, as was understood so well by the partisans of Naturalism, which is dead. That was a great category, Naturalism (was it not you, my friend, who did the first Swedish translation of Zola's *Le Roman Expérimental*?).

I remember exactly where I was when I realized that Post-Modernism had bought it. I was in my study with a cup of tequila and William Y's new book, *One Half.* Y's work is, we agree, good—*very* good. But who can make the leap to greatness while dragging behind him the burnt-out boxcars of a dead aesthetic? Perhaps we can find new employment for him. On the roads, for example. When the insight overtook me, I started to my feet, knocking over the tequila, and said aloud (although there was no one to hear), "What? Post-Modernism, too?" So many, so many. I put Y's book away on a high shelf and turned to the contemplation of the death of Plainsong, 958 A.D.

By the way: Structuralism's tottering. I heard it from Gerald, who is at Johns Hopkins and thus in the thick of things. You don't have to tell everybody. Frequently, idle talk is enough to give a movement that last little "push" that topples it into its grave. I'm convinced that's what happened to the New Criticism. I'm persuaded that it was Gerald, whispering in the corridors.

On the bright side, one thing that is dead that I don't feel too bad about is Existentialism. Which I never thought was anything more than Phenomenology's bathwater anyway. It had a good run, but how peeving it was to hear all those artists going around talking about "the existential moment" and similar claptrap. Luckily, they have stopped doing that now. Similarly, the Nouveau Roman's passing did not disturb me overmuch. "Made dreariness into a religion," you said, quite correctly. I know this was one of your pared-to-the-bone movements and all that, but I didn't even like what they left out. A neat omission usually raises the hairs on the back of my neck. Not here. Robbe-Grillet's only true success, for my money, was with *Jealousy,* which I'm told he wrote in a fit of.

Well, where are we? Surrealism gone: got a little sweet toward the end, you could watch the wine of life turning into Gatorade. Sticky. *Hélas!* Altar Poems—those constructed in the shape of an altar for the greater honor and glory of God—have not been seen much lately: missing and presumed dead. The Anti-Novel is dead; I read it in the *Times.* The Anti-Hero and the Anti-Heroine had a thing going that resulted in three Anti-Children, all of them now at Dalton. The Novel of the Soil is dead, as are Expressionism, Impressionism, Futurism, Vorticism, Regionalism, Realism, the Kitchen Sink School of Drama, the Theatre of the Absurd, the Theatre of Cruelty, Black Humor, and Gongorism. You know all this; I'm just totting up. To be a Pre-Raphaelite in the present era is to be somewhat out of touch. And, of course, Concrete Poetry—sank like a stone.

So we have a difficulty. What shall we call the New Thing, which I haven't encountered yet but which is bound to be out there somewhere? Post-Post-Modernism sounds, to me, a little lumpy. I've been toying with the Revolution of the Word II, or the New Revolution of the Word, but I'm afraid the Jolas estate may hold a copyright. It should have the word "new" in it somewhere. The New Newness? Or maybe the Post-New? It's a problem. I await your comments and suggestions. If we're going to slap a saddle on this rough beast, we've got to get moving.

Worrying about women. Woman is an imaginary being, a fabulous animal kin to the manticore, the hippogriff, the ant-lion. Woman does not exist. What exists in the space "woman" would occupy, if she existed, is a concatenation of ideas about women. Throughout history men and women have attempted to zoo the animal. Imagine an immense net, woven of paintings, epigrams, laws, courtesies, lies, clothing, Polaroids, aggression, desire, and dreams. Imagine a net as big as a sea, stretching from the Advanced Palaeolithic to the present time. Imagine human beings standing along the circumference of the net, doing their best to support it—the mighty effort, the colossal straining. Yet the animal escapes. And a strange thing happens. The net becomes the animal.

The nonexistence of woman has occasioned a certain anxiety among women. Some feel that it is the result of a male conspiracy perhaps twenty million years old. Others contend, with Hegel, that there is in consciousness itself a fundamental hostility toward every other consciousness and that this adequately accounts for the scandal. All would probably agree that *looking* is crucial.

"The looking at a woman sometimes makes for lust," says Thomas Aquinas, in one of the great understatements of the thirteenth century. Philosophers of the gaze, that terrible regard which can illuminate or cxtinguish its object, are part of the net. Simone de Beauvoir, whose work on women is definitive, finds that a man's gaze is in all cases a loss of value for a woman. "The eye is a secret orator," says Burton, "the first bawd."

Women now demand a presuppositionless regard, one into which are wound no definitions of woman. The disembawdiment of the eye will not be easily achieved. The kind of mystification from which women wish to free themselves may be seen, for example, among enthusiasts of concavity/convexity. The traditional view, based on the morphology of the sexual organs, is that women "are" concave. Convexity, with its connotations of assertiveness, imperialism, domination, is said to be male. Woman, in this formulation, is a dish containing "the statically expectant ova" (Erik Erikson). Theories proliferate from this slender base, insights accumulate, conclusions are drawn. Such thinking makes objects of us all.

Moods change. Men, exhausted by the accomplishments of reason, whose processes undergo further refinement even as its products are discovered to be often pernicious, realize that something is wrong. With reason suffering a partial discredit, with science increasingly suspect, there is a turning toward other ways of knowing, the nonrational, the "feminine," feeling-with. Women choose this moment to mobilize. If, as Oretga says, the core of the feminine mind is occupied by an irrational power (he intends this positively), the next hundred years are going to be wonderfully different from the last, in ways which no one has contemplated.

The question of Beauty disturbs the Movement, as beauty disturbs. Its very discussion, in the vocabulary of the revolution, is somehow inappropriate—like the startling appearance, in the 1572 edition of the Bishops' Bible, of a woodcut of Jupiter visiting Leda in his swansuit. When art enters the dialogue, the situation is further confused. Women in the gallery, literally on pedestals, or hanging on the walls, like skins, like trophies—perfect objects at last. One does not know how to behave. The slightest perusement of the mesial groove is done guiltily. As in life.

Art, touching mysteries, tends to darken rather than illuminate them. Artists enrich and complicate (whatever else they may also be doing). In terms of sexual politics, this means adding to the mystification. But more than politics is involved. Women as a subject, a pretext, for art, become momentarily free. Art's refusal to explain itself translates into a refusal to explain women. They are, for a moment, surrounded by a blessed silence.

Because the government isn't very good and the New York Cultural Center is being sold and there is so much pornography around, many people are persuaded that these are dark times. I don't yet have a firm opinion, but I've been asking folks.

I went to a bomb scare with Sweet Georgia Brown. At the bomb scare, everybody stood around on the sidewalk looking up at the tall, tall building, figuring out a favorite place for the bomb to be. Mr. Ryan's office, Mr. Kineally's office. Mr. Costelli's office. The police bringing in squads of those big, specially trained, bomb-loving dogs. And I said, "Sweet Georgia Brown, do you think these are dark times?"

And she said, "Well, they sold the cemeteries and they sold the fire-alarm boxes and they sold three-quarters of the College of Municipal Knowledge where I got my degree in Excellent English from, and I *hear* they 'bout to raffle off the World Council of Churches. The Mayor done seen a bright, bright star in the sky that said sell, sell, and a afreet appeared to the Governor out of a burning bush with much the same message. But let's us split this bomb vernissage," she said, "and go ask my wise old daddy, Blind Lightnin' Lemon Howlin' Brown, what is his position. He is the Elder Statesman of Pulling Your Coat to What's What, you dig where I'm comin' from?"

So we left that bomb scare getting itself ready to become a paragraph on the ball-score page of the *News,* and went down into the subway. We walked down the tracks where the sold subway cars used to run, making our way by the light from the manholes where the sold manhole covers used to be.

"Thank God no rats no more," said Sweet Georgia Brown.

"The last one auctioned off in May," I said, "at the Parke-Bernet."

Blind Lightnin' Lemon Howlin' Brown said, "Good morning, dear children. How was the bomb scare?"

"Average," said G. Brown.

"Well, what you been up to?" he asked. "You ain't been out in the park playin' that monkey music, have you?"

"No, Papa," said Sweet Georgia Brown.

"Mister Blind Lightnin' Lemon Howlin', sir," I said, "do you think these are dark times or is all this darkness merely the creation of the media?"

"What's a media?" he said.

"The TB and like that."

"Well, I don't watch the TB so much since they sold off the electricity. I don't find it fruitful," he said, lighting another candle. "But lemme lay this on you: The President's gone save the situation, 'cause he loves and cherishes us and thinks we're just as good as any other Americans, even though we do live in wicked, sinful New York City."

"Naw he don't," said Sweet Georgia Brown.

"He wants us to pull ourselves out of this morass by our own bootstraps," I said.

"All the bootstraps been sold," said Georgia Brown. "Ain't a bootstrap between here and Toronto."

"You a little slippy in the head, chile," said B.L.L.H. "He got to help out. All he have to do is go into his missile-money jar that he keeps his missile money in. And everything's cool, just like that."

"He vetoed the school-lunch bill," said Georgia Brown.

"He just bein' *prudent,*" said her father. "Some of them non-needy chirrun might sneak in there and grab some of that chicken potpie."

"Well, you are my wise old daddy," said Sweet Georgia Brown, "but I think you a little oversanguine in this matter. What the people of this city of dark times gonna do now? What they gonna sell?"

A beautiful and malicious smile illuminated the countenance of Blind Lightnin' Lemon Howlin'. "Why, sweet chile, they gone sell the onliest thing they got left to sell. Votes," he said.

Spring in the Village! Sunlight roaring through new green leaves! On West Twelfth Street, I pause to count the books stacked in Ramsey Clark's big second-floor bay window. Many, many books! Hardcovers, at that. I lose count and begin again, but am distracted by a bulldog the color of steel wool who wanders by with a red plastic poinsettia pinned to his collar. We are not afraid of what people think. I follow the bulldog and his owner to Ray's Pizza, at the corner of Sixth Avenue and West Eleventh. Ray's Pizza is expanding into the space formerly occupied by Casual Kids (which has moved to 2 Bank Street). Young artists from P.S. 41, across the street, have filled the empty Casual Kids window with Magic Marker variations on the theme "Ray's Pizza Is Getting Bigger." And, indeed, one of these works displays a pizza as big as a model railroad, loomed over by a giant pizza freak in a parrot-green coat. Down Sixth Avenue a bit, at Igor's Art Foods restaurant, Igor has filled part of *his* window with "Igor's Book of the Month." Choices for the month include two Irving Howes, the new Bruno Bettelheim, and *Lazy Stories* (for children), by Diane Wolkstein and James Marshall. (Igor democratically refuses to indicate which are alternates and which are full selections.) We are a bookish community.

And, in fact, here is Norman Mailer, strolling! Mailer is wearing a powder-blue safari suit and looking very good, very healthy—struggling with that immense novel must keep him in top shape. What does it feel like to know that your novel must be worth a million dollars, more or less, before you write it? He is a brave man. He walks past an old, old woman dressed in a black rug who is writing something on the wall with a black crayon, screening her operations from passersby with a *News* held aloft in a shaky hand. When she moves on, I read, "Philosophy tells us sex only for procreation." We are a community of writers.

Around the corner, on Greenwich Avenue at Tenth Street, Sutter's bakery has gone out of business after fifty years. Today, the fixtures are being auctioned and there are tables piled with silverware, cups and saucers, sugarers and creamers, stainless-steel pots and pans, and five sets of spun-candy wedding bells in their plastic wrappings. People are staring through the big windows, estimating. At the curb is parked a classic car, British (I can't figure out what make), shiny black, late nineteen-twenties perhaps, on the open rumble seat a book, *Graham Greene on Film.* At the Elephant & Castle, farther down Greenwich, the menu offers a Love Omelette (hearts of artichoke, hearts of palm) for $3.05. Love and grub are important to us, both.

Change, renewal. The three-story brick house at 240 West Eleventh has just been painted a blazing white—what a vote of confidence in this sooty city! The old Your Father's Mustache (beer, banjos), at Tenth Street and Seventh Avenue, has become Settebello (Beautiful Seven), after an Italian card game in which the seven of diamonds is the winning card. The entrepreneur is Alfredo Viazzi, who already operates two of the Village's pleasantest restaurants; the new place will offer cabaret (directed by and starring his wife, the actress Jane White), chamber music, dance, and classic films of the forties and fifties, and will be open from 11:00 A.M. to 2:00 in the morning—a *stufato* (stew) of the arts, no less. Good luck, Settebello, and welcome to the neighborhood!

But spring is not without its new dangers, which we will form new committees to meet (we are forever forming committees). The budgets of the Jefferson Market and Hudson Park Libraries may be cut another 10 percent in July by the city, and an especially strong commando has been mustered (forty-nine members, from Catherine Angle to Marguerite Young) to rush into the breach. Good luck, Friends of the Jefferson Market and Hudson Park Libraries!

I tarry a bit before a bulletin board inside a Perry Street laundromat (we have thousands of bulletin boards, the jungle drums of the Village). Nelson Algren is reading from his work at Greenwich House. A flyer from the International Committee to Reunite the Beatles, headquartered in Merrick, N.Y. Send one dollar to Let

It Be. Has anyone any information about the two men seen scuttling down the street carrying the commemorative plaque honoring pioneer filmmaker D. W. Griffith, pried from the front of 7 East Fourteenth (site of Griffith's early studio) last Friday morning? "Runaway wife sought by female reporter for indepth interview," and a telephone number. We are forever taking each other's temperature.

Meandering down Hudson Street, thinking about lunch, I see in the back seat of a Dodge with Tennessee plates a sleeper who has wrapped himself in Reynolds Wrap to ward off the fine midmorning Village light. I am happy and know myself to be happy—a rare state. Good luck to you, traveler from Tennessee!

Reviews, Comments, and Observations

ACCEPTANCE SPEECH

NATIONAL BOOK AWARD FOR CHILDREN'S LITERATURE

Writing for children, like talking to them, is full of mysteries. I have a child, a six-year-old, and I assure you I approach her with a copy of Mr. Empson's *Seven Types of Ambiguity* held firmly in my right hand. If I ask her which of two types of cereal she prefers for breakfast, I invariably find upon presenting the bowl that I have misread my instructions—that it was the other kind she wanted. In the same way it is quite conceivable to me that I may have written the wrong book—some other book was what was wanted. One does the best one can. I must point out that television has affected the situation enormously. My pictures don't move. What's wrong with them? I went into this with Michael di Capua, my editor at Farrar, Straus & Giroux, who incidently improved the book out of all recognition, and he told me sadly that no, he couldn't make the pictures move. I asked my child once what her mother was doing, at a particular moment, and she replied that mother was "watching a book." The difficulty is to manage a book worth watching. The problem, as I say, is full of mysteries, but mysteries are not to be avoided. Rather they are a locus of hope, they enrich and complicate. That is why we have them. That is perhaps one of the reasons why we have children.

1972

ON "PARAGUAY"

I would be reluctant to say that "Paraguay" is the best of my stories because I hope that there are others that come as close to achieving whatever it is that I'm trying to achieve. But neither do I think it the worst of the eighty-some-odd I've written. A cab driver in Boston last week told me a bit of Georgia folklore, the story of a father coming to the hospital to look for the first time at his newborn son and saying, "That boy's so ugly we gone have to tie pork chops to his face to get the dawg to play with him." I don't feel this way about "Paraguay." Ordinarily I would have used the pork chop story in a story, but since the cab driver was himself a writer, a Yale graduate in English, as it happened, I'm sure he will want to use it in one of his own beautiful works but probably won't mind if I borrow it, temporarily, here.

What I like about "Paraguay" is the misuse of language and the tone. Mixing bits of this and that from various areas of life to make something that did not exist before is an oddly hopeful endeavor. The sentence "Electrolytic jelly exhibiting a capture ratio far in excess of standard is used to fix the animals in place" made me very happy—perhaps in excess of its merit. But there is in the world such a thing as electrolytic jelly; the "capture ratio" comes from the jargon of sound technology; and the animals themselves are a salad of the real and the invented. The flat, almost "dead" tone paradoxically makes possible an almost-lyricism. I think my Paraguay is an almost-beautiful place, and a better writer would probably have lingered longer there, perhaps abided at book length. But I am extremely nervous, and had to hurry on.

Every writer in the country can write a beautiful sentence, or a hundred. What I am interested in is the ugly sentence that is also somehow beautiful. I agree that this is a highly specialized enterprise, akin to the manufacture of merkins, say—but it's what I do. Probably I have missed the point of the literature business entirely. But "Paraguay" is for me a hint of what I would like to do, if I could do it.

1974

A SYMPOSIUM ON FICTION

DONALD BARTHELME, WILLIAM GASS, GRACE PALEY, AND WALKER PERCY

In October 1975 the Glasgow Endowment Committee at Washington and Lee sponsored a two-day Symposium on Contemporary Fiction and invited a group of distinguished American writers to give readings and talks, lead classroom colloquia, and hold an informal, day-long panel discussion. What follows here is a much-abbreviated version of that discussion.

DONALD BARTHELME: I'm only beginning the discussion because yesterday there was a philosophy colloquium at which Mr. Percy and Mr. Gass talked about various issues at insufficient length and I had at that time a 44-part question which I did not get an opportunity to ask and I'll give you a short form of that this morning. The issue yesterday, unless I've misperceived it, was what kind of knowing is peculiar to literature. The question is for Bill Gass and it is "What does a painter know?"; the answer that a painter knows how to make something that is beautiful is not allowable.

WILLIAM GASS: How about "He knows how to paint"? I think that what a painter knows is increasingly the qualities and properties of his medium, the exploration of relationships between certain kinds of qualities, which he lifts out of his medium. What I find painters know is that kind of exploration of the qualitative relational possibilities of color, shape, and all of the things can be constructed with them. If, as I suspect you're suggesting, they might know something else about the world, this frequently happens if they have been observant about the world, but I don't think it's necessary. I would want to suggest that the knowledge an artist really possesses is that he can formulate, at least, and I think knowledge has to be formulated to be called knowledge. It is a kind of skill—the manipulation of a medium and an understanding and responsiveness to it. That's why I think what writers know is language and how to fiddle.

WALKER PERCY: I'd like to continue our disagreement there. I find myself always in sympathy with the esthetics, first of Suzanne Langer and people as different as Maritain and going back originally to Thomas Aquinas, who said, in different ways, that art is a form of knowing. It's a kind of knowledge which is quite different from discursive knowledge and mathematical knowledge. My own feeling is that it's primarily cognitive, whereas emotional transactions may take place in both the creation and reception of a work of art. I think, as Langer said, that what is transmitted primarily is not feelings but the forms of feelings and that involves an act of cognition.

GASS: The problem with saying that art is in some sense a special form of knowing is that in order to make a knowledge claim, a number of conditions have to be met which art rarely does meet, if ever; in order to make a knowledge claim you have to be able to translate it into a number of different ways. It can't be so tied to the form of expression that it's unique to that and secondly, it seems to me that it has to be put in such a way that the kinds of conditions necessary to ascertain whether the claim is true or false are specifiable, and the third is that these conditions then must be in principle possible of execution. What tends to happen is that if you claim, for example, that the poet or the novelist gives us knowledge that can't be got in any other way, then the demand ought to be "What is it, state it," while the answer is of course "it's stated in the book, you can't translate it out" and so on. And the second problem is that if you could state it, it probably wouldn't be in testable form. I'm not demanding a particular kind of test here though I probably would if pushed, but it has to be open to verification of some kind or other and usually this is left to the intuitive response to the work itself. So I feel that in general the claim that art has some particular kind of knowledge peculiar to it ends up being an unverifiable hypothesis put in such a realm where you can't really get at it, and that bothers me a good deal. So my feeling is that if someone says that it's possible to make a knowledge claim, the fist thing I might want done is that claim rephrased. Now of course if I bring my own prejudices to it, I want it rephrased in mathematical language.

PERCY: Of course you imply a definition of knowledge which is positivistic, namely that truth is, must be, testable.

GASS: Yes, not necessarily a positivistic criterion of verification, but some principle of verifiability. Yes.

AUDIENCE: It seems to me that when you say that in order to be verifiable or to establish truth, you want a kind of mathematical testability. Is that right? Some kind of data processing, with procedures of the sort that would provide the testable material in the verification procedure.

GASS: Yes, I think it's true that ultimately the expression of scientific knowledge is done in this way. Not so much to achieve verifiability but to achieve clarity and place your knowledge in the system. I think what's happening is that now scientific development and mathematical development have reached a point where it is simply no longer possible without terrible falsification to try and translate mathematical expressions into material form. The kind of mathematical moves now made are in a sense removed from what we normally call understanding, a verbal understanding. It simply can't be done any more and I think it's going to get more and more that way. As a consequence, of course, we're going to develop a whole group of people whose understanding of the world is so mathematical and our sciences so complex that it won't be possible for the ordinary person to follow them at all. It seems to me this condition has already been achieved, and in that sense the most advanced contemporary science is already past language. It isn't spoken in words any more, and I don't see any halting that process.

AUDIENCE: If language constantly betrays truth, which is what I understand, in one sense, you seem to be saying, why not abandon truth as an ideal?

GASS: Well, I think we ought to abandon truth as an ideal as artists. I think it's pernicious. I think it gets in the way all the time. That sounds sort of odd to some people but actually you'd say that to a mathematician. Mathematicians aren't interested in truth, they're interested in formal coherence. That's how they develop their systems. That's the way poets work, I think.

PERCY: What bothers me is the question the young lady asked you yesterday, that is, why do you write novels? And I'm hard put to imagine what kind of motivation you would have other than the fact that in writing you must be converging on some approximation of the way things are or the way you think things are, either in the realm of ideas or in the realm of the way things are in The Heart of the Heart of the Country or the heart of the heart of the American consciousness. It's hard for me to imagine any novelist not being motivated by some desire to approach some kind of truth or what he thinks to be the truth. If I didn't think that I don't think I'd bother to set pen to paper. I can't imagine what I would be doing if I wasn't doing that.

BARTHELME: I think when you are writing you are inevitably making statements of one kind or another, however much you may strain to avoid doing so, and I do not think that they are statements about beauty or necessarily about writing itself. They are statements about the world. They are not mathematically verifiable statements, but they are statements of some kind. How do you deal with that?

GASS: Well, I don't think they are statements; they *look* like statements. If you say "the center cannot hold, mere anarchy is loosed upon the world" it sounds like you're saying something about the world, and that has the quality of statement you want. Yeats is a great statement poet. The fact that most of the statements he made aren't true, if you were to translate them into intelligible statements, doesn't matter at all. Certainly I wouldn't be suggesting, for example, that literature is about itself or that it uses mathematical means for testing. I'm just thinking of an analogy between the two kinds of things. I don't think it's about anything in that sense. If you reduced what Yeats said to something that could be true, you would say something like: There's a lot of disorder in the world. And then you would wonder why you had bothered to say so. If you detach from the mode of speech what could be reasonably assented to or even reasonably denied, I think you'd get mostly clichés of various sorts and nothing very profound. You might, for example, say it's a kind of feeling people can legitimately have. That's about things. They can have that attitude and this is what, of course, Plato thought poets did. They dealt with beliefs, opinions, and so you might say, it may not be true but a lot of people feel this way about things and that's something true. But that isn't the statement of the poet, that's the statement of the critic who is looking at the opinions and making the connection and saying, yes, lots of people say things like that. There are lots of theosophists in the world. To respond to Walker's question about a story I wrote which is taken to be about, as people frequently to my dismay suppose, an Indiana town, then it's false. It falsifies the real conditions of life in a town I was living in. It wasn't that way at all. The first thing I had to do was to get rid of any intention to be truthful about the place. That would have been exceedingly difficult and would have required all kinds of other operations. What you could say is, yes, something like certain of these things happened in a town like this but that was only part of what happened, not the whole thing, and I frequently get letters that dismay me which say, "You really captured how it was to live in this small town in Utah, in Indiana." That just means they weren't seeing their town fully enough because it isn't the way it was. Again, they are doing something people frequently do, taking the complexities of experienced reality and bringing them down *not* to the complexities of the language which is, I hope, a rival, but to the complexities of something they then lift out of that language, simplify, and then suppose that they have got a picture of their world. I find that dismaying.

BARTHELME: There is another area of reality beside the actual geography and demography of this place in Indiana which is just as real and that is Gass's consciousness of the place and of the people, and that is a legitimate object of knowledge.

GRACE PALEY: I think what you're forgetting, what you're underestimating, are the readers. It's true to write one part of that town but they bring something to it and they hear and they understand and they make that whole town and that's what happens when you write. It's perfectly true I can't say *everything* about my block in the city. I never can, but I can say enough so that anybody who is anywhere out there who lives or who understands or who guesses at it can build up enough of the rest of it and recognize that block, maybe even in a better way than a kind of quantification of events and people and paving stones and rubble and pieces of brick. I think that is art, and I think it's been omitted from a lot of our talking and it is two things, it's the reader and the writer, and that's the whole of the experience.

GASS: You want the creative reader.

PALEY: You got 'em. I mean, he's there.

GASS: I don't want them.

PALEY: Well, it's tough luck for you.

BARTHELME: I have to disagree absolutely about what Bill wants. He does want the creative reader. He could not possibly write in the way he does without positing a highly intelligent and rather wonderful reader, totally docile, whom we all want to go out and drink with. You do posit such a reader, or you could not write the way you do.

GASS: What I mean by this is that I don't want the reader filling in anything behind the language.

PALEY: Right, that's what's wrong with you. You don't leave him enough space to move around.

GASS: Anymore than I would suppose that somebody did a sketch, did a few lines, and left out the rest. You could see the face there but what the viewer then is supposed to do mentally is continue all the lines and fill it in. I think that the principle, ideally, that I would hold to is Valeryan. For example, if you want to write something where you want a particular, it's not in the direct text but it's intimated or suggested—then that suggestion you want the reader, of course, to discern in exactly the correct words. Ideally the suggested meaning has to be in an exactly particular order because at that point the suggested other sentence isn't written down directly. You can't just throw in a number of words any old way. So the implications have to be as completely written out, yes, you've got to get the implications.

BARTHELME: The ultimate case in point being obviously Joyce, who wrote every sentence in three languages and four times and left the reader the least possible space for participation.

PALEY: Yes, but that reader moved in, by God, where there was space, and he always will.

GASS: Oh, yes, it can't be helped.

PALEY: Well, I'm glad.

AUDIENCE: Mr. Gass, I was wondering as you were talking whether Robbe-Grillet would be a kind of ideal of this reduction of space.

GASS: I don't particularly care for the theoretical approach there because I think he's far too old-fashioned. He's content oriented. He's really writing about what he conceives reality to be, and I find that conception rather uninteresting. I think that's my objection to the whole so-called New Wave. But my view is very old-fashioned, of course, it's just the symbolist position, really.

PERCY: I think Robbe-Grillet, like so many of the French, tends to fall victim to theories. He develops theories for fiction, which can be fatal. His theory was to get rid of all the appurtenances of fiction, namely plot, characters, narrative, theme, and so on, and reduce it to geometry. As someone said, the only good novel he ever wrote was a novel called *Jealousy* and that was because he was jealous of his wife at the time.

GASS: He uses (as a number of other writers do, Barth for instance) as a kind of metaphorical constructive principle things borrowed from geometry.

BARTHELME: The effort there is also to get rid of psychologizing the novel, and as with every heroic effort, the French new novelists, so-called, have managed to do this and the effort is considerable. In doing this, it seems to me, they miss much else, they pay far too little attention to language, although many of them write beautifully.

GASS: Yes, I would certainly agree with that. When Borges suggests that all novels are written by one mind, in a sense one writer, one author, I think that raises a similar kind of question that occurs in Kantian aesthetics and also bothered Gertrude Stein later in her life: what does make a masterpiece a masterpiece? What does allow works to transcend cultural and personal limitations and appeal universally? The catch of course with Borges is that he is supposing that all works of literature are written by human beings and that if we understood fundamentally the nature of human beings we'd have a single theory. That it's written, in short, by what Gertrude Stein called the human mind as opposed to human nature, human nature being, of course, what Kant would call the phenomenal self, the self that exists in the experienced world and has particularities of time and place. She finally concluded that it wasn't Gertrude Stein the celebrity, the particular person, that wrote her books, that made them so great, she modestly insisted; rather that they were written by the human mind for the human mind. Now I don't particularly like the characterization "mind" here, but if you follow that kind of reasoning then you do conclude that it is a creation of an object to be appreciated in that abstract sense. I wouldn't want to suggest that the reader isn't allowed any liberty. If one gives birth to a daughter there are certain points at which you can no longer follow her around to make sure she's treated properly. She goes out in the world and gets screwed like everybody else. Well, what your responsibility as an author is is to make that object as perfect as possible. Again, to revert to an analogy with the mathematician: his responsibility is to the total validity and coherence of his system. The scientific enterprise has enormous problems, but they're problems, real ones. They're problems that arise out of real attempts at solutions and the chance to solve them. That's what's so strikingly different about a great many scientific problems as opposed to traditional philosophical ones. Some of the traditional philosophical problems can only be understood as neurotic symptoms. They're not soluble in the ordinary sense, they're not problems, objective problems.

PERCY: I think there are other scientific statements that can be tested by other ways. For instance, the Freudian analysis of dreams. Freud proposes that certain dream symbols stand for certain things, say you dream of a house with a balcony, the house with a balcony stands for a woman. Well, there's no way to quantify this by pointer readings or otherwise, but there is a canon of verifiability in which the dreamer can be told this theory and then he can all of a sudden recognize it. He can say, yes, sure enough, I can verify it by the context of the dream, it makes sense. So that's one kind of verifiability which maybe the positivists would not accept and yet which, I think, maybe most psychiatrists would accept. And I would extend that to fiction because I think the main transaction which takes place in the reception of a work of art, a mysterious work of art, like fiction, is also a kind of verification which takes the form of recognition. I think the main thing that happens and the main source of pleasure in the reader is a sense of recognizing something, something that he knew, but which has been verified to him and affirmed for him by the writer. To me that's quite as respectable a kind of verification as a physicist's pointer reading.

BARTHELME: Harold Rosenberg said, I believe of Jasper Johns, that Johns was dealing with things the mind already knows. That's a nice phrase and I think to the point. What I tend to worry about in this kind of discussion is, what is left to the writer? What can the writer do? If I go up to a reader, grab him firmly by the lapel, look him straight in the eye, and say "Eating people is wrong," well, I've told him something, as we would all agree, but nothing new. I would suggest, on the contrary, that there is a realm of possible knowledge which can be reached by artists, which is not susceptible of mathematical verification but which is true. This is sometimes spoken of as the ineffable. If there is any word I detest in the language, this would be it, but the fact that it exists, the word ineffable, is suspicious in that it suggests that there might be something that is ineffable. And I believe that's the place artists are trying to get to, and I further believe that when they are successful, they reach it; my painter friend, for example, reaches an area somewhere probably between mathematics and religion, in which what may fairly be called truth exists.

GASS: Well, maybe. I began by objecting to describing these ineffabilities as cognitive. I see no ground for that claim. If it's ineffable, silence is the response, not claims about cognition. In a certain sense my argument is a Kantian one: that the aesthetic experience is not mediated by concepts, is not basically cognitive. Therefore, of course, I wouldn't want to make any cognitive claims for it. It's an intellectual operation in lots of ways, but I don't see why one couldn't very well suppose that one's experience of a work of literature was indescribable. In a sense, ineffable, but also not knowable then.

BARTHELME: I'm suggesting, of course, another way of knowing.

GASS: I know, yes. I want to find out what it is that is known and whether I should believe it and on what grounds, and I would be a little reluctant to accept Walker's suggestions because there have been so many assents, people say "That's right!" The angel did appear, et cetera, and I'm not inclined to follow that. For example, in the case of psychoanalysis, I think one has to go a little further, not just the assent of the patient, but also then a carrying out of investigations to see whether or not and to what extent that recognition yields a removal of symptoms, a change in behavior, and so forth, and to that degree one might begin to support the hypothesis, because Freud himself indeed had his patients on occasion assenting to certain interpretations as a screen to hide still others. The only way you could find that out was a continuous process of investigation which led to changing behavior, and I think I'd want to go further in the verification process.

PERCY: When I speak of recognition and verification and cognition in fiction, I'm thinking, say, of passages in certain novels which have given me great pleasure. For example, the passage in James Agee at the beginning of the prologue to *A Death in the Family* in which he describes the quality of life on a summer afternoon in Knoxville and the quality of the consciousness of the boy who's with his father and living and seeing the life and smelling the smells of Knoxville. What I experience is a recognition and a formulation, a concept, if you like, of something which I have been vaguely aware of but which had not been formulated by me by such exquisite symbols and sentences. I cannot describe this transaction in any other way than a cognition, a reception of a formulation from a writer to a reader. I can't think of it as simply a transaction of stimuli, giving pleasure, or a transaction of feelings, or in any other way except as a cognitive process.

AUDIENCE: It seems to me that the panel is made of two halves, what we would call extremely experimental and rather more traditional writers in their attitudes toward the conventions of fiction. I have a sense that Mr. Percy's response to the idea of characterizing a figure in fiction or drawing a character might be quite different from Mr. Gass's attitude. I've had some difficulty in getting into contemporary fiction because I am bound by or brought up on certain conventions. Are there such things as conventions in fiction, say analagous to mathematical formulae, that are so important for verification?

PERCY: I remember when I made an ill-conceived venture into philosophy and wrote an article which I was not prepared to write and Flannery O'Connor, who was alive at the time, read it and sent me one of her laconic postcards in which she said, "Well, Walker, this was pretty good but why don't you go back and make up a story." I think she was saying something very important; fiction is, if nothing else, making up stories, telling a story, and narration is probably an essential ingredient. I don't want to read a piece of fiction if there's not a story involved, and Caroline Gordon is right, I think, when she says that both the reader and the writer, in a sense, have to be five or six years old, and that there has to be a sense of something happening and expecting something to happen, and wanting something to happen.

PALEY: People don't know how much they know. You know how women and men live in this world, by God, or how they don't and how hard it is. You know by now enough about that. Yesterday we heard a story in one of the classes about two small boys on a raft, two medium-sized boys on a raft (I'm very particular), and their kind of risky journey. I thought I didn't know anything about that country at all and that part of it was very interesting to me, strange country and the river and water moccasins and so forth, but then I've written a story about medium-sized boys in a city, about four boys on a subway train which I didn't think of while I was listening to the story, but certainly that experience was very similar. So you really know a lot.

AUDIENCE: To what extent do you think there is a search on the part of the powers that be, by which I mean the literary establishment, book publishers, magazine editors, and so forth, to accept unconventional experimental fiction? Do you think that the publishing powers are interested in unconventional material, or are they interested only in conventional material? Do you think many good writers really have a lot of trouble getting their work published?

PALEY: I think the publishing world has nothing to do with literature and I think that's a fact you have to face immediately. The publishing world is really not interested in literature.

BARTHELME: To say that the publishing world is not interested in literature is to overstate it. They are extremely interested in it, they just don't want to publish it, you see. Publishers are very brave, as brave as the famous diving horses of Atlantic City, but they're increasingly owned by conglomerates, businesses which have nothing to do with publishing and these companies demand a certain profit out of their publishing divisions. They take very few risks and they publish an enormous number of things which look like books, sort of feel like books, but in reality are buckets of peanut butter with a layer of whipped cream on top.

PALEY: That's what I meant.

BARTHELME: Now to turn to the other part of the question: Is there an underground of people who are not being published but who are dynamite experimentalists?

PALEY: I don't know how I can answer that except that it's always hard in the beginning to have your work published and with me it was entirely accidental. There has to be such an underground, if you want to call it that. I also think, though, that people should get together and publish themselves, each other, and that's a lot healthier than the real state of publishing. If in some way writers could really move away from the publishing centers—New York, Boston, San Francisco—then literature in this country would be in a lot better shape.

GASS: I think as a writer you have to forget about the problems of publishing, the distinction between traditional and experimental fiction. I don't like the distinction. I think the real problem is between quality and dreck. There's a lot of experimental stuff, so-called experimental writing that gets a comparatively wide audience and it does so because it isn't any good. Even those writers who are excellent, who do get a wide audience, happen to have the illusory whipped cream there, somehow, they're misread, read for the wrong reasons. Quality has always had a small audience. If you're interested in quality you're underground automatically even if you're published. There's nothing like being published and being totally misread, praised for the wrong reasons, and admired for this and that. There are plenty of outlets. Lots of people are writing and there are lots of magazines and lots of chances to get published. I think the problem for an individual is not so much getting published, though it may be, initially, but all through one's career getting published where you want to or in the way you want to. You might as well forget it. I can't get published, not where I want to. If I wanted to go to certain smaller magazines, that would be fine. I could get published there. There must be at least a million of them. I can probably send a word to each one and they'd print it, maybe.

AUDIENCE: Aren't you demanding too much? You want to be published where you want to be, you want the reader to read you exactly as you want him to read you. Isn't it enough that you are published and that people read you and find pleasure in it?

GASS: Yes, up to a point, but that's the motive one has when one first starts, you know. Your first story, you don't care where it's published. It can be in a urinal, and then after a while, one of the advantages of publishing enough is that you don't have to care about being published so much.

BARTHELME: On the question of enough, I must remind you that there is never enough of anything. On the question of this distinction between conventional and experimental writers, experimental always seems to me to mean that which is not successful. One does not choose to be a "conventional" writer or "experimental" writer. One writes as he or she can. It's not a conscious choice. I agree with Bill that the reason a lot of this material is not being published is because it's no good. There is a large and quite vociferous small magazine culture in the country, and much of what is published in these magazines I cannot recognize as anything I care to describe as literature.

PALEY: I wonder whether you're really also asking another question, apart from publication, a question you have to think about. If you are grown up in the world and have responsibilities and you have a twenty-four-hour day, you just live a certain amount in a day and a certain amount of life in your life. Can you make a living at writing? Which is a very important point, and I would say, along with almost anybody here, I think, you can't. The reason I talked about people getting together and publishing their own work as they may in their own communities was because I think it's very hard for writers not to have anybody to read their work or any kind of community of writing people. And I say this as someone who really shunned writers, stayed away from writers for many, many years. I think young writers need other young writers or other old writers or readers: it's very painful to live for years alone with your own work and then to try to make a virtue of it.

AUDIENCE: Do you find yourself at the mercy of the best-seller list and critics?

BARTHELME: Well, they can't hurt you in any way except in terms of making you cry, for example, or in terms of sales. But what they say doesn't matter at all. I have just published a book and if everybody in the world comes around and says it's a lousy book, Uncle Don, I can't do anything about it; and I still will persist in the idea that that book is a book of some value, otherwise I wouldn't have published it. The further point is that in any week, if you look at the best-seller list, nine books on the list are not going to be in any way books of literary merit. One might be, in a good week.

AUDIENCE: But if the critics put down this one, isn't it going to influence your publisher not to publish the next one?

BARTHELME: I happen to have what I consider one of the few literary houses, Farrar, Straus & Giroux, which, as a matter of fact, publishes three of us here. I think Roger Straus might look at me a little narrowly but he would probably go ahead and publish the next book anyhow.

PERCY: You know the success of selling books is a great mystery to me, that's why I've said nothing about it. One reason I take comfort from my ignorance is that Mr. Alfred Knopf told me once, "I've been publishing books for fifty years and to this day I do not know what makes a book, a good book, sell or fail to sell." So if he doesn't know, God knows I don't know.

AUDIENCE: I'd like to return to what we were talking about before. In the reading Mr. Gass gave Tuesday night from *The Tunnel,* the chapter in *The Tunnel,* I'm trying to understand the way you look at how you write, your understanding of what truth is or isn't. That chapter has, for me, a sort of scientific elegance, if you want to call it that, in the way it was constructed, in the different techniques you used—like repetition of various phrases and descriptions—and I can use all those things for my enjoyment of the chapter itself, but I don't know what Germany is like, I don't know what the character of the teacher is like, I can only deal with what you give me there and I take that as truth for the moment, or the truth of your story for the moment. But is that praising your book for the wrong reason?

GASS: Well, because you said "for the moment," within the text it's got to seem legitimate, I mean it's got to work within the text, but if you said, I didn't know what Germany is like but now I do know, I would be very upset. I haven't the vaguest idea what Germany is like and so I wouldn't want you to suppose that I was informing the reader about Germany, because if that were the case I would be misinforming the reader. Within a particular construction that you're making, you want things, of course, to seem genuine, so that people are willing to follow and regard what's going on as a real thing inside the scheme. That's what you hope for, otherwise you're not going to carry any weight at all.

PALEY: But you picked Germany for a reason. Why didn't you say Luxembourg or Italy or something?

GASS: Oh well, yes. You have certain kinds of problems. But one of the kinds of things that interests me as a problem, in fact this may have been a debate some years ago, was the matter of the moral relationship to literature. The question was whether you could write a good, aesthetically good, anti-Semitic book. That's a nice problem. Now I want to create a character who is going to be, among other things, basically anti-Semitic and a lot of other bad things, and I want to get the reader to accept that. That's a problem, an abstract problem. It's a problem to see whether it can be done. It's a problem to write about a particular thing that happens in the world that is so powerful and overwhelming that the difficulty is itself in using the material, coming close to the material. So one of the first things, of course, you have to do, would be a kind of apocalyptic event, say the murder of the Jews. Very hard to write about that. So it's a problem. How can you do it? That's what moves me. If I thought, for example, that I was going to expose the Fascist character, then I would certainly be presumptuous. I don't know anything about that. What the chapter's about is rhetoric. If someone were to say to me, do you know anything about rhetoric, I would confidently say I know a hell of a lot about rhetoric. I'm a rhetorician, I know a lot about rhetoric. About Germany? People may know about Germany. I've read books about Germany, sure. But if you saw any knowledge being displayed in the chapter, it would be my knowledge of rhetorical forms, devices, techniques.

AUDIENCE: Then that's the truth of the chapter?

GASS: It's not the truth, it's just whether you make it work well. It's like being a carpenter, you know how to put a table together well or you don't. When you put it together that indicates you know something about how to put tables together. On the other hand, a table doesn't exist exactly just to tell people how to put tables together. So I'm not writing in order to inform people how to monkey with rhetorical structures.

PALEY: I can't say that I'm presenting a truth when I write. I'm trying to understand something which I don't understand to begin with. I begin by not understanding, and the tension and the excitement for me and the tension that the reader may get also is in that not understanding and that pull away from not knowing to knowing. So I got very interested in this way of trying to understand what happened in Germany, although that's not what you're interested in. You're interested only in rhetoric, maybe, but you're interested in that move from rhetoric to extreme action, to the destruction of the people. It's interesting, just there by itself. And also, I think you know more than you say you know about Germans, Fascism, and so forth. Also I think that what happens is the reader will come in to your book, and he isn't a total dummy. That reader has been alive and has been reading the papers and books, or they're as old as me, they've lived through that whole period and they know a good deal about it. The whole business is joined and more knowledge occurs in your work, or more truth, if you want to put it that way, than you know, or than you planned, or than you even wished.

GASS: Well, of course, there's a certain ironic possibility. If you're concerned for example, as I am, with the way people are bamboozled with language and you bamboozle them, you prove something.

PALEY: I don't believe that at all. I don't think people are completely bamboozled. I think if that's what you're going to do, that book is not going to work.

GASS: This is the old technique of the Marquis de Sade, you know. What he said was in effect, people are sexually stirred by a lot of things they deny, so I will write a philosophical work to prove this by putting in scenes and when the erection occurs, you know he's made his proof and that's in a sense a certain kind of proof. You prove, for example, the power of a rhetorical scheme by moving an audience with it. You do this in class all the time. Anybody who's doing philosophy has constantly to work with illegitimate, invalid arguments which you quickly discover are much more persuasive than good ones and part of the exercise is to persuade people with arguments that are rotten.

BARTHELME: A member of the audience has raised a question by quoting a statement of George Steiner's. The statement is as follows: "A good deal of what is representative in modern literature from Kafka to Pinter seems to work deliberately at the edge of quietness. It puts forward tentative or failed speech moves expressive of the intimation that the large, more worthwhile statements cannot, ought not be made." Then Steiner quotes an entry from Ionesco's diary: "If through becoming involved in literature, I have used up all possible symbols without really penetrating their meaning, they no longer have any vital significance for me. Words have killed images or are concealing them. A civilization of words is a civilization distraught. Words create confusion. Words are not The Word. The fact is that words say nothing, if I may put it that way. There are no words for the deepest experience. The more I try to explain myself, the less I understand myself. Of course, not everything is unsayable in words, only the living truth." Anybody care to respond to that?

PERCY: I think Steiner expresses something metaphorically and poetically and rather mysteriously, which I think can be said much more simply. It's the simple fact that words get worn out, and instead of conveying meaning they act either as simulacra to conceal meaning or as if they were transparencies with no meaning, which I think brings up the question of the vocation of the creative writer, the novelist, or maybe particularly the poet; I think it's his job to create new language by way of metaphor, which is the way new language is created, avoiding the worn-out words and using fresh words, fresh metaphors. And I think a cultural thing is involved here. I think there are periods when the language does wear out; something happens and there's an explosion of new language such as happened in Elizabethan times; a real explosion of metaphor and new meanings and the language is almost literally created afresh. I think there are two things involved: there's a cultural decline and a cultural refreshment, and it is the vocation of the artist, the fiction writer, the playwright, and the poet, to create new language.

PALEY: I would go a little further and say that being Americans and living in the United States we really have a much better opportunity to do that than people in other countries. This language of ours, here in this country, is always being refreshed and scrambled up and knocked around. It's always coming up from the bottom, again and again, and I don't think that's a problem in a sense. It's just an event.

BARTHELME: I tend to see it not as a problem but as an opportunity. We were talking here earlier about experimentalism and one of the funny things about experimentalism in regard to language is that most of it has not been done yet. Take *mothball* and *vagina* and put them together and see if they mean anything together; maybe you're not happy with the combination and you throw that on the floor and pick up the next two and so on. There's a lot of basic research which hasn't been done because of the enormous resources of the language and the enormous number of resonances from the past which have precluded this way of investigating language. I wrote a story once called "Bone Bubbles" which did just this—put together unlike things—and everyone who has ever read it has loathed it. The editor of the book in which it appears didn't want it in there. I insisted that it should be in there. I am still interested in that story and intend to work more on this rather simple-minded principle of putting together more or less random phrases—but not so random as all that. This particular piece—which is only about eight pages long—was not easily written, was not whacked out, it was rewritten and rewritten and rewritten, and in one sense it still is as nonsensical at the end of this rather arduous process as it was in the beginning except that to me it seemed right. The writer in the twentieth century who went farthest in this direction is of course Gertrude Stein, for perhaps other motives, but it's part of her enterprise—she's a greatly misunderstood writer, and that's where I would locate experimentalism.

GASS: I agree with you entirely, and indeed—mothballs-vagina, I thought only too true, besides being very good. With regard to what Steiner says—the study of language has been very intense in our time. The study reveals more and more problems: people feeling hemmed in by language, their views about the world being linguistically oriented. There's a great deal of skepticism emerging out of the study of language, just as in the eighteenth century a great deal of skepticism about the power of reason emerged from a close scrutiny of it. That's one kind of problem. The other kind of problem has to do with the general cultural changes. It has become increasingly difficult for people to think they could make large general statements, and I don't think this is necessarily the fault of a weakening language. The feeling is now that large statements cannot any longer be sensibly made. Now I think that those two subjects Steiner tends to mix up, though both kinds of things have happened. The people he cites are very treacherous in this respect. It's true that Beckett uses silence, for example, a great deal. He uses inarticulate speech gestures a great deal, but the only thing that keeps his characters alive is the flow of language. Not a flow of experience but a flow of words. So what's really happened, and it's something I certainly welcome, is that language is seen in all its deceptiveness in making statements about the world. Language is seen to be itself the symbolic response to experience (not just the English language or some other particular language), and it's more powerful as an experience of things than the experience of things. Signs are more potent experiences than anything else, so when one is dealing with the things that really count, then you deal with words. They have a reality far exceeding the things they name and so I certainly don't agree very much with Steiner's suggestion that we'll have to fall silent, because the very experience of symbols is now the important experience. When we think about our own life, it's surrounded by symbols. That's what we experience day and night. In conversation, on the radio, the television, in newspapers, the main things that we respond to much of the time we are awake are these symbols and not the pretty leaf on the tree or the daffodil on the hill. In the old days we might have supposed that the daffodil was much, much more interesting than the word daffodil, but I simply would deny that. The word daffodil is much more interesting than daffodils. There's much more to it.

PERCY: I've always been interested in metaphor and the extreme potency of metaphor as a creator of meaning, and along the line of what you were saying when you oppose very different nouns, you get all kinds of reverberations of meaning between the two that generates a new kind of meaning which sheds light on both terms. I come from Mississippi and the black people in Mississippi are very inventive about language. They often mistake the correct word and use another word which is close to it but not the same, and always better. For instance, we used to have coin record players made by the Seeburg Corp. and black people call them "seabirds." I always thought seabird was a tremendous name for a coin record player. Now don't ask me why, except some sort of interaction of meaning takes place between the noun seabird and this object, the coin record player, which I think enhances the meaning on both sides. And I remember another example: I was hunting a long time ago with my father in south Alabama and saw a beautiful bird. I had never seen anything like it. It flew very fast and it suddenly folded its wings and fell like a stone into the woods. So I asked the Negro boy what it was and he said "That's a blue dollar hawk," which I thought was an entrancing name so I was aware of my mind trying to put the two together. How is this bird a blue dollar hawk? This is the name of the bird and all sorts of meanings came up, so I asked him why was it a blue dollar hawk. He said something like "Well, it's the way he balls himself up and rolls when he balls," and so it helped me perceive and formulate in my own mind the motion of the bird, but what happened later was that I asked my father if the guide was right and he said, No, he got it all wrong. He made a mistake. It was a blue darter hawk. The correct name was accurate and it described what the bird did and what he looked like. He was blue and he did dart, and yet the correct name was much less revelatory of meaning than the guide's metaphor. The opposition of these two opposites generated much more meaning for me than the so-called correct term for the bird, which I think has something to do with the way metaphor acts, whether it's deliberate or done by mistake. I think that's the way language renews itself.

BARTHELME: In terms of large statements which Bill suggests are increasingly difficult to make, I have only heard one in the last ten years that I thought was any good, a large statement about life, and this comes from my friend Maurice Nathanson who's a philosopher and he was quoting a Hasidic scholar, and the statement is as follows: "It is forbidden to grow old."

PALEY: As we've been talking I've really been thinking about what it means for writers not to make large statements or to make large statements. We haven't liked to say we like to make truthful statements since Bill has scared us on that a little bit and it may open up further discussion about it. But I think I look at this stuff a little more politically maybe, and it seems to me that large statements are made and we don't notice they're being made. There's a large statement being made right around the corner from you and you don't know it.

AUDIENCE: Can we imagine a writer now, whom we respect, who isn't an ironist? I think it's really hard to think of a writer who is straight, who is direct. Doesn't this have something to do with the fear of large statements and fear of worn-out language?

GASS: Yes, it's a connected thing. I'm not sure that I would want to be called an ironist, though. I suppose I'm one of the few writers still trying not to write funny. I'm interested in tragedy, which is really old-fashioned.

PALEY: Well, all humorists are.

AUDIENCE: Isn't there a suggestive analogy between contemporary writing and contemporary modes of painting? Is that something you could explore? I mean abstract expressionism in painting and in literature.

BARTHELME: I've been told by a neurologist that writing comes from the left brain in right-handed people and painting from the right brain, so I'm glad our brains may be getting together. I think there is an analogy. I have said this too many times to make it interesting even to myself, but the principle of collage is one of the central principles of art in this century and it seems also to me to be one of the central principles of literature. *Finnegans Wake* and *Ulysses* are obviously the chief cases in point, Joyce is the great collagist, literary collagist, of the century.

GASS: I think not only his methods of composition, which resemble certain techniques in painting, but a theoretical retreat from the world, in Ortega's famous examples, a retreat from natural objects is also present: spatial forms, as opposed to temporal, the traditional temporal or linear composition. Again Joyce is a famous example and *Finnegans Wake* is probably as obvious a case as any, connected in part with the phenomenon of the book itself and the increased stress upon the fact that you're composing, as Joyce does, with the idea that you haven't really got a temporal object except in the immediate presentation. The notion that you read straight through a book in the ordinary sense of hearing a piece of music played straight through, where you have no interruption, is simply no longer the case at all. Contemporary literature is filled with concepts of spatial form. Partly this is a discovery too, or the increasing belief that what the writer works with are words, in the sense that they descend into flesh, into sound and shape and that in the West we have neglected shape for sound for a long time because of the linear tendency. But the basic material of the writer is concept. The concepts are neither spatial nor temporal. The reversion, therefore, to a spatial form is not necessarily commitment to space, but a disinclination to be committed to time, a movement in the direction of neither one nor the other.

AUDIENCE: You say the basic material of the writer is a concept? Rather than the word?

GASS: Yes. The word, of course, is essential. But the fact is that he is really working with words, and I prefer that because it stresses the fact that you're working with given units and whether you want them read as word after word, you're working with that and you're working also with things that have sound and have physical space. But increasingly one begins to suspect that those things are first of all arbitrary with respect to their sense, and that what they're really carrying is conceptual. If you put together a nonreferential use of language, that is, denotative, instead of thinking, let's say, of the word *ashtray* as denoting this particular ashtray, you indicate primarily the concept-idea ashtray. Concepts, of course, are not spatial or temporal, and if you start switching and insisting on spatial form, it doesn't follow necessarily that you've decided simply to do calligraphy rather than music. But behind that and connected to it, but arbitrarily, probably, is a series of concepts. There's also, of course, the referential one which I've been trying to beat down all day. The medium of poetry and fiction is fundamentally, not entirely, but fundamentally concepts.

BARTHELME: We do have one immense advantage over our dearly loved colleagues, the painters. Painting is normally an object on a wall, and you go up to it and look at it and you don't look at it for very long; whereas we, if we are successful, get somebody and hold on to him for a certain length of time. This is not to say that the painting might not deserve the same amount of contemplation, it just usually doesn't get it. The great example of this is the Guggenheim Museum which is, as Harold Rosenberg described it, "a machine for not having seen paintings." He says nobody contemplates a painting anymore and I think he's right. So at least we have something going for us in that direction.

AUDIENCE: How much of this emphasis on shape can be attributed to the influence of the film on contemporary fiction?

GASS: It depends on which comes first, whether collage influences montage or the reverse. Certainly films have a lot of influence on all sorts of writers. Since it's had no influence on me it's hard for me to figure out when it appears in other people, whether it came from some other direction, but I'm sure that it has had great influence on French writers. That's partly involved too with Steiner's remarks. We've committed to the word, it's our business and we're not likely to say it's a sinking ship. But for audiences it very possibly is, and it would be perfectly natural if writers began to try to borrow from the areas that matter, and of course novels don't matter now, movies do.

BARTHELME: I think films have been very helpful in that they've taken over an immense amount of territory, they've forced us to think about what we've been doing very much harder than we might ordinarily have done. It's the exact same situation as with the invention of the still photograph, which revolutionized painting, and forced the painters to do something other than literally render landscapes or nudes or whatever. Painters didn't have to do that anymore because you could take a picture of something and it was, if fidelity is a criterion, probably going to be better at one level of truth. Therefore, the painters had to go out and reinvent painting because of the invention of photography and I think films have done something of the sort for us.

AUDIENCE: What about the new journalism? Has that influenced fiction?

BARTHELME: Should I tell the story of how Tom Wolfe killed my tree? I sublet my apartment one year to Tom Wolfe and had a very flourishing tree out in front and when I came back the tree was dead and the story was that Tom had been looking out of the window a lot.

PERCY: I don't like it.

BARTHELME: Could you tell us, Mr. Percy, why you don't like it?

PERCY: Well, it's journalism, bad journalism.

PALEY: I think one of the things about Don's work is that he is a kind of a cross between a poet and a journalist, I mean in his work and not in his job experience. But the new journalism—I think it's just an invention of publishing and the media. That kind of prose writing always existed, more or less, and it just got itself a fancy name and a way of publicizing itself. I don't see any difference between that and what went on when I was a girl.

GASS: You get a kind of interaction, frequently, between media, but the "New Journalism" isn't like that at all, really. I think its just a fancy name to excuse self-indulgence. It is neither journalism nor fiction.

BARTHELME: I have to disagree there. It is sloppy and I am not fond of it either, but what it is is a reaction to the old idea about journalism that the writer has to be objective and keep himself out of his story. Now he's urged, it's even demanded of him that he put himself in the forefront of whatever story he's working on. That is what's technically going on.

PALEY: With as much malice as possible.

BARTHELME: Yes, that's right. The writer's personality becomes a very important factor in the writing and so you get stuff that most of us don't like a lot.

GASS: Yes, so partly it's still the same old thing, only instead of looking, as the journalist used to say, at the burning building he's looking at himself looking at the burning building, but it's still this notion that he's got to take a hard look at himself looking at the burning building, so that he's objective about himself while being sloppy about what he's seeing, which I think is a contradiction. You can't do that.

BARTHELME: I would like to ask Grace Paley a question, which is, what do you want to say about storytelling?

PALEY: We were talking about this before and I said I would like to answer the question about storytelling. When you talk about new forms or different forms, it seems to me this non-linearity has really run its course, played its game out. I understand it, it has been my way of working too. I haven't moved dead ahead except once in a while in that sense, and I wonder about our need for storytelling in its most simple linear sense of *what happened then, and then what happened, and what came next.* I wonder to what extent that isn't going to make a very vigorous comeback and if it isn't necessary. I think a lot of it has to do with speaking aloud and with the word as a said thing, not as a written word but as a spoken word. I am simply interested in it, you have to come at things not knowing. I come at that too, in a sense, not knowing, and yet understanding that I probably know more than I think. I've heard lots of stories and I've told lots of stories, and it seems to me a very honorable business to be a storyteller and to tell stories to people. Just as language rises again and again from new voices, from black people, as Walker said, and in my own world, from foreigners of all kinds. So do new forms come or old forms turn round on that wheel, come again and again as new people tell stories. I think particularly at this point of women. I might say that this is the first place that I've been in for five years where women haven't been mentioned until this moment, and I'm nervous about it. Different people, new people are telling stories, and women haven't told stories yet, not really. I think of myself as a woman who has been a writer and who has been in a tradition which is largely male.

PERCY: I agree with you, Grace, and I'm ashamed to say that I require of other writers what I do not require of myself, namely, that I want to be told a story and I think a narrative tension is necessary, that it's good to want to know what is going to happen next. Yet when I write I find myself drifting off into what I consider beautiful descriptions, long things about clouds, and character studies, which I wouldn't tolerate in anybody else, but that's a matter of self-indulgence.

BARTHELME: Walker has a passage in, I think, *The Moviegoer,* where a bird flies nearby and Walker says the bird came so close that you could hear the gristle in his wings creak. One of the most beautiful descriptions of anything I've ever read from anybody.

AUDIENCE: I remember having grandparents tell these stories, but I think the storytelling tradition is dead.

PALEY: I don't think it's a dead art form at all. I think that women do tell lots of stories and I think they're probably among the last of a great oral tradition, and it's called gossip. When men do it it's telling stories and when women do it it's gossip. Except that men don't tell stories anymore, they talk shop. But I think that's where it's going to come from, the great oral tradition that women have of handing down stories from grandmother to granddaughter and speaking together wherever they are.

We all live in a society in which everybody says the word *alienated* (that's only the second time I've used that word in my life, by the way, and I feel sheepish about it) but people do live alone and are competitive from a very early age, brothers and sisters are, and it's supposed to be natural but I think that's bunk. What happens to them is that they're supposed to fulfill themselves and develop themselves and not one of us, really, can really labor to refine and cultivate and develop ourselves, our single self, without being hurtful to others. This kind of life is extremely painful to people. I think it hurts everybody that this is how they were brought up. Every person here feels a little sick about it and I think that people (even if you don't know it) really are moving now more and more toward real experiments with different ways of life and many of them I can't imagine because I don't have a very good imagination. But I think that storytelling and people telling stories to other people and the experience of paying attention and listening in some way relate to that former loss of a community.

BARTHELME: Doesn't a book create a community, not the kind you're talking about, but doesn't the fact that I've read Marquez and you've read Marquez and most of the people here have read Marquez, create a community of Marquez readers? I know you're not trying to get rid of the book because you'd never do such a thing. I trust you. You're not trying to get the tribal storyteller back, or are you?

PALEY: I'm not against him. I wouldn't get rid of the book, just because I love it and I do love literature. But I think that the community we have had in all having read Marquez is very nice if we all get together, really, and talk about him and talk about the book and deal with that.

GASS: A similar kind of thing happens when you start with a record and music. What was once almost inevitably a public experience, in the sense that people had to congregate to have it is increasingly now no longer necessary, and everybody can go home with his own Bach and play it in his own room and thus it becomes a private kind of experience, and increasingly as one composes directly to tape, you can bypass the performer altogether and go straight to your lonely listener and that will have a similar kind of effect of dissolving the musical community. And you now find that replaced by a different kind of musical community increasingly, that is to say the record fanciers. Now I think one of the consequences of this kind of development is the fact that because of records the quality of hearing has gone up enormously. There are two different things involved: there's the recreation of aurality and the emphasis on oral reading which one has to do when one is reading alone. If you don't read Henry James by hearing every sentence go, you're missing Henry James, it seems to me. It's a long performance and somewhat tiring for the internal vocal chords but it's got to be sung and if it isn't sung and if it doesn't sing it isn't worth anything. But this doesn't have to be done in a group. So there are two ways in the oral tradition: one is to bring people together in a group with a performance and the other is an orality that needn't take place that way.

AUDIENCE: I remember when I was in high school, my sister and I one summer read *Return of the Native* and *Mayor of Casterbridge* aloud to each other. But could you conceive of my sister and me reading *Gravity's Rainbow* aloud to each other?

BARTHELME: I know a married couple who live across the street from me who do read difficult modern works aloud to each other. Grace and her husband.

PALEY: Yes, we read aloud all the time and certainly I think Henry James is much improved by being read three, four pages at a time aloud. In fact, he becomes quite bearable to me that way. I want to agree with Bill for once that when I talk about telling stories I assume that the language is beautiful and I don't care who tells the story. I don't mean it has to be a fantastic writer. It can be my aunt or someone like that who doesn't like to write at all and doesn't. But storytelling has more to it than that narrative drive. It does have that, but it ought to speak beautifully. I would not be interested in a writer that I couldn't read aloud. But the real point that I wanted to make is this: I consider that as a writer I have several obligations and one of them is to write as damn well as I can. I take that very seriously and responsibly and write as truthfully as I can, as well, and I do really feel responsible for the future of literature. So that I'm saying a funny kind of thing. The moral word is "ought to be" which people don't like to use too much these days. Something ought to be. What ought to be? People ought to live in mutual aid and concern, listening to one another's stories. That's what they ought to do. I'm not doing that, I'm very much a person in my time, but I'm saying that that's the next thing that interests me. The next thing that interests me is the last thing to have interested anyone. I want to find out a way. Is there a way for people to tell stories to one another again and to bring one another into that kind of speaking and listening and attending community?

Published 1986

MR. HUNT'S WOOLY UTOPIA

A REVIEW OF *ALPACA* BY H. L. HUNT

One of the disadvantages of being the richest man in the country (or the second or fourth) must be a profound sense of political frustration. No matter how many billions you command, you are given under the Constitution only one vote. The insult is personal; in the voting booth, you are brought at a stroke to the level of the poorest citizen. Worse, you must abide by decisions which are not your personal choices. In his Utopian romance *Alpaca,* H. L. Hunt of Dallas sets out to correct this gross equity.

As a novelist Mr. Hunt quickly brushes aside a mildly hilarious love story ("You have my devotion, but I must tell you that I love my country more") to get down to business: the establishment of a perfect state where the number of votes a man has bears some reasonable resemblance to his financial status. In the process of drafting a constitution for Alpaca, a tiny, vaguely South American republic, he has tidied up some other loose ends that have been worrying him, such as curbing the power of the unions, getting the citizens off the dole, abolishing confiscatory taxes, and generally cleaning up the mess in which old-style voters have chosen to leave things. It is hard going, for Mr. Hunt's prose combines the virtues of Anthony Hope and Michael Arlen; but it is an earnest effort, and very much in the public interest. With General Bullmoose, the author believes that "what is good for the possessor of the greatest wealth in the Nation is good for the poorest citizen or the citizen in any degree of prosperity between these extremes."

His hero is a young man named Juan Achala, handsomely

endowed with "flashing eyes beneath shapely brows" and "an innate persuasiveness and power." Like the hero of the conventional quest novel, Juan journeys through the world in search of wisdom; unlike characters in more complex works, he finds exactly what he is looking for. Surrounding himself with a quorum of the leading thinkers of his day, he forms a Plan Team. The product of their joint ratiocination is the Alpaca constitution.

With this instrument Mr. Hunt is revenged upon our Founding Fathers, for whom he nevertheless professes the greatest admiration in a special chapter on the U.S. Constitution, which is offered side by side with his own, presumably for purposes of comparison. Its most revolutionary provision is a system of graduated suffrage. Citizens of Alpaca who are eighteen through twenty-one and sixty-six or older get one vote; citizens twenty-two through sixty-five get two. Bonus votes are added based upon the amount of taxes paid, or the citizen's "contribution to the Nation." Those who are among the top 10 percent of all taxpayers get seven additional votes; those among the top 20 percent, six additional votes; and so on down to the top 60 percent, who get one additional vote. There are also bonus votes for waiving retirement payments, government salary, and government per diem, and for paying a voluntary poll tax. "Exhaustive discussion by the Plan Team led them to the conclusion that the graduated voting system offered the best hope of preventing 'share-the-wealth' and treasury handout excesses which are only too often the end result of 'voting by head' suffrage." Mr. Hunt warns darkly that such measures have "frequently forced the responsible property holders to turn in despair to a dictator or some other desperate expedient in the hope of warding off national ruin."

The "voting power" of a taxpayer is figured with close attention to such matters as his pro rata share of the taxes paid by companies in which he owns stock. The rationale of this system, according to the Plan Team, is unimpeachable: "In efficiently operated corporations the largest stockholder naturally has the greatest voting power." But the heavy taxpayer is not merely the biggest voter; he is also the best. "It was also pointed out that while the big taxpayers could not be expected to see eye-to-eye and vote together, those who paid little or no taxes could be expected to vote alike and constitute what is often known as a 'bloc' vote." Furthermore, "the recognition that he has a direct stake in the government and its spendings gives him [the large taxpayer] an alertness and caution in the exercise of his citizenship which is seldom found in the non-taxpayer or the very small taxpayer."

This alertness and caution are admirably present in some of the other provisions of the plan. The taxing powers of the Alpacan government are severely restricted, "to prevent confiscation." Income tax cannot exceed 25 percent, property taxes 1.25 percent, the inheritance tax 24 percent. For labor, there are several attractive clauses. The "sacred right to work" is zealously safeguarded; unemployment insurance is forbidden, as is "a guaranteed wage for a future period of time." Aliens, who have a tendency to "consort with intellectuals to build and join subtle organizations . . . for the overthrow of their host governments," are severely scrutinized, and are not admitted unless they are wholly self-supporting. And "the government shall conduct its affairs so as to compete as little as possible with private industry."

In Alpaca, under the new constitution, public issues are fearlessly debated by chosen representatives of the two major political philosophies, the Liberals and the Constructives. For this only the printed word is permitted; discussion via radio and television or "before more than 200 persons" is outlawed as inflammatory. The plan is presented to the people, and after a debate carried on "without hysteria." Alpaca accepts the inevitable. Here Mr. Hunt himself enters a disclaimer: the Alpaca Plan, he says, is peculiarly fitted to small, compact countries, and might not work so well elsewhere.

The novel proper ends in a burst of exclamation points. "Alpacans wanted to be compelled to do the just, honorable and right thing, and they wanted desperately that others be required to do the same. Then there would be Peace! It was as simple as that!"

What is remarkable about the book is Mr. Hunt's modesty. Why should he be content with a mere ten or twelve extra votes when he could, by adjusting the scale, have hundreds? It may be that political power is not what touches him most. Perhaps he is only interested in re-establishing the view, somewhat tarnished in recent times, that money is something more than bonds and banknotes—it is manna, a mark of wisdom, and a sign of grace.

1960

THE TIRED TERROR OF GRAHAM GREENE

A REVIEW OF *THE COMEDIANS* BY GRAHAM GREENE

"Mounting suspense," the jacket says, but in fact there is no suspense, not a whisper of it, only a long, disintegrating slide to a puffy resolution, an extended demonstration of exhaustion. The exhaustion is Mr. Greene's; after nine novels, seven "entertainments," three plays, and six assorted other works, this is a ghostly self-parody, placing in question all that has gone before.

Haiti and the terror of which Dr. Duvalier is the proud proprietor supply the background, and there is voodoo, murder, adultery, Tontons Macoute (the regime's bogeymen in dark glasses), insurrection, imposture, treachery. The promise is of a novel as exciting as an "entertainment," but also "serious," significant, not an entertainment at all but a large, important book with a religious, even a philosophical dimension. No. It is an entertainment, and not a very good one.

The chief actor is Brown, a dull, remote half-Englishman and the owner of a Port-au-Prince tourist hotel left him by his flamboyant mother. The girl is Martha, daughter of a German hanged for war crimes, married to a South American diplomat who doesn't seem to care whether she sleeps with Brown or does not sleep with Brown. There is a Major Jones, a shabby, shady British con artist who proposes himself as an expert in guerrilla warfare, a Clausewitz of the small-group action, first to Dr. Duvalier's henchmen, then to the pathetic revolutionary movement. A couple of eminent American vegetarians enter, muck about for a bit having their innocence shattered, then depart. When Jones switches allegiance, Brown helps him make a getaway to the hills. A good Haitian doctor, a communist, opposes the regime and is murdered. Brown loses his hotel and takes up the mortuary business in Santo Domingo. The love affair between Brown and Martha, surely the most pallid in recent literary history, fizzles out. Everyone is tired, tired, tired, including the villains. Not even the forces of evil put up a good show.

It may be that the confusion of genres has always been ruinous for Greene in a way that now becomes obvious. The apparatus of the thriller, employed in his serious works, may always have been an adulteration of their seriousness. In the earlier books, that miasma of meanness, drabness, and distemper hanging over the territory the critics call Greeneland has served to validate the work, to stand for its genuineness. Here the Greene atmosphere merely seems a trademark, like the "Klein blue" of the painter Yves Klein, a color he slathered over everything, or the holes in a Henry Moore, without which you don't have a Henry Moore. The feeling of terror Mr. Greene could once produce from these materials has leaked away. We are left with the manner.

The writers Mr. Greene most admires are probably Conrad and Henry James, and in his earlier books, aspects of Conrad and James, of *The Secret Agent* and *The Princess Casamassima,* work quite successfully for him. In *Brighton Rock* (1938) and *The Power and the Glory* (1940), the plots made of violence and hysteria seemed a satisfying artistic equivalent for the terror abroad in the larger world. Now, however, they have begun to pall, not because the world is any less violent and dangerous, but because Mr. Greene has apparently had no new ideas about it: Is there really nothing more to say than this? The fatigue and despair evident in both *A Burnt-Out Case* and *The Comedians* seem something the writer brought to the work rather than an artist's response to the world. And by clinging to the form, he throws into sharp relief the inadequacies of the present effort vis-à-vis its predecessors.

The writing is poor. On the first page Mr. Greene is speaking about London monuments. ". . . who cares for dead politicians sufficiently to remember with what issues they were identified? Free Trade is less interesting than an Ashanti war, though the London pigeons do not distinguish between the two." Cosmic irony? On the same page: "There is a point of no return unremarked at the time in most lives." Villains depart "laughing hollowly in an attempt to heal their wounded pride." Martha, apparently unable to resist, tells the narrator, "It's a dark Brown world you live in," and the narrator himself is given to such musing as "Death is a proof of sincerity."

Pseudoprofundities struggle with worldly wisdom of a Somerset Maugham-ish sort: "Like some wines our love could neither mature nor travel." The notion that the uncommitted are comedians, playing a part, is unsubtly introduced: ". . . if one can describe as serious the confused comedy of our private lives" and "Life was a comedy, not the tragedy for which I had been prepared." These crudities argue exhaustion at the deepest level, at the level of feeling.

The movement of the plot is hardly more encouraging. The love-making between Brown and Martha takes place, most often, in a Peugeot (Brown owns a motel, remember), and is, for plain joylessness, remarkable. "The back of her neck was against my mouth and one leg spread-eagled across the radio." "We'll get in the back of the car. It will be all right there." "She had drawn up her knees and I was reminded of Dr. Philipot's body under the diving board." ". . . a year later she changed her Peugeot for a newer model." "Sometimes I wonder whether it was not the happiest moment we ever knew together." (They had been discussing her hanged parent.) The net effect is to thrust one into a sort of mad optimism, a state in which one goes running through the streets shouting, "A merry heart maketh a cheerful countenance!" and, "A merry heart doeth good like a medicine!"

The maneuverings of Jones, on which the action turns, are barely sketched. We encounter him first on a Dutch cargo steamer headed for Port-au-Prince, a vessel on which Brown is also a passenger. The captain receives a cable: watch Jones, it says, and we shrewdly surmise that there is something sticky about Jones. And indeed, the next time we meet him he is in jail, beaten up but conducting some sort of negotiations with his tormentors, and shortly after this he is installed as an honored guest of the regime, planning unspecified dirty work for Dr. Duvalier. But abruptly, the regime discovers that Jones is a charlatan, and he takes refuge in an embassy, the very embassy presided over by Martha's husband. Brown, jealous of Jones (the Brown-Jones business is a minor stylistic annoyance, and the eminent American vegetarian is, of course, Smith), decides to get him out of the embassy by putting him in touch with the revolutionaries. These latter see Jones as a heroic figure, a potential leader, and Jones, who cannot bear to have his disguise peeled away, dies in a rear-guard action, thus becoming the hero his comrades suppose him to be. In fact, the death of Jones parodies that of Robert Jordan in *For Whom the Bell Tolls*, lacking only the dialect and a wineskin or two.

What I take to be the philosophical core of *The Comedians* is reached in the last pages, neatly packaged in two telegrams (not really telegrams, they only seem like telegrams). The first is in a sermon delivered by a priest conducting a memorial service for the slaughtered revolutionaries: "The Church condemns violence, but it condemns indifference more harshly. Violence can be the expression of love, indifference never. One is an imperfection of charity, the other the perfection of egoism." The kindly communist doctor writes: "Catholics and communists have committed great crimes, but at least they have not stood aside, like an established society, and been indifferent. I would rather have blood on my hands than water like Pilate."

What is operating here, it seems to me, is the desire to be complex and bloody at any cost. It is not enough to say, simply, indifference is reprehensible; that is platitudinous, it lacks the dark glamour of evil. The chief modern literary expression of this position is T. S. Eliot's, in his 1930 essay on Baudelaire: "So far as we are human, what we do must be either evil or good; so far as we do evil or good, we are human; and it is better, in a paradoxical way, to do evil than to do nothing: at least, we exist." Mr. Eliot's remarks, unfortunately, are themselves at the mercy of an unexamined assumption, that it is better to exist than not to exist. This, to say the least, has not been proved, and it is the genius of a novelist like Beckett that his characters act precisely in the area of the unexamined assumption: they yearn toward nonexistence. Beckett's pessimism makes Greene's pessimism look amateurish.

One can imagine a group of Greene's characters gathered together to regard the new book, perhaps on such a television show as David Susskind's *Open End*. Here are Pinkie, from *Brighton Rock*; Arthur Rowe, from *The Ministry of Fear*; Major Scobie; Querry; the Whiskey Priest:

DAVID: Well, what do we think of Brown? How does he stack up? Pinkie?

PINKIE: Well, it's that he doesn't have *size*, like. I mean he's lacking, in a way, *scale*.

DAVID: Arthur Rowe. In *The Ministry of Fear*, Mr. Greene put you through some pretty unpleasant experiences. What do you think of Brown? Do you think he is, as Pinkie says, lacking in scale?

ARTHUR: I'm wanted for a murder I didn't do. People want to kill me because I know too much.

DAVID: Yes, yes, Arthur, we understand, but what we want to know *now* is, how do you regard the new book? Is Brown a . . . fit companion for the rest of you?

ARTHUR: Well, I'm not even sure that Brown is *there.* I seem to sense an absence.

MAJOR SCOBIE: Yes, the blighter seems to be walking through the book with his eyes closed.

QUERRY: I'm not sure.

DAVID: Querry. In *A Burnt-Out Case* you were a famous architect who abandoned a successful practice to work in a leper colony in Africa. What do you feel about the milieu in the present book?

QUERRY: I'm not sure. I'm not sure what I think, I *may* think that it's simply *used.* Do I know what I mean? I don't know.

DAVID: What do you think of the quality of the guilt here? Mr. Greene is justly applauded for his manipulation of guilt. Is the guilt up to standard?

THE WHISKEY PRIEST: I think it's guilt of a rather low order. Low-grade guilt. Back in the 1930s we had *real* guilt. When a man was guilty he was *guilty*.

DAVID: Anyone else?

MAJOR SCOBIE: I am the only guilty one. Because I've known the answers all the time.

DAVID: The answers?

MAJOR SCOBIE: The same old questions and answers.

DAVID: The same old . . .

MAJOR SCOBIE: The same old questions and answers.

1966

THE ELEGANCE IS UNDER CONTROL

A REVIEW OF *THE TRIUMPH* BY JOHN KENNETH GALBRAITH

In his preface John Kenneth Galbraith says that he hesitated to call "this small fable" a novel. Truman Capote, he says, would perhaps wish to call it a non-novel novel. (There is a lot of winking in the book. Aside from Mr. Capote, Averell Harriman and Arthur Schlesinger, Jr., are also winked at.) Mr. Galbraith states further that he would not wish to have it thought that he was using a fable to say things he would not otherwise put in print. "As some will be aware, I have not, in recent years, been wholly reticent as a critic of our foreign policy."

The book is, then, critical of our foreign policy. It draws attention to the fact that our manipulation or attempted manipulation of the affairs of other countries is often self-defeating. It further suggests that we are over-concerned with the menace of Communism. These propositions are, I think, true.

The story involves a change of governments in a small Latin American republic. A dictator is replaced by a reformer of sorts. Our State Department withholds recognition of the new regime on the grounds of possible left-mindedness. Eventually the reformer is turned out by an army coup. There is, finally, a plot twist which probably ought not be revealed.

The story is dandy, or dandy enough. What is surprising about the book is that it's so stuffy.

The stuffy as a literary category has not been explored. In fiction, stuffy characters are often encountered, stuffy authors less often. In the stuffiest possible way, Mr. Galbraith tells us things we already know.

Some examples: "The Washington protocol that requires the lesser of two officials to get on the line and await the pleasure of his superior in rank is, on the whole, more binding than any legislation enacted by the Medes, the Persians, or the combined empire of the two." "They rewarded visiting Congressmen and Senators from the United States, including men of long tenure and great influence from the rural South in whose hearts the democratic passion is under adequate control." "A government crisis has this in common with a sex orgy or a drunken bat: The participants greatly enjoy it although they feel they shouldn't." "Such store does our culture set by useful toil that not even the employees of a Congressional Committee can afford to seem totally idle."

There are occasional traces of aristocratic disdain: "It is told that once the magnificent new wife of a washing machine magnate attended such a White House gala in an exceptionally low-cut evening gown. While conversing expansively with an elderly Senator, her breasts fell out." The messages here are that washing machine magnates (1) should not be invited to the White House, (2) should not have new wives, (3) should not have wives who can be described as "magnificent," (4) should not have wives who wear exceptionally low-cut evening gowns. Violate any of these rules and your breasts fall out.

Mr. Galbraith is uneasily ribald, the rump rampant being his chief literary enthusiasm. "Once years before when she still worked at Commerce, she had opened a door wide to announce that people had arrived for a meeting. All assembled had seen the acting head of the Bureau of Foreign and Domestic Commerce stroking, among other things, the bare bottom of a lady editor of 'The Statistical Abstract.' " "When the time came to go back to his hotel his trousers had disappeared and so had his undershorts. Everyone was helpful. But it was clear that so vast the area of masculine flesh to be draped that no substitute could easily be found. While the problem was being canvassed from all angles in two languages by a highly mixed company. . . ." You see the range.

The language of the book is a minor irritant. Elegance is here, as Mr. Galbraith might put it, under adequate control. People feel twinges of annoyancc. People have glints in their eyes. People are natty. A muffled burst of small-arms fire is followed by a hideous burst of laughter, with only a sentence between them. Poverty is abject, rifles crack, years are halcyon. Needs are urgent, rest much-needed. Expanses are limitless and vegetation, lush. A glittering assemblage hears the earsplitting music of a brilliantly uniformed band. Brawls are drunken, breasts firm. Confidence is exuded. The gloom is pierced. In a notable auctorial tic, about fifty things in the book are described as "small." One assumes this is the view from the top.

The Triumph will probably have a great sale. It is already a Book of the Month Club selection for some sorry month. What is the appropriate response to this news: A hideous burst of laughter, clearly.

1968

AMPHIGOREY ALSO

A REVIEW OF *AMPHIGOREY ALSO* BY EDWARD GOREY

Edward Gorey, whom I've never met, did the cover for the paperback edition of my first book, *Come Back, Dr. Caligari.* The illustration presents handsomely detailed jungle foliage from which various pairs of wildly waving hands emerge. The Gorey touch was to clothe each pair of hands in cotton work gloves, white with a wide blue band at the wrist. Rarely have the raw and cooked been so neatly joined.

Amphigorey Also is the successor to two previous collections of Gorey's grimly risible moral instruction. Consider for a moment "The Broken Spoke," from the new book. Ostensibly it is a series of nineteenth-century postcards with a common subject, bicycles. Several sorts of parody are in play. Magritte, for example, is clearly the father of the famous Unreflecting Bicycle of M. Bandage-Herniaire, who stands by the edge of the pond, proudly supporting the bicycle. M. Bandage-Herniaire's reflection appears in the pond, the bicycle's doesn't. (Can Gorey's funny names be quoted twice? I think not.) *The Crumbath Cyclery by Moonlight* is Magritte again, a commonplace little building topped with an immense (woman's) two-wheeler, itself topped with a half-moon in a moody, stormy, brown-orange sky.

There's a good Lascaux joke (mastodon on wall of cave surrounded by spear-wielding hunters on bicycles) and a deft send-up of allegorical painting (*Innocence, on the Bicycle of Propriety, carrying the Urn of Reputation safely over the Abyss of Indiscretion*) and a nod to Max Ernst (*Les insects Cyclistes*) and a Japanese stencil, bicycle and bats, that might be from the hand of Hiroshige. *The Martyrdom of St. Egfroth,* billed as an eleventh-century drawing, gangs the chorus hastening the saint to his fate in the upper left in uncanny imitation of drawings of the period, as the saint goes over a cliff tied upside-down to a rudimentary bicycle whose wheels echo the shape of his halo. In the title piece, the broken spoke itself, wispy, bent, pathetic, is presented by the well-dressed traveler to an obviously not very well-off Sicilian family obviously unable to appreciate the dimensions of the tragedy. A tot in the corner of the picture clutches a skull, a *memento mori.*

Gorey's texts are as startlingly original as his drawings. One of the properties of language is its ability to generate sentences that have never been heard before. Surely "They spent the better part of the night murdering the child in various ways" in such a sentence (from "The Loathsome Couple"). "The better part of the night" is both the longer part of the night and the *better*—the most murdering fun part. "In various ways" in its demure vagueness springs open a devil's hoard of possibilities. Are we to believe that the child was murdered repeatedly, or by degrees, as a meal may have twelve courses? It's a dazzling sentence, partnered by a drawing of an open door, a chair in the room beyond, a black box on the chair, a bloodstained towel over the back of the chair; it's a sentence that ranks with Gertrude Stein's best. You'll be reassured to know that the Loathsome Couple are apprehended, Harold's cold turns into pneumonia and he expires in jail, and "Mona failed to such an extent that for most of her life she did nothing but lick spots on the walls."

In "The Sopping Thursday," one of a pair of umbrellas says this to the other: "Last night it did not seem as if today it would be raining." The meeting of the "it" which did not seem and the "it" which would be raining is inspired. There's a dog vowing to "succeed" in several of the drawings: "I know I am going to succeed," "I feel I shall very soon succeed . . ." Things dark, dire, and mysterious ("The Toastrack Enigma," "The Blancmange Tragedy") are for Gorey cozy as teakettles. "What the murderer failed to realize is that there is *no* Fourteen, Bandage Terrace."

Gorey is so quotable that one is tempted to neglect his draughtmanship, which is never less than admirable. Individual illustrations reward study, are not to be taken in at a glance. The heavily swathed old man to the left of the woman in black is holding a crooked stick, and the stick is the essence of crookedness. Why is that man to the right of the thug in the Norfolk jacket wearing a top hat? And the fellow with his back to us—did you notice that his right hand terminates not in a hook but a harpoon? What the murderer failed to realize is that *Grumblotch's salts are not soluble in lemonade.*

1983

THE MOST WONDERFUL TRICK

One has a wide choice of what to admire in the work of John Hawkes; beginning at the beginning, I admire his sentences. Consider this, from *The Traveler:* "Early one morning in a town famous for the growing of some grape. . . ." Not even a full sentence, yet the conscientious reader has already tripped, as was intended, over the phrase "some grape." Does it imply ignorance: "This poor clod, meself, who don't know Beaujolais from beanwater"? Or indifference: "Although Riesling is the region's raisin d'être, I don't give a fig"? Or contempt: "Some grape wildly inferior to that grand grape that we grape-kenners ken"? Or something other? It is characteristic of the good reader that he notes and worries about such problems. Not-knowing, most wonderful of our cheap tricks, blinds him into the story as a screw binds wood to wood.

Mr. Hawkes does well with mornings. "Monday morning, bright as the birds, and there he stood for the first time among the twenty-seven girls who, if he had only known, were already playing the silence game." The rhythms of the sentence are perfectly in place: two quick phrases, a long declamatory statement, a hesitation, and another statement. The twenty-seven horrible girls who will shortly assault the teacher in *The Universal Fears* are, rhythmically, poised to leap. "Among the twenty-seven girls who" hangs over "if he had only known" like a cartoon boulder over Road Runner. The bright, noisy Monday-morning birds (English slang for girls, we recall) are balanced against the silent, sullen hardcases at the sentence's conclusion in a fine, uneasy equilibrium. Rhythm is not always the contemporary sentence's stronger attribute; Mr. Hawkes is unerring in knowing where to place what.

"There is nothing like an empty grave to betray the presence of a dead king in all his lechery," Mr. Hawkes writes in *Travesty.* Cautiously, we test the proposition. The king is quick again, has clawed his way out of the clay in pursuit of some tender passing rumplet. 'Tis lechery, 'tis lechery, that makes the world go round. What is here with which a prudent man would disagree, and what's the French for "fiddledeedee"? It's one of the writer's virtues that his formulations throw us back into the whole corpus of English literature, that doors (or graves) are continually popping open, that dead kings hotfoot once more along disorderly paths, and that our attention is focused, in the same sentence, on first and last things. Stuffing the mort monarch into his safe-deposit box is a task for armies of the circumspect, and the suggestion is that they will not be able to achieve it. Mr. Hawkes's sentences, like the larger designs they advance, are splendidly not-simple.

1984

A NOTE ON ELIA KAZAN

The work of Elia Kazan and of the actors and playwrights associated with him has been variously described as the salvation and the final affliction of the contemporary stage—sometimes by the same critic and in the same breath. The half-dozen immensely successful plays and films that have defined these craftsmen as a group, almost a movement, have also made possible an attempt to perceive a unifying thread, a view of the world, in their work. What kind of a theatre, then, does Mr. Kazan represent and what is the substance of its vision?

The theatre of Elia Kazan, if we may call it that, is among other things a response to the crucial problem posed for imaginative literature in general and the drama in particular by the widespread public acceptance of the "new sciences" of sociology and psychology. Sociologists and psychologists have long since invaded areas of investigation once the private domain of novelists and playwrights, and have made these fields their own. In a practical sense, they have deprived the makers of imaginative literature of a considerable portion of their audience, or at least of that audience's attention. It has been said that David Riesman offers more exciting reading, in terms of what he is able reveal to a reader about himself, than any novelist now at work; with the added virtue of presenting his insights clothed not in ambiguity, symbol, and myth, but merely in sociological jargon.

Grossly misperceived as the nature of these disciplines may be, their special terms are now firmly imbedded in the language, and the concepts behind them a part of the consciousness of every novel-reader and playgoer. The immediate reaction, in the theatre, to the popularization of these sciences was something called psychological drama. Seriously-intended theatre became for a time a giant sanitarium, almost exclusively the realm of the mentally ill; and the last of these adventures in pathology has not yet been unveiled. But it rapidly became clear that there was no profit, for the theatre, in simply rehearsing case histories from the textbooks.

At the moment there exists an uneasy liaison between psychologist and playwright. The latter, in most cases, draws freely upon the resources of psychology in sketching his characters (sound motivation is now required even for song cues in musical comedy), but refuses to present man in purely psychological terms. He reserves the right to transcend science, if he can, in attempting to fix the meaning of man in the world. And this is precisely the point where Mr. Kazan and his associates enter, for in the contemporary American theatre it is, more than any other, their view of man, world, and meaning that prevails.

The complex of ideas, impulses, theory, and doctrine for which we are using Mr. Kazan as a symbol has many tributaries. Among them are the Stanislavski-based theory of acting, with its emphasis on "inner truth" and ensemble playing, which, via the Group Theatre, has come to be promulgated by Lee Strasberg through the Actors' Studio; the plays of Tennessee Williams, Carson McCullers, William Inge, and their contemporaries; the peculiar interaction of literature and the films represented by John Steinbeck—who wrote the script for one Kazan film, saw another adapted from one of his novels—and Budd Schulberg, who accomplished both operations with a single property, *On the Waterfront*, which appeared first as a film, then as a novel. There are other influences—the postwar Italian film realism of Da Sica, the documentary approach to fiction of De Rochemont—but the above seem most noteworthy.

Whatever its validity in contrast to other schools of acting, the Kazan-Strasberg-Stanislavski attack—"The Method," to its partisans—is perhaps the most rewarding of the approaches to the art currently being offered on American stages. Often criticized, The Method undoubtedly has its limitations; Method actors do not fare well, for instance, in high comedy or expressionistic drama, where manner is valued above psychological realism. There are frequent complaints that these actors are presenting the truth not of American speech, but of a rigidly defined metropolitan area, ethnic group, or social stratum. On the other hand, it is impossible to reproach Marlon Brando for not being Edwin Booth; Booth, after all, would be ludicrously wrong for this time, as Brando, in a way, is eminently right. And neither Brando nor The Method can be blamed for the fact that the playwrights in whose dramas they find themselves employed seem most interested in (or most at home with) the less privileged members of society.

Mr. Kazan has said that he searches, in an actor, for "the ability to capture inner contradictions." This ability is theoretically part of the equipment of every actor; that he has singled it out may suggest its significance for the kind of theatre he represents. In the same interview, he praised Tennessee Williams for "emotionalism—he doesn't clean things up." A surrender to unfettered emotion is fundamental in the writers Mr. Kazan admires—their most reliable dramatic device is, uniformly, the outburst. Tennessee Williams' people are forever bursting forth in a blaze of invective, remonstrance, anguish, or entreaty. At the other end of the forensic scale there are inaudible mutterings, growls, and tugging at clothing. These are the effective limits of the Actors' Studio performer; between them lies faithfully rendered banality. Mr. Strasberg, a sort of Belasco of the soul, insists not on real scenery, but on real anger, ecstasy, boredom, and tears.

Aside from a serious commitment to naturalism, the only characteristic the playwrights in this circle share is a wholehearted belief in poetry as a medium of dramatic statement. But the poetry of these dramas is of a very special and peculiar kind, the almost-lyricism Clifford Odets found in a general poverty of speech touched by the not-quite-magic manufactured in quantity by Maxwell Anderson. No one disputes the fact that these writers, with the appropriate players and skilled direction, can offer the shock of recognition, a clear and distinct grasp of life in progress. What they conceive to be poetry, however, is more often than otherwise simply inflated rhetoric, embarrassing rather than moving, as a glance at the text of almost any of their plays will reveal. This kind of "poetry," in other words, is sadly inadequate for the burden of meaning it is expected to bear.

As to Mr. Kazan himself, it is particularly difficult to assess the work of a director, to distinguish his special contributions from those of author, actor, and a multitude of technicians. But in general we may assume that a director is responsible for the sense of the whole, and within the framework of this responsibility, for a synthesis of the efforts of his colleagues. To compare his task with that of the conductor of an orchestra is not quite accurate: for although like the conductor he neither evolves the theme of the work being performed nor stands with the players, his responsibility exceeds interpretation. He is, rather, the orchestrator, concerned above all with the most effective possible statement of a theme, and creatively engaged in its realization. In the case of Mr. Kazan, as Eric Bentley has pointed out, the contributions frequently approach co-authorship.

Tennessee Williams has noted, in reference to *The Glass Menagerie,* that "because of its considerably delicate or tenuous material, atmospheric touches and subtleties of direction play a particularly important part . . ." This is rather an understatement. Mr. Kazan at work, busily amplifying and elaborating the images which the playwright has contrived, is essential to the realization of the drama's total meaning. And his talent, like those of the writers and actors around him, seems to find its highest expression in moments of "inner contradiction" or plain silence: no one else has made so much, in the theatre, of instances of the inadequacy of speech in dealing with the world about us.

The young hero of Budd Schulberg's *On the Waterfront,* attempting to convey his feelings to Eva Marie Saint, mumbles, chews a lip, coughs, gives it up; the problem of making his emotions known is too rough for him. If extraneous considerations—a murder and waterfront racketeering—were not present, he would never get it out, and the girl would never know. As with many of the characters in the dramas of this school, for him possibility is realized only by accident.

Blanche DuBois, in Tennessee Williams' *A Streetcar Named Desire,* chatters endlessly if somewhat nervously in a fine approximation of easy Southern speech of the type intended, more than anything else, to preclude the disaster of a conversational pause; but the instant she must make a statement, she chokes—or moves into "poetry." The dramas of William Inge are filled with people who have difficulty with the simple declarative sentence until required to present a message, whereupon they are suddenly struck with the gift of tongues. Carson McCullers' characters are in the same predicament, alternating between wordlessness and flights of spurious affirmation.

These are, of course, precisely the kind of images which Mr. Kazan's actors are best equipped to render, and in the plays of his associates they assume a pattern, a design which is nothing so much as an elaborate structure of frustration. In *The Glass Menagerie* no one (including the author) solves any problems; at the conclusion the characters stand in exactly the same relation to one another that they assumed in the beginning. Even those who seem to break out of the pattern discover themselves, at the finish, more tightly bound up in it, as Tom, the narrator, confesses in his curtain speech. In the film *Viva Zapata!* the liberator-hero, made chief of state after a successful revolution, finds that his land has merely exchanged one dictatorship for another—his own. At his death, the country is still firmly in the grip of totalitarianism. The pattern is repeated over and over, and is presented as unbreakable.

What we have, finally, in the body of work to which we have linked Mr. Kazan's name, is a theatre in which the actors, at the summit of their powers, explore the limits of speechlessness; in which the playwrights, strive as they may for a positive statement, can present such a statement only in terms of a "poetry" that falls under its own weight; and in which the most accomplished director, half-author, surpasses himself in revealing the hidden outlines of a labyrinth where there are no silken threads leading back to the light.

If we accept as a principle that a particular kind of theatre is inseparable from what it expresses, it will be seen that what we have been investigating in relation to this theatre has been not two questions but one, the concept of form as a structure of meaning. The form of these dramas *is* their meaning; an interplay of silences, it speaks in accents that are eventually unmistakable.

The ultimate meaning of the portrait of the modern world which these craftsmen present us is subject to a number of interpretations. But in this context wordlessness and frustration seem overwhelmingly images of helplessness, a universal lostness in the face of an existence that is complex and unforgiving. For all its quasi-poetic rhapsodies, it is this view of the world that the theatre of Elia Kazan presents, almost against the will of the people involved. Uniquely dumb in the history of a medium whose reason for being is communication, plays and performers have nevertheless said what they have been fashioned to say.

1956

THE EARTH AS AN OVERTURNED BOWL

The extravagant German director Werner Herzog has made a remarkably selfless version of Georg Büchner's prescient 1830s drama *Woyzeck*, a work that, in itself and especially by virtue of the Alban Berg opera drawn from it, has been an emblem of modernism ever since it was first staged, in 1913. Herzog gives us a dutiful, responsible rendering, perhaps not the best choice. The play, after nearly a century and a half, requires something more. Already in the early 1930s Antonin Artaud may be found proposing it as raw material for Theatre of Cruelty exacerbation, "in a spirit of reaction against our principles, and to illustrate what can be derived theatrically from a formal text." The pile of scenes and fragments left in no particular order by Büchner at his death in 1837 has become for Artaud canonical, something to be acted upon or against, a pretext. For many people, the opera was and is exemplary shock, bright and howlish as Kandinsky, a quick definition of the new. The overhang of Berg's music is so strong that a *Woyzeck* without it seems truncated, partial.

Herzog's is a hands-off treatment, a *Woyzeck*-for-the-schools, a Standard Authorized Version. For a director capable of producing an all-dwarf feature (*Even Dwarfs Started Small,* 1970), or hypnotizing most of his cast to simulate sleepwalking (*Heart of Glass,* 1976), or rushing off to Guadeloupe to embrace an imminently erupting volcano (*La Soufrière,* 1976), this is uncharacteristic restraint, and probably the wrong occasion for it. Perhaps it's a course correction, a pendulum swing. (It was one of two films Herzog made last year, the other being a remake of Murnau's *Nosferatu,* which will be shown at the New York Film Festival.)

Woyzeck has been called the first modern play, the first to place the "ordinary man" at the center of the action, the first to tear away conventional stage notions of motivation, cause, and effect. Büchner based it on a celebrated real-life murder case, that of Johann Christian Woyzeck, a common soldier who killed the woman with whom he was living in Saxony in the 1820s. There were doubts about his sanity—he complained of having visions and hearing voices—and he was examined at great length by a court physician named Clarus, who credited him with extensive disturbances but finally found him sane. He was beheaded in Leipzig in 1824, festively.

Büchner, an extraordinary writer who was barely twenty-four when he died, was a student of medicine and natural history as well as philosophy, active in radical politics, a gifted pamphleteer fascinated by the French Revolution (his other major play is *Danton's Death*). His "ordinary man" is lost to himself, an object of utility for others when he is not a lodestone for casual humiliation. "At the top of the uniform is situated the head, to inform the soldier of the height to which his salute should be brought," wrote Bruno Paul in *Simplicissimus* in 1904. The soldier is a paradigm of the thing, endlessly replaceable, not more significant than a coin or a brick. Shaving his Captain, Woyzeck is given a lecture on the delights of morals (Fischer-Dieskau's sombre "Jawohl, Herr Hauptmann!" from the Deutsche Grammophon recording of the opera intrudes here) with the clear implication that he wouldn't know what to do with a moral if handed one by the archangel Michael on a flaming sword. The Doctor sees him as a specimen and has him on retainer, a few groschen a week on condition that he eat only peas and present regular urine samples to further the Doctor's spurious scientific work. His *aberratio* is praised ("a most beautiful *aberratio mentalis partialis* of the second order!"). The strutting Drum Major forces schnapps on him and squeezes the breath from him in a tavern scuffle. Marie, the mother of his child, allows herself to be seduced by the Drum Major.

Throughout, Woyzeck can make only fragmentary (though sometimes startlingly shrewd) objections, defenses. He cannot *explain himself,* and the others can: the Captain is a military man, the Doctor has his "science," the Drum Major has his mirror, Marie her child. Woyzeck sees "white fire" over the town, he wants to read what's written on the toadstools, a voice is telling him something he doesn't want to hear, there's such a thing as a being with a "double nature" . . . But he cannot say what Woyzeck is. "You're running through the world like an open razor," the Captain tells him, and when he has stabbed Marie, at the finish, one feels that he is pure instrument, that murder has been done and it is the knife that will be punished.

"Yea, verily I say unto you: How should the farmer, the cooper, the shoemaker, the doctor live, had not God created Man for their use?" asks a drunken hanger-on in the tavern scene. It's possible that the idea of man-as-victim-of-society or man-as-victim-of-the-conditions-of-existence has minimum dramatic life left in it, cannot be taken unmediated—thus the efficacy of Berg's music. "This timid man," as Berg's teacher Schoenberg called him, allows us to feel the proposition rather than think it. Herzog is content to have us deal with it directly, and the film suffers for the lack of emendation or challenge or contradiction. Like the birth trauma, victimization as a given doesn't take us very far.

Klaus Kinski, Herzog's Woyzeck, has such strength on the screen that it's difficult to see him as the butt of everyone else's cruelties and inadvertencies. It's as if George C. Scott were playing not Patton but Patton's batman. Dressed in a gray fatigue uniform with a little round cap that makes him seem more convict than soldier, he appears in a mock manual of arms behind the titles wearing a truly memorable rictus, which he never relinquishes thereafter. The stamp of this mask on the mind is very strong (it's what you see in advertisements for the film), but it also robs the picture of any possible dynamics; Kinski is not more anguished murdering Marie than he is shaving the Captain. His body seems at perpetual attention, perpetually quivering. He gets Woyzeck's frantic money-haunted busyness, and his fear of Marie's sexuality after the Captain and the Doctor (Wolfgang Reichmann and Willy Semmelrogge) have dropped their leering catastrophic hints, but it's hard to imagine that he ever had much to do with her, and although there is a baby around, it's barely noticed. Kinski is successful in making us believe that *something is wrong* and murders Marie on schedule (balletically, approximately four minutes), but for all his undoubted skill and presence he tends to undermine rather than enforce the film's argument.

The candy-pretty Czech town where it was shot, the costuming and set-dressing, the sketchy quality of the few crowd scenes all suggest the stage rather than film. Eva Mattes, as Marie, does not; she's ordinarily human, round and busty and down-to-earth, almost a visitor from another reality. The English titles miss some opportunities. Of Marie it's said that she can stare her way through a pair of leather pants; in the original it's seven pairs of leather pants, a finer image by a factor of seven. No amount of reverence can dim or blanket some of Büchner's poetry: the speech, for example, in which Marie relates a story about a child all alone in the world, without parents or friends, everyone dead, and because the moon looks friendly she journeys to the moon and finds it to be a piece of rotten wood, and the sun a faded sunflower, and the stars little golden bugs, and the earth an overturned bowl, and she sits down and cries, and sits there to this day, all alone. . . . In the context, this sings.

1979

PARACHUTES IN THE TREES

There's been a clear shift of emphasis in war movies in recent years, from faith to doubt. Where our own military is not seen as potential enemy, as in *Seven Days in May* or *Fail Safe* or *Dr. Strangelove,* it's presented as a locus of megalomania, as in *Apocalypse Now* and, to some degree, *Patton*. Even a rather straightforward epic like *A Bridge Too Far* finds its subject in a military disaster, Operation Market Garden, in contrast to *The Longest Day* (the Normandy landings), also made from a Cornelius Ryan book, fifteen years earlier. Some of the pleasures of simplicity are forfeit. One remembers Bogart, for instance, in *Sahara* (1943), wandering the desert in his tank, Lulubelle, forever banging on it, tinkering with it, whispering to it, picking up stragglers, a South African, a Frenchman, a Sudanese, a German—watch out for that German, *he understands English. . . .*

Soldier of Orange, a new Dutch film, is reliable terrain; there's no confusion as to which side we're on. Based on a true story, the memoirs of Erik Hazelhoff Roelfzema, it deals with the occupation of Holland at the beginning of the Second World War and has a fine central actor in Rutger Hauer, who plays Erik. The film opens with a small group of young men in Leiden in 1938, some of them going through a university hazing; under the impact of the war, the group splinters in various ways, physical and moral; at the end only two are alive.

Hauer, who is tall and bespectacled, looks a bit like a younger Prince Philip with perhaps the faintest hint of Harold Lloyd. His

Erik is slightly bemused, slightly off to one side—Fascism seems not an issue for him, anti-Semitism still less so, merely a tic of boors. The news of war between Germany and England interrupts a garden party, but only for a moment: "A spot of war would be quite exciting," someone says, and then it's back to tennis. Erik becomes an authentic hero but he's initially fastidious, choosing his occasions. All those white parachutes hanging from the good Dutch trees come as a shock, the first in a brutal series. When the paratroopers arrive, he's motorcycling home from another party, in white tie. The Dutch capitulation is so swift (four days after May 10, 1940) that no one has a clear idea of what action is appropriate—how to be "occupied." Erik's friend John (Huïn Rooymans), a Jew, is captured by the Gestapo in a botched attempt to escape to England. He's tortured, then shot. Impossible things are now possible, quickly routine. The transformation of everyday reality into unprecedented ghastliness is like being in bed in an earthquake, the bed falling beneath you.

Erik gets away to England, through the good offices of a Swiss freighter captain, and is enlisted in underground schemes aimed at bringing Resistance leaders out of Holland to shore up Queen Wilhelmina's government-in-exile. These are guided by a British colonel (Edward Fox, quite as knowing-fatuous as he was as General Horrocks in *A Bridge Too Far*) and mostly fail—Erik's friend Nico is killed on the beach in one mission, and his friend Guus cut off from hope of rescue. Another of the group, Robby, is caught operating a clandestine radio and becomes a double agent; another, Alex, joins a unit fighting for the Germans on the Russian front and is blown up in a latrine by a small Russian boy with a potato-masher grenade. Robby, the traitor, is shot by Guus, who attempts a getaway on his bicycle but is caught, tortured, and guillotined.

Torture and the possibility of torture, in fact, provide the film's emotional tension—unthinkable behavior repeated and repeated, foreshadowing the extermination camps. To be killed in the course of ordinary military operations is almost to be privileged. The sense of ordinary life as fragile, subject to irruptions of the most monstrous kind, is very strong. There are some good quick glimpses of Hollanders who have made accommodations: a farmer who tips the Gestapo to Guus's photographing of coastal installations and then complains about his payoff ("It's the tariff," he's told, and looking at the money in his hand he says doubtfully, "Well if it's the tariff . . ."), Mercedes full of drunken Dutch girls on their way to Nazi revels, an Iron Cross (Alex's) thrown from hand to hand to hand at a dance.

Jeroen Krabbé, as Guus, is especially fine; his mustache and jaunty hat and funny in-on-the-joke smile play nicely against the slightly prim and straight-arrow Hauer. There's a casual wartime bawdiness coloring the film, and that's convincing, too. Susan Penhaligon, as a British military aide, is, like Fox, working a little too hard, but Andrea Domburg's Wilhelmina is first-rate (and said to be especially meaningful for the Dutch for the way she has reproduced the late Queen's mannerisms). Paul Verhoeven's direction and Jost Vacano's photography are both calm, unfancy. There are intimations of historical dimensions that are scanted—one of the Resistance chiefs refuses to be brought out because he feels that Wilhelmina has just discovered democracy and he doesn't want to be part of her conversion, for example—but in general the film covers an immense amount of material with admirable economy.

Erik eventually enlists in the R.A.F. as a pilot flying bombing missions over Germany, then becomes an aide to the Queen. There's a short scene at the end when he's back in Holland for the liberation, celebrations raging everywhere, and looks up Jacques, who has more or less sat out the war and is the only other survivor of the original group. Jacques tells him how hard a time he's had completing his degree, how he's had to take his prelims secretly and so on, and Erik, for a moment, can't believe just how much there is that Jacques doesn't know—his slight hesitation about whether to have a drink with Jacques or not is sadly telling.

The unfortunately titled *Run After Me Until I Catch You,* a new French offering, is an elaboration of the truism that nobody loves a tax man. The revenue agent in question is Jean-Pierre Marielle, as Paul, and the woman who does not love him, at least at first, is the beautiful Annie Girardot, as Jacqueline, here an employee of a pet-grooming establishment. The jokes are on the order of large-dogs-in-bed and are sometimes marginally funny. The principal dog is named Gaston. Paul has a loutish layabout son (Sylvain Rougerie) who has a super-vacant girlfriend (Christine Laurent); the young folk manage to be present whenever the not-so-young folk want to be alone, etc. The picture is a rush of misunderstandings. Paul takes Jacqueline to a film on their first date and it turns out to be X-rated; Simone, a female colleague, locks him in her office and he can't pick Jacqueline up for a scheduled weekend. Conceptually, it's the Theatre of Pique. Send it a retrofit package containing a few litres of *grand mal.* There's a bit about the supposed viciousness of tax people which has some zest ("I'm going to cut them to shreds," says

Simone of a part of her clientele), but fundamentally it's large-dogs-in-the-dahlias, large-dogs-in-the-pistou. The director was Robert Pouret, from a screenplay by Nicole de Buron. Charm, as Goethe said, is the dead green bug on the golden leaf of occasion.

1979

SPECIAL DEVOTIONS

In *The Films in My Life,* François Truffaut reflects upon his own writing about films: "Was I a good critic? I don't know. But one thing I am sure of is that I was always on the side of those who were hissed and against those who were hissing; and that my enjoyment often began where that of others left off." American audiences don't hiss overmuch, but *The Green Room,* Truffaut's seventeenth full-length picture, has been so greeted, I'm told, at some European showings. If this is true, I think it's because the film from the beginning excludes the viewer, shuts him out, and although that may be appropriate to a story about obsession, it's as likely to provoke hostility as any other exclusion. This most ingratiating of directors (*Jules and Jim* was at one time the deadliest contrivance in the seducer's filthy arsenal, in dozens of languages) deals here in closed doors.

The Green Room is drawn from Henry James, principally *The Altar of the Dead,* not one of the Master's merriest tales. The script is by Truffaut and Jean Gruault. Truffaut changes the locale from England to France, ten years after the First World War, and plays the lead himself. James's "poor Stransom" has become Julien Davenne, a provincial journalist whose real career is the preservation of the memory of his wife, killed in an accident shortly after their marriage. He maintains a shrine in his home (the green room of the title), decked with candles and photographs of the dead woman, and lingers in the cemetery. He's angry with a friend who's delighting in a new wife, horrified that the friend's dead wife can be, in any sense, replaced. He commissions a wax mannequin of his own lost love, then flies into a rage when he finds that the artisan has produced an imperfect image; it's chopped up. Tracking down objects that once belonged to his wife, he visits an auction house in search of a particular silver ring; there he meets Cécilia (Nathalie Baye), a pretty young woman with commanding griefs of her own.

His obsession enlarges to accommodate others of the Dead (irritatingly capitalized in the film, as in James), friends and heroes. Stumbling upon an disused chapel, he conceives the notion of refurbishing it, ostensibly an act of piety but in fact a perversion—the chapel will be used for his own special devotions. The ecclesiastical authorities are suspicious but in the end acquiesce. Cécilia is enlisted as co-religionist, although Julien doesn't know whom or what she's mourning. The place fills up with candles, each candle a Dear Departed, the camera enjoying, or trading upon, the flames. Truffaut permits himself some private *hommages* here; the icons in his chapel include Henry James himself, Oscar Wilde, I thought I saw Cocteau, and Oskar Werner (the Jules of *Jules and Jim*), representing the German war dead of 1914–18. Julian exhibits slides of slaughtered soldiers to the young ward of his housekeeper, a boy with speech difficulties (an echo of *The Wild Child,* Truffaut's treatment of the Caspar Hauser story). This cross-referential filigree, which suggests that the truly worthy filmgoer must have paid attention over the span of the director's whole filmography, is less fun than it used to be. Julien eventually discovers that the man for whom Cécilia is carrying a taper is none other than a certain Paul Massigny, once his own best friend, who betrayed him in a shockingly vile, although unspecified, way. Can he bring himself to allow a candle honoring this person in his sanctum? A bean I won't spill. What does *not* happen, of course, is a love affair between Julien and Cécilia; she is, as May Bartram is in *The Beast in the Jungle,* what the man misses.

It's the solemnity with which all this is parsed out that is discouraging. From the moment Truffaut appears in his poilu's uniform before blue-green First World War newsreel clips, looking sad and serious, the dolor is unrelenting. The journal Julien writes for is itself dying; the editor shows him bundles of returned copies addressed to deceased subscribers. When the editor says of him admiringly that he knocked out thirty-one obits the previous year, this is funny, but it's not meant to be—you're not allowed to smile. The film becomes stuffy. Its central idea, that obsession with the past can stifle life, is painfully commonplace. Dressed in Jamesian overtell, the story works because of the mad virtuosity, the insistence, of the telling. Without it, there is only a certain amount of beautiful candlelight.

Love and Bullets is entertaining whenever Rod Steiger, as a stammering, resplendently bathrobed Arizona mob chieftain, is on the screen, which is not often enough. He lives in an enormous Edward Durell Stone palace on the side of a hill, with a screening room where he shows Nelson Eddy–Jeanette MacDonald movies and fulminates against the exigencies of his métier. Steiger is always first-class or better (I've admired him ever since he walked into Jack Palance's lavish movie-star layout in *The Big Knife,* in 1955, and pronounced, exquisitely inflected, the words "This . . . is . . . an . . . unhealthy . . . environment"), and Charles Bronson, too, is good at what he does, as solid as a tool-pusher on a Texas oil rig. In the present instance, Bronson is a Phoenix detective charged with the recovery, from a hideout in Switzerland, of Steiger's paramour (Jill Ireland), with the hope that she will then sing to the Feds. Steiger, pressured by colleagues and with a reluctance that actually seems real, orders the lady cooled; Hotshot Hitman Vittorio Farroni (Henry Silva, in his familiar iron mask) gets the assignment.

In defending his prisoner, Bronson is called upon at one point to sink a hatchet in some poor fellow's spine; at another, he fashions a blowgun from a lampstand and with it blows away three or four heavily armed enemies. Ireland is fine in a Dolly Parton wig, issuing country-girl squeaks and squeals. A lot of bright-red Swiss machinery is involved—trams, ski lifts, cable cars, which function to slow rather than speed the action. The exteriors, in Zermatt, Kandersteg, Montreux, and Geneva, are grand. Lord Grade (formerly Sir Lew Grade), first cause uncaused of this production, is said to have spent three hundred thousand dollars on a replica of the Stone edifice, which is blown to flinders at the film's conclusion. Antonioni's exploding house at the end of *Zabriskie Point* was better.

1979

DEAD MEN COMIN' THROUGH

"Corn-pone jiveass peckerwood" is what Jimmy Smith, a black petty thief, calls Greg Powell, his white counterpart, in the early moments of Joseph Wambaugh's *The Onion Field,* and although the description is accurate as far as it goes, it's a horrific understatement. It's amazing how much of his book of the same title Wambaugh, who formed his own company for this project, got into the movie, and how good the movie is, with a startling performance by James Woods as Powell. Powell and Smith are involved in a cop-killing (the story is a true one, based on a notorious California case of the sixties), and Woods makes the leader of the pair so thoroughly odious that he's actually painful to watch. In the beginning, he's smarmy-friendly, trying to buy the black man (Franklyn Seales) with small gifts and large boasts. "I'm kind of a virtuoso sexually," he confides, and he's also a top marksman and master criminal and philosopher of family life. What he is, in fact, is a world-class sociopath.

Neither of the two police officers who become his victims is exactly what he set out to be: Ian Campbell (Ted Danson) is a former pre-med student whose father was a doctor, and Karl Hettinger (John Savage) had wanted to be a farmer ("Police work is so noisy; tomatoes are so quiet"). Patrolling on a Los Angeles Saturday night, they stop a suspicious-looking car; it's Powell and Smith, cruising for a liquor store to knock over. Powell manages to get a gun on Campbell, and the unbelieving Hettinger is forced to surrender his own weapon. Then the two officers are placed in Powell's car and taken to the farmland near Bakersfield, to the onion field. They're told they'll be released there; instead, Powell shoots Campbell in the face. Hettinger, in shock, runs. Powell and Smith are quickly picked up and charged with the murder.

The ensuing series of trials, the longest criminal case in California's history (the transcript, Wambaugh says in the book, eventually ran to nearly forty-five thousand pages), is a judicial quagmire. Judges are replaced, new juries impanelled, new lawyers engaged, testimony is repeated and repeated, ever more fantastic motions are gravely considered. The defendants quickly become pseudo lawyers. You can see Powell slipping into the role, becoming lawyer-polite and lawyer-sarcastic, playing with a pencil, citing the D.A. for misconduct. Smith, noticing that time is being won, emulates Powell.

Meanwhile, Hettinger, the surviving officer, deteriorates. He has nightmares, headaches, a stiff neck; he drinks. He's forced to attend all the roll calls and explain to the other cops what happened in the onion field; they're skeptical. The department circulates a memorandum implying he was wrong to give up his gun. He's assigned to the detective bureau, and one day, while looking for shoplifters, steals a watch. He can't stop stealing, and he's caught. The department gives him a choice: resign or face possible prosecution. No attempt is made to understand his behavior in terms of what happened in the onion field. He's out of work, with a pregnant wife. He backhands his crying baby in her crib, and is almost a suicide.

John Savage, as Hettinger, has a small-town look; it's easy to believe that farming is what he's meant for. But he's a powerful actor. His utter disbelief at the moment Powell has a gun in Campbell's back, his terror as he runs and rolls over the fields, the later, shrunken, bruised Hettinger as the years of trials drag on are all beautifully done. Danson's Campbell, playing the bagpipes in an empty station-house holding tank or driving Powell's Ford coupé to the murder site while enduring Powell's compulsive chatter ("How big are you?"), is thoroughly likable, and even though we know what's coming, the shock of his death is thunderous. Seales makes the poor loser Smith immensely real, and there's a fine actor's invention toward the end of the film when Smith, suddenly resigned and almost debonair in a new mustache and shades, has a friendly colloquy with a guard in the prison yard. All of the supporting parts are thoughtfully acted, a vindication of the casting director's art (in this case, it was Lynn Stalmaster).

Wambaugh knows what things are called, knows the tags and

lines appropriate to the milieu he deals with. ("Dead men comin' through," says a guard ushering Greg and Jimmy onto death row.) In the book, he gives us the sociology, the "explanations," first, then the crime—we are led through Powell's miserable family life and Smith's lack of anything of the kind, then presented with what happened. In the film, the process is reversed, the murder first, then, as Greg assumes his own defense and Jimmy's auntie is placed on the stand, something of the background. The picture is rich in ugly knowledge—for example, Powell smoothly advising the cops interrogating him that if they want to grab his partner they should spread mug shots of him around Bakersfield's black area (this, in fact, is how Smith was caught), or an impervious defense attorney droning through obfuscatory motion after obfuscatory motion as the prosecutors sink into despair. The idea that the law is an idiot is emphatically endorsed—we last see Powell, in horn-rims and new curls, operating what amounts to a flourishing law firm from his cell.

The film is perhaps a bit too long and ends at least twice—once with a scene between Hettinger, made whole by time, and his wife frolicking by a lake, and again with Campbell's mother (Priscilla Pointer) in a hopeful dialogue with a young piper at a Highlands festival. Mr. Wambaugh, who wrote the script, knew what he wanted to do and went out and recruited his own producer, Walter Coblenz, and director, Harold Becker, and they've made a rare picture together.

Some of the duffelbags carried by the soldiers in *Yanks,* which has to do with Americans billeted outside a small English town in 1942–44, dangle limply from their owners' shoulders as if containing maybe a couple of shirts or something, like no duffelbag that ever was. The duffelbag is always fatly packed. And Richard Gere, as a mess sergeant, wears his SFC's stripes sewn to his cook's whites, which is like having them sewn on his arms—are we to assume he's insecure? And the trucks are wrong, Korean-era trucks rather than Second World War trucks, and the trumpet solo played on "I'll Be Seeing You" at the films big New Year's Eve dance couldn't have been phrased before Art Farmer. God is in the details, as Mies van der Rohe put it.

Director John Schlesinger, who did *Darling, Sunday Bloody Sunday, Midnight Cowboy,* and *Marathon Man,* is very skilled yet seems to be having a little trouble here. The impact of what amounts to an invading army, ours, on a friendly country *in extremis* is his subject, and in many ways he deals capably with it.

The sense of American plenitude in men, matériel, and most especially optimism is carefully laid in. The Yanks think everything is possible, not only victory but love, too; the British wish they could be as certain. The Colin Welland-Walter Bernstein script posits three affairs between visitors and cousinly hosts, at varying levels of social class. The first involves Vanessa Redgrave, as a lady of the manor whose husband is away at war, and William Devane, as a wry and gentle Chemical Corps captain whose hanging about is not unwelcome. The second is between Gere and Lisa Eichhorn—the daughter of shopkeepers, who's affianced to a Ken in the British ranks—and is given the most emphasis. The third, and lightly sketched, liaison has Gere's friend Danny (Chick Vennera) hand in hand with a lively bus-ticket puncher. "I'm pregnant!" she cries as she's pushing through a crowd at the station when the troops are shipping out. "So's half the bloody town, love," someone replies.

There's severe story anemia despite the three stories. The Redgrave-Devane saga is mostly pale loitering, and the Gere-Eichhorn pairing has its high moment in a scene in which, Ken having been reported dead, the girl's mum is allowed a you've-killed-him-the-both-of-you-with-yer-dirty-sneakin'-around tirade. The new permissiveness in film language lets the soldiers speak a bit more flavorfully than in the past, but nobody has anything very bright to say. One hankers for a generalization, such as "The English are thus-and-such, the Americans on the other hand . . ." We don't get beyond Devane explaining to Redgrave that America is a young country. The film is really a hundred-and-forty-minute rendering of the overpaid/oversexed/over-here joke, and although all of the principals, Gere, Redgrave, Eichhorn, Devane, Vannera, and Wendy Morgan, as the bus lady, are endearing and accomplished, we learn not very much from it.

Nest of Vipers, directed by Tonino Cervi from a story by Roger Peyrefitte, is more a muff of ninnies. After Carla (Senta Berger) has her head bashed in with a handy object d'art by Elena (Ornella Muti), the next shot is of Elena dribbling raspberry syrup over her ice cream at a family dinner. How's that for ironic counterpoint? We are in Venice between the wars, and Carla and her son, the beautiful Renato, are more or less competing for the affections of the upright Mattio (Christian Borromeo, slightly pop-eyed, in a slicked-back Valentino hairstyle). Carla enjoys this likely lad for a while, until Elena, who's younger and richer, engages his attention; Carla then seduces Elena, nibbling feverishly on her knees, and when this is accomplished announces that she's going to tell *the whole town*, and thus put the kibosh on Elena's marriage to Mattio. Then, the bashing. It's just as Richard Gilman suggests in his useful new book on the subject; strain as we may, we *still* don't have any damn decadence.

1979

THREE FESTIVALS

The seventeenth New York Film Festival opened with a disappointment, Bernardo Bertolucci's *Luna.* This remarkable director, begetter of *The Conformist, The Spider's Stratagem, Before the Revolution,* and, most recently, *1900,* slips badly here: the film is near-ludicrous. Jill Clayburgh is present as Caterina, an American opera star in high career, clustered about with managers and coaches and avaricious fans. Early on, her husband, played by Fred Gwynne with Herman Munster peering over his shoulder, dies; she gathers up her young son (Matthew Barry) and flees to Italy. At a party celebrating his fifteenth birthday, she finds him shooting up, and discovers that he's been a druggie for a good while. What's the therapy of choice? Why, mother love, of course, and for the balance of the film she slathers it on, not even drawing the line at the dread i*n*c*e*s*t taboo itself.

The star is pictured as crazy about Verdi. "He's like a father to me," she says, absurdly, when she takes her son, whom she has named Joseph (that is to say, Giuseppe), to visit Verdi's house. The son's not interested, nor is he sufficiently interested in her handsome body, when she finally gets around to proffering it—a development we've been teased with for what seems like hours. "You never loved me, you hate me," he shrieks, and runs off madly to listen to the Bee Gees.

The boy as written is a shade on the detestable side; he has lost any possible audience empathy before the first third of the picture is over. As things progress, or unravel, the diva reveals to him the whereabouts of his *real* father, an earnest Italian teacher (Tomas Milian); he has been in the presence of this new father only briefly before he's off into a song-and-dance about the father's being responsible for his addiction—an "I mean *H,* man, these are *tracks,* man" bit that leaves Milian quite justifiably bewildered. (The boy has earlier kicked in the face of a television set and given other evidence of unease.) Then Clayburgh decides that she can no longer sing, that her voice, as her old vocal coach had warned her it would, has become an enemy. We see her walking through a rehearsal of "Un Ballo in Maschera" speaking her part rather than singing. The teacher-father appears. The boy looks at the father. The father looks at Clayburgh. Clayburgh looks at the boy, then the father. The boy looks at Clayburgh, then the father, then Clayburgh again. Somebody smiles, and we have a deafening Verdian finale, with Clayburgh singing to beat the band.

Bertolucci is never entirely without interest, and there are some good backstage scenes of opera mechanisms and rehearsals, as well as a rather funny encounter between the singer and an Italian who picks her up and says he's a Communist, and that he knows, because she's an American, she is shocked by this. He once went fishing with Fidel Castro, and caught a bigger fish. Meanwhile, the boy is sitting at a nearby table, drumming paradiddles amid the glassware with knife and fork. Clayburgh works very hard and is, as always, a tremendously appealing performer, but nobody could jump all the hurdles placed in her way here. Barry, as the young man, is obviously gifted but similarly hampered—in a drug-conscious city like this one, where even cats and dogs may fairly be suspected of addiction, his withdrawal symptoms and drug panic were common theatrical coin as long ago as Jack Gelber's *The Connection* and Michael Gazzo's *A Hatful of Rain,* and that's long, long ago. The film's opportunism—incest was recently a vogue subject—is dated, too. *Luna* gives new meaning to the epithet "codswallop." The script was by Giuseppe Bertolucci, Clare Peploe, and the director.

American Independents, offered as a sub-festival under the umbrella of the New York festival, was devoted to features that had somehow got themselves made outside what is called "the industry." Nine were "classics," like Shirley Clarke's *The Cool World,* Paul Morrissey's *Trash,* the Mekas brothers' version of Kenneth Brown's *The Brig,* and Terrence Malick's *Badlands* (a main-festival choice in 1973). Six were new. Of the latter, *Heartland* was billed as "A National Endowment for the Humanities Presentation," a credit I'd not seen before. A spokesman for the Endowment says there was six hundred and eighty-two thousand dollars of public money invested, that this constituted almost the film's entire budget, and that fourteen more feature-length pictures, fiction and documentary, are now in production with comparable Endowment support. On the basis of *Heartland*, this must be considered good news. (*The Wobblies*, to be shown during the parent festival, also had Endowment aid.)

Directed by Richard Pearce from a screenplay by Beth Ferris, *Heartland* is set on a Wyoming ranch circa 1910, and is a true story drawn from two books by Elinore Pruitt Stewart. A widow (Conchata Ferrell) arrives with her small daughter (Megan Folsom), having contracted to keep house for the ranch's owner, a phlegmatic Scot played with greater than usual reserve by Rip Torn. She comes to the place in summer, plump and responsible and determined, and says of cows, "I only met three I ever liked"—she's from Denver, and the exigencies of ranching are foreign to her. Nevertheless, she digs in and takes over sizable amounts of the brute labor required to keep the ranch going—just how much labor that means is one of the film's major themes. It's crushing, an endless round. She thoughtfully files a homesteading claim, at a cost of twelve dollars, on land adjacent to her employer's, and in time they are married, she so flustered by the preparations that she wears apron and work boots to the ceremony.

Then, a killing winter. There's no money to pay the hired man and not enough hay for the animals; half of them are lost. She has a baby and the baby dies. Stewart, the rancher, carpenters a coffin, as he has previously knocked together a house on her homestead land. He plays dominoes in the evening with Jerrine, her daughter, by kerosene light, one of the few times we see him relaxed. Most of his stock ends up as hides strung out along a fence; fluctuations in beef prices make sure he's kept poor. A measure of new hope is intimated by the birth of a calf at the picture's end. It's dragged out of the mother with a rope looped about its forelegs—the dragging, not the birth, is the important part of the metaphor.

Pearce, who was the cameraman on Peter Davis's *Hearts and Minds* is matter-of-fact with this potentially sentimental material. The drudgery, for example, is stated rather than agonized upon, as it is, for my taste, in Olmi's *Tree of Wooden Clogs*. Fred Murphy's photography is perceptive; he locates a tilting abandoned house in its landscape or allows the camera to spot, from a considerable distance, an approaching flivver with a nice sense of what these things mean to the participants. Ferrell, as Mrs. Stewart, is formidable.

There's never a moment when the viewer's belief in her flags, and she brings to difficult scenes, such as the birth of her child, a rigorous authenticity. Rip Torn does not have the advantage of being relatively unknown—you see him and the mind says, "There's Rip Torn in a big beard"—but he is in good form here, too, and Folsom, as the young girl, is real and serenely beautiful.

Another use of "independent" is to avoid saying "experimental" or "avant-garde"—the term is thought less a libel on the work. Thus the Whitney Museum's tenth "New American Filmmakers Series" is subtitled "Exhibitions of Independent Film and Video." This world has been in an intense dialogue with the world of painting and sculpture since the early sixties, with such artists as Andy Warhol, Les Levine, Richard Serra, Robert Morris, Vito Acconci, Lynda Benglis, and Dennis Oppenheim involved, to name only a few of the most prominent. Their aesthetics, the questions they have chosen for themselves, have touched their colleagues in film, as have conceptual and performance art. The two offerings on the Whitney's opening program both reflect this.

Rebecca Horn's *Der Eintänzer* (the word means "gigolo," but in this case also denotes solo dancing) was made last year and uses Horn's loft as its setting. The forty-five-minute piece is more or less "about" the loft space itself—its prior life as this affects new arrivals, the possibilities, physical and psychic, it holds for them. A ballet mistress (Geta Constantinescu) is giving a lesson to some young dancers; twins (Kathleen and Mary Marten) show up and ask if they can stay, since they've no place else. A blind man (David Warrilow) appears next and requests lessons; soon he's tangoing with Constantinescu. There's a man who plays the theme from *The Third Man* on a toy piano and who's given to making aggrieved phone calls, and a Japanese who pops in to make sushi, bearing a big bundle of knives. One of the women is swinging in a rope swing; suddenly she flies through an open window, and we see, in a subsequent shot, the top of a police car pulling up to her body far down on the street.

Horn is unforced and casual about all this—she doesn't hit us over the head with an entire Arts Council. There's no feeling of large statements being made, engendering film guilt if rejected; rather, we're being given a series of studied hints. If the film is possibly more pleasurable in memory than on the screen, that's because while watching we are burdened with the expectations that it is part of the artist's strategy to play against. There are some mild jokes: the

Japanese sushi-maker is called Nada, the ballet teacher wears red shoes. The camera at one point dwells suggestively on a young dancer's groin, but it's a Weight Watchers eroticism, lightly stressed.

The individual tableaux—the woman in the swing, the man seated before the toy piano—suggest performance art, the suave inanity of Gilbert & George, but elsewhere the film's effects derive from classic Surrealism. There's a dancing table, a presence in an earlier Horn work, that's charming; at another juncture one of the twins regards herself in a glove that has mirrored fingers, an object that is pure Meret Oppenheim. Mirrors, a bouquet of elaborately worked hatpins, ostrich feathers, ostrich eggs—the clutter to be found on any good Surrealist's workbench—are amply present, but so, too, is a contemplative sense of time suffusing space, space coloring time.

Altered to Suit, a twenty-five-minute 1979 film by Lawrence Weiner, seems to come more from a conceptualist's severe atelier. Some of the credits are stuck into the middle of the film, and there's a concern with words as objects throughout—a girl lettering on a wall using a twirler's baton as a maulstick. There's a strangely pleasant moment with a man and woman looking out a window, the man's hand caressing the woman's (clothed) back in husbandly fashion; the moment is protracted, goes on and on, the man's hand moves to the cleft of the buttocks, in husbandly fashion—a good and true observation. The Whitney's fest runs on into December, and steam screens, computer-generated images projected onto steam in the Sculpture Garden, a project of Stan VanDerBeek and Joan Brigham, are promised, among other rarities.

1979

PECULIAR INFLUENCES

The director James Ivory and the writer Ruth Prawer Jhabvala have collaborated on eight films, notably including *The Householder, Shakespeare Wallah, Autobiography of a Princess, Roseland,* and *The Hullabaloo Over George and Bonnie's Pictures,* and they've now attempted *The Europeans,* from the Henry James novel, with financing from Britain's National Film Finance Corporation (they were turned down by our own National Endowment for the Humanities). The James novel, published in 1878, is an early one, done in what is for James a most economical prose; the setting is the countryside around Boston in 1845. The shrewd, charming, and energetic Eugenia, Baroness Münster, played by Lee Remick, and her handsome bohemian brother Felix (Tim Woodward) have come from Europe to seek out distant American cousins, the Wentworth family. The visit is not entirely unmotivated by the fact that the Wentworths are exceedingly well off and Eugenia and Felix almost on their uppers. She's married to a German princeling of not very great resources and he's a portrait painter of no extraordinary distinction. To dissolve her morganatic marriage she need only send a certain document back to Germany; thus, she's on a shopping trip. The impact of this dazzling pair on the solid, God-fearing Wentworths is the burden of the story. James clearly had great affection for both the Americans and the "Europeans" (Eugenia and Felix are the children of Mr. Wentworth's half sister, who had run away to Europe); while the latter are, strictly speaking, fortune hunters, they are also quite remarkable human beings, as strangely flavored to the Wentworths as sauce aïoli. "We are to be exposed to peculiar influences," says Mr. Wentworth, and indeed they are.

Felix falls in love with Gertrude, a Wentworth daughter (Lisa Eichborn). Eugenia attracts Robert Acton (Robin Ellis), a family relation who's the wealthiest man in the immediate vicinity, and undertakes, as well, to tutor the Wentworth son, Clifford (Tim Choate), in certain worldlinesses he's not used to. The cousins are established in a small house across the way from the Wentworth house, and Gertrude, her sister Charlotte (Nancy New), Clifford, Mr. Acton, and a young Unitarian minister, Mr. Brand (Norman Snow), who is a part of the family circle, begin a parade of visits to the fascinating newcomers, with only Mr. Wentworth, the patriarch, exhibiting a degree of reserve: "He looks as if he were undergoing martyrdom, not by fire but by freezing," Felix comments.

Felix is at length able to persuade Gertrude, who's been understood to be involved with Mr. Brand, to marry him. Eugenia is not so fortunate with Acton, who can't make up his mind whether he's in love or not, and is in addition experienced enough to be slightly skeptical of her. She makes ever more explicit attempts to capture him, dropping handkerchiefs big as bedsheets, finally announcing that she's going to return to Europe. She asks him for a reason she should stay, and he replies that she is widely admired. "I'm admired also in Europe," she snaps back, but that's the best she can get out of him, and she departs.

The film is handsomely mounted, considering the relatively small ($1 million) budget, and the beauty of the New England autumn is fully exploited. Lee Remick and Lisa Eichhorn are both excellent, and Wesley Addy is an admirable Mr. Wentworth; some of the other performances are less than distinguished. Mrs. Jhabvala has boned the novel most skillfully, giving a strong sense both of the limitations and goodness of the Wentworths and of the very different ethos of their guests. But the direction severely compromises the picture. There's a feeling of amateurishness that is surprising—actors waiting a beat too long to respond to others' lines, scenes running cuttable seconds after their points have been made, people having trouble getting in and out of doors. A particularly clumsy episode has Clifford, the Wentworth son, hiding in Felix's studio when Acton has come calling. He knocks something over in the dark, Acton doesn't hear, he knocks something else over, with an especially loud crash, Acton doesn't hear, he knocks something *else* over, with a still louder crash, and Acton finally reacts. The film is stiff, with not enough going on in some of the two-shots to fill the screen; the only time its pace approximates what it should be is when everybody's going to church, and then rain is falling and they're running. But it's good to have James on film, even in an imperfect rendering, and the work's many felicities almost outweigh its defects.

The vampire myth as a literary growth stock may be said to begin with Byron and the famous houseparty at the Villa Diodati in 1816 which also produced Mary Wollstonecraft Shelley's *Frankenstein.* Byron's contribution to this elegant storytelling competition was *The Vampyre,* sketched by him and later actually written and published by his friend John Polidori. It appeared, through a misunderstanding, under Byron's name, and Goethe immediately declared that it was the best thing Byron had ever done. Whether Bram Stoker, whose *Dracula* was issued in 1897, had read *The Vampyre* is debated, but Byron's enthusiastic Don Juanism and his penchant for things satanic are amply present in the countless variations on the theme which followed. In films, these range from F. W. Murnau, Tod Browning, and Carl Dreyer to the modern Hammer Films series, to the accomplished camp of Andy Warhol and exoticisms of the French Jean Rollin, to *Blacula*—an enormous and amazing life. The historian of vampires David Pirie estimates that there were almost two hundred vampire films made in ten countries during the period 1957–72 alone. Recently, there have been new American versions utilizing Frank Langella and George Hamilton, and now there is Werner Herzog's *Nosferatu, the Vampyre.*

Ask a vampire what he's all about and he'll tell you sex, death, and religion. The basic component of the story is thought to be sexuality asserting itself against Victorian mores (although Steven Marcus's *The Other Victorians* argues that the Victorians were not exclusively Victorian). The vampire's stated insatiability is thought to reflect a human possibility, that of being limitlessly, indiscriminately sexual, and a fear of the consequences. Bound into this is the notion of sex as a threat, as capable of shaking the individual's world in a fundamental way, of changing one from *this* to *that.* These elements are certainly present, but there's another way of thinking about the myth, a sense in which it's a critique of sexuality, a lament that sexuality is inadequate as an affirmation of life, as a palliative for the fear of death. In this case, the vampire stands for a failed or deficient sexuality. The vampire is a paradigmatic failure; the point is not that some of his fell purposes are achieved but that he is forever unsatisfied, forever questing.

In *Nosferatu,* Herzog has desexualized the story, in two ways: first by a stress on the classic 1922 Murnau version which gives his own film an air of pious re-creation, and, second, by a bothersome uncertainty of tone. The film is very much of a piece with his *Woyzeck* (they were both shot in 1978), as if he had set out to make a pair of salon paintings to be placed at either end of some vast museum gallery. Herzog makes abundant references not only to Murnau but to his own previous films. A shot of coffins on a raft immediately recalls the voyaging raft in *Aguirre, the Wrath of God,* and Klaus Kinski, as the vampire, seen surrounded by rats suggests the wonderful last images in *Aguirre,* with the camera circling the raft in great looping arcs as Kinski stands upright amid hundreds of tiny hopping squirrel monkeys. Here Kinski is playing not so much Nosferatu as Max Schreck, the actor famously used by Murnau, with the same long, vegetative fingernails and the same dress and makeup—a new reading of the role would have been preferable.

It's a cleanly drawn picture. Even the rats are good-looking—they're white-gray lab rats from Hungary. (Herzog is said to have had great difficulties with the municipal authorities in Delft, where it was shot, over his schedule in general and the rats in particular.) There are some memorable set pieces: a scene of the plague ship with its load of coffins crossing a calm sea (Herzog's given it blood-red sails) and a sort of Last Supper with the inhabitants of the plague-stricken city carousing in the square while acres of rats boil about their ankles. Too often, however, the actors slip into an absolutely disruptive burlesque, perhaps realizing that, after all, they're making a vampire picture. Why Herzog allowed Roland Topor, the French artist and writer, to gibber and leap about so broadly as Renfield, Nosferatu's familiar, is beyond me. Some of the lines, on the other hand, are underimagined; my favorites were "Lucy is in danger" and "Death is overwhelming." As Lucy, Isabelle Adjani is beautiful but perhaps too mannered. What she's not is sexual, although this is always smashingly subjective. The problem here is that Herzog was unable to bring new life to his much-handled material. I assume he thought he had a viable approach in conceiving of the film as being "after," as it's phrased, Murnau. He's better at creating new myth; at this, he has few peers.

1979

EARTH ANGEL

Q: Do we really need *Superman III*?

A: Clearly not.

Q: Yet it's here. Must be a response to something, some kind of need. . . .

A: Financial exigencies undiscussable on the plane of the cultural slash aesthetic.

Q: To which we shall stalwartly adhere. Would you like to be able to fly?

A: I've always wanted to fly. In the air.

Q: A basic human yearn. To fly.

A: A conquering of dailyness. Whoosh!

Q: How is Christopher Reeve? In the picture?

A: Christopher Reeve is perfect. For the third time, he's perfect. That's hard to do.

Q: How is Richard Pryor?

A: Richard Pryor is very, very good. He plays this black guy.

Q: Yes.

A: This unemployed black guy who is sent to computer school and finds out that he has very, very hot hands, computer-wise.

Q: He can make that devil stand up and whistle "Dixie."

A: Your imagery is somewhat insensitive, but that's the idea. He then falls under the sway of this evil rich guy, Robert Vaughn. Very rich and very evil. Tops in the rich line and superbo in the evil line.

Q: How is Robert Vaughn?

A: Very good. He's essentially playing William Buckley—all those delicious ponderings, popping of the eyes, licking of the corner of the mouth. I mean he may not actually do these things but the totality, the grammar of the performance, strongly suggests William Buckley. The author.

Q: So what is Robert Vaughn into?

A: Socks. He has never worn the same pair twice, we are told—a nice detail. Also, control. First, coffee beans, then oil. World domination, in fine.

Q: Are there any women in this picture?

A: Margot Kidder. Annette O'Toole. Pamela Stephenson.

Q: How are they?

A: Very good. Kidder is once again Lois Lane but this time around she's sort of being phased out, if you know what I mean, doesn't have too much to do. Stephenson is Vaughn's "psychic nutritionist," or toy. She's very sexy. Also has eyes for the Supe. The O'Toole is a high school inamorata of old Clark's, from back home in Smallville.

Q: Might the O'Toole's qualities be further commented upon?

A: Freshness. Simplicity. American beauty. Believability. Directness. A certain sexual smolder not entirely disguised by ricky-tick Smallville couture.

Q: You may advance the plot.

A: Robert Vaughn builds or causes to be built this incredible computer with which Richard Pryor is able to synthesize about six pounds of Kryptonite, the same being employed to whack out Superman so that his, Vaughn's, incredibly evil plans for domination of the entire world may proceed apace. But the computer doesn't quite get it right. The Kryptonite. There's a little flaw in the Kryptonite.

Q: What does six pounds of Kryptonite look like?

A: Like six pounds of green liver.

Q: The film displays a certain animus toward computers.

A: Yes. Tech-dread is abundantly in evidence. Also, dread of great wealth. The themes reinforce each other.

Q: Big is bad and rich is bad. Do you believe this?

A: Like the good proletarian noodle that I am. Let us press on. Superman, coked to the gills on bad Kryptonite, suffers a personality change. He begins doing bad things. Malicious mischief. For example, he straightens up the Leaning Tower of Pisa, thus lousing up the tourist trade in half of Tuscany. He begins to let himself go—his cape gets dirty and he forgets to shave. He manifests an untoward interest in the heavy-bosomed Ms. Stephenson. He's a stone mess.

Q: Dreadful.

A: Quite.

Q: But Clark Kent still has his feet on the ground, as it were.

A: Thank God. And things get sorted out eventually. But it's pretty nerve-wracking there for a while. I mean, we're not used to seeing Superman screw up, you know. We're not used to seeing Superman *behave badly.* It's a bit of a shock. I mean, we don't have the context for it.

Q: So this psychological *frisson* is the core experience of *III*?

A: In my judgment.

Q: It's sort of a warning to us. That we can't take anything for granted. That the verities are not, after all, eternal, or may not be. That the earth is shifty under our feet. That the terrible combination of run-mad technology and big-buck-malefaction is terrible. That if you fly too near the sun you can get your wings burnt off.

A: All true. Mythic and grand and true.

Q: How is Richard Lester, the director?

A: In very good form. Many nice bits. A dynamite scene wherein Superman picks up a lake, *a whole lake,* which he has frozen into ice with icy blasts from his icy breath, and flies through the air with it to put out a chemical-plant fire. Scene's got a lot of sizzle to it, beautiful. Once in a while Lester maybe goes off, a trifle. Some business with a guy and his wife at the breakfast table and something goes wrong and the guy pushes a grapefruit into the goodwife's face à la the famous Cagney-Mae Clarke grapefruit-pushing in *The Public Enemy* that doesn't quite play, seems a little. . . . Pryor does a George C. Scott *Patton* takeoff that should have been better. But in general, excellent, excellent.

Q: Is *Superman III,* then, the finest of the Superfilms, in your view?

A: Perhaps the second-finest.

Q: And the first-finest?

A: The first, I think. Or perhaps the second.

Q: You think the first might be the first-finest and the second also might be the first-finest?

A: When Clark Kent goes back to Smallville for his high-school reunion, at which he re-encounters the grand O'Toole, the music playing, at one point, is "Earth Angel." I liked that a lot.

1983

CULTURE, ETC.

It is frequently painful for a Texan to decide that he is, after all, not a cowboy. The role is glamorous, sanctioned by the community, and not difficult to play. Adults can manage it far more easily than they could, say, Spaceman. But there are some serious disadvantages.

The trouble with being a cowboy, even a counterfeit cowboy, is that although exquisitely sage in matters of horses and cattle, the cowboy tends to be somewhat limited outside these areas. This has more to do with the ritual demands of the role than with his innate gifts. Certain important areas of thought and feeling are closed to him; like a cloche hat or an interest in the United Nations, they are simply not becoming.

A number of talented improvisers have attempted to enlarge the role, giving us, for instance, the scholar-cowboy: "All I eat is beans cooked over a mesquite fire but I also speak Chaucer." The role is legitimized by the cachet of scholarship, and we are made more comfortable in it. It is not necessary that we speak Chaucer; it is enough that we are told that Chaucer and mesquite fires may safely coexist.

A community of largely bogus cowboys, or cowboys who are uneasy in their roles, provides interesting examples of amateur or do-it-yourself schizophrenia. Thus we have the moneyed cowboy whose money proceeds not from cattle but from a nice little plastics plant. To complicate the picture insanely, let us say that he is also, in his rough-hewn way, a patron of the arts. Note that the drama here is generated by the delicious incongruity he presents—and savors—in his role of the cultured cowboy: "I died with my boots on in the Art Museum." When we remember that he is in fact not a cowboy at all but a plastics engineer, the multiple level of the charade is revealed, the lostness of the leading actor established.

These charades are sometimes played on a grand scale, with the entire community taking part. This can be seen in the recently advanced proposal, apparently seriously intended, that Houston's new Museum of Natural History be built in the shape of the state of Texas. When we begin building things in the shape of other things (hot-dog stands in the shape of giant wieners, tourist courts à la Indian tepees) we immediately betray a desperate inadequacy of the imagination. Not content to let the thing be what it is, we insist that it pretend to be something else—usually something we can despise. Luckily, the Houston museum will escape this fate. But the appropriateness of this maneuver in regard to a museum, which usually despises us, is clear.

Role-playing is a complex business, and the role of a cowboy is certainly both gross and obvious; all of us are involved daily in dozens of subtler impersonations. What is significant, for the moment, is our choice of models, what we select from tradition and other sources as images of what we are and what we can be.

Most of these models come today from the mass media. The rather proprietary interest displayed by the press, radio, and television in certain agreed-upon objects of admiration—Dr. Albert Schweitzer, the United Fund, General de Gaulle, urban renewal, Mr. Bang-Jensen, juvenile delinquency, Gamble Benedict's grandmother—solicits our sympathy without really involving us. My admiration for Dr. Schweitzer is considerable but it is also almost meaningless, because I do not believe that he is real; he has approximately the same status in my world as that other celebrated physician, Dr. Lionel Barrymore, and sometimes I am not sure that they are not one and the same. In this way the mass media siphon off our powers of concern; the models they propose, as proper subjects for thought and feeling and emulation, are if not spurious at least safe, distant, and "approved."

The influence of the media is not altogether pernicious. We tend to accept the attitudes they impose even when these conflict with some of our most cherished and wrongheaded notions. I recently read an account of the troubles of Southern conservatives who, in attempting to bring their arguments against integration before the public, found themselves barred by the mass media. Almost entirely, the mass media have accepted and are urging, at least tacitly, racial equality. The conservatives felt, with perhaps some justice, that the nonavailability for their purposes of the largest publications and the greatest networks constituted an abridgement of their freedom of speech. In a sort of wonderful way, this is probably true. The ideology of the mass media is by definition national rather than sectional; this is implied in their efforts to reach every last one of us, in their ferocious desire to please. Where the rhetorics of American idealism and Southern tradition are mutually exclusive, the latter must give way. The Law of Bilateral Good Fortune ("there is always some truth on both sides") does not apply here.

My complaint about the ideas and attitudes received from the media—as well as such homegrown myths as the myth that every Texan is in some sense a cowboy, or capable of being one, or should possess the cowboy virtues—is that they are secondhand, weak, and flat. In the choice of such models is to be found the meaning of provincialism.

Not long ago I heard a local jazz group among whose obvious merits was a distinct resemblance, in style and attack, to the Modern Jazz Quartet. The latter is the most accomplished, most original jazz unit in the country. I know that this is so because I read it in *The New Yorker,* and because I have heard their records. What I felt while listening to the local group, along with pleasure in their proficiency, was how much I missed having heard the Modern Jazz Quartet.

What made this clear was both the excellence of the imitation and its imperfections. For one thing, the musicians had hands and faces. For another, the drums were a little loud, the bass a little dim, the vibes a bit hasty—as is absolutely never the case when listening to music in the comfort of your own living room, where everything is always cool, meticulous, perfect. The quality of the experience was fresh and vivid; it made listening to records seem a very pale enterprise indeed.

I rehearse all this in order to place myself in a postion to say that I think we know what we know of the principal sources of innovation in our culture in pretty much this pale, unsatisfactory way. This too is part of the definition of provincialism. John Crosby recently remarked that although he'd been pleasantly surprised by the number of legitimate theaters he'd encountered on his trips around the country, he did wish they'd all stop doing *Bus Stop.* Like the cowboy, Dr. Schweitzer, and Leopold Stokowski, *Bus Stop* is a piety—a lovely myth that enables us to avoid the arduous business of seeking out and experiencing The New.

In a way, this is simply a function of one of our traditional obligations in our role as the public, the obligation to neglect artists, writers, creators of every kind—or to patronize the wrong ones. In this way a Starving Opposition is created, and the possibility of criticism of our culture provided for. Neglect is useful; consider what *La Bohème* would be if, in the second act, Rodolfo entered and declared, in a passionate aria, that he had just received a two-year grant from the Ford Foundation.

I think that on this score we may consider ourselves safe. As far as I can see, neglect is proceeding at appropriate levels. But those of you who are contrary, cross-grained, and generally unruly might give some thought to Cyril Connolly's acute insight that to a writer whose work one has admired, one should send money—"anything between half-a-crown and a hundred pounds." I suggest that a dollar in the mail to Tennessee Williams, for having written that remarkable line "I have always depended on the kindness of strangers," would not be amiss. Better still, find a Tennessee Williams of your own.

1960

THE CASE OF THE VANISHING PRODUCT

A REVIEW OF THE *39TH ANNUAL OF ADVERTISING AND EDITORIAL ART AND DESIGN*

The surprising thing about the best contemporary advertising is the way in which The Product is being shunted into the background. In the *39th Annual of Advertising and Editorial Art and Design,* a remarkable number of the advertisements give not so much as a clue to what is being advertised. An amazing reticence seems to have overtaken our advertisers; a new discretion veils their efforts to whip up the consumer's flagging will to consume.

The *39th Annual* displays an intense preoccupation with objects: keys, clocks, corkscrews, kiosks, balloons, musical instruments, stones, telephones, birdcages, wineglasses, eggs, chairs, cups and saucers, pinball machines, Greek statues, old buildings, whisk brooms, candles, dice, giant strawberries. None of these things is being offered for sale. Instead they are the means by which we are to conceive of other things which *are* being offered for sale—typically nowhere in sight. The very high level of abstraction in contemporary advertising both confers a new freedom upon designers and increases the possibility of ambiguity in its use.

How does *The New York Times* present itself to the public, once it has decided to advertise? By means of a handsome Robert Frank photograph of children playing in Central Park. What has this to do with the *Times*? The copy strains to make a connection: "New York is up in Central Park. New York is out in the suburbs. New York is five million families, growing, wanting, needing, buying. New York is *The New York Times*. . . ." This nonsense is dignified, if that's possible, by the illustration; the product is seen through the photograph (which is, appropriately, both good and gray). It is a case of gilt by association.

It might be argued that this is an "institutional" piece, which must be constructed after different laws than those governing "selling" pieces. But the fact that there are institutional ads at all is itself an instance of the disappearance of the product, of the new prominence of the sideshow, the diversion. In more than half the pieces, institutional or otherwise, illustrated in the advertising sections of this collection, what is being offered for sale is not identifiable at a glance. Instead there are symbolic constructions, many of them very nearly opaque.

One presents a huge cup of coffee, dominating two-thirds of the page. The legend reads: "What ever happened to the nickel cup of coffee?" The product, however, is not coffee but a gasoline called Speedway 79 Super Regular, and the idea seems to be that in these days of higher and higher prices, Speedway 79 is a bargain. The ad (by Saul Bass) is a model of careful design and clean typography: the product is deftly concealed until the last possible moment. Another piece, done by the Doyle Dane Bernbach agency for the ILGWU, institutional in character, displays a grandmotherly woman with a baby on her lap. The photograph is arresting, harsh, and full of contrast. What is being pushed here? Grandmothers? Babies? Not at all. The product is unionism, and the copy, in a spectacular imaginative leap, makes the point: "From Babyhood On. This Is the Label That Will Be Sewn Into Your Life."

Examples of product concealment abound. A full-page ad for Dee Sportswear, done in primer style with a trumpet, a bird, a carriage, a tree, a fly, and other objects named in three languages, also contains, almost as an afterthought, a solitary item of sportswear. Another, for the same concern, is illustrated with a huge hotel key and reads simply: "Be Our Guest." We are left to speculate as to why we should accept this eager hospitality; perhaps because our hosts are such classy, casual advertisers.

Probably the most secretive of all big-budget space buyers is General Dynamics, which in a few short years has built an enviable reputation in a field that, I suspect, few readers of its advertisements could define. What does General Dynamics *do*? Perhaps the information is classified. The ads are masterpieces of their kind. One juxtaposes what looks like the central cortex of a computer with a photograph of a soaring rocket. We are left to infer that General Dynamics is beautiful and important (the ads are beautiful and important) and that we are lucky to have it around. But sometimes unpleasant side effects intrude. The tone of these glittering affairs is so disinterested, costly, noble, and high-minded (another shown in this collection mentions Gandhi and the peaceful uses of atomic energy) that we perversely suspect a bad conscience. What's going on over at General Dynamics, anyhow?

I don't mean to imply that product-less advertising is the norm, only that it seems to be increasing, that advertisers seem less and less interested in getting right down to the dog-biscuit-and-cornflakes of the thing. This is a break for those to whom the fascination of cornflakes muttering to themselves in a bowl (with fresh fruit and plenty of milk) is less than total. These people would probably rather go for a romp with, say, the Whimsey Distillers of Ireland, who give you a bit of a run for your money.

In these pages entertainments of the latter type are well represented. IBM explains how Blaise Pascal fathered the science of probability; American Cyanamid ushers us around Cyanamid-Land; we eavesdrop as two Tennielish tigers converse about I. Miller ("Marvelously exciting . . ."); Bernard Buffet pops up with one of his skeletal paintings for Verve Records; and there are puzzles to solve from Whitehouse & Hardy ("The crime in room 60S"), Girltown ("Where have you been, Emily Ann?"), and CBS ("How do you get to New York?"). As Robert Benchley remarked of the headlines in French newspapers, not only do they not tell you anything, they ask you questions. De Beers Consolidated Mines has produced one of the book's most forthright entries; it shows a diamond growing on a tree.

One question remains. Why is there diffidence about the product? Why is it being kept under wraps? Perhaps it is simply that selling by indirection has been found to be effective; certainly larger, more poetic statements can be made if the product is not dominating the picture. The professionals themselves may be bored with the crudities of the past. Artists and art directors, with their sophisticated attitudes toward communication, may be running away with the business of advertising, leaving copy writers, account executives, and the like to trail along behind, lamely making what sales points they can.

Perhaps there is another reason. The Canadian anthropologist Edmund Carpenter has suggested that selling in advertising is frequently a side issue. "If we think of ads as designed solely to sell products," he says, "we miss their main effect: to increase pleasure in the consumption of the product. Coca-Cola is far more than a cooling drink; the consumer participates, vicariously, in a much larger experience. In Africa, in Melanesia, to drink a Coke is to participate in the American way of life."

If this is so, the current shyness of our advertisers becomes somewhat easier to understand. It is not so surprising that, living in a land of plenty within a circle of poverty and near or actual starvation, Americans should be self-conscious about their fabulous consumption, and that advertisers should be cautious in reminding us of it.

1961

SYNERGY

(A SPEECH DELIVERED TO THE HOUSTON FORUM FOR THE HUMANITIES, 1987).

In November 1982, twenty-six of the world's most distinguished architects gathered at the University of Virginia at Charlottesville for a conference. The press was excluded, although the proceedings were later published under the title *The Charlottesville Tapes.* The architects were among the the most prominent now practicing, including Philip Johnson, Cesar Pelli, Frank Gehry, Léon Krier, Stanley Tigerman, Richard Meier, Paul Rudolph, Kevin Roche, Rem Koolhaas, Peter Eisenman, Michael Graves, and Robert Stern. Each presented a project which was then critiqued by the assembly. Let us listen for a moment to the architects talking, for they speak most sweetly:

PHILIP JOHNSON: I am a whore and I am paid very well for building high-rise buildings. I think that going into an elevator is one of the most unpleasant experiences a man can have, and I do not see why we need them. We have all the room in the world. If you fly over this country, you wonder where all the people are.

KEVIN ROCHE: When you speak about the building as a "village," you seem to be suggesting that the people of the village are simply the occupants of the building. However, this village does not contribute to the city of Boston.

JOHNSON: It is a problem of isolation and how to design two million goddamn square feet that should not be built in this part of Boston.

A bit later, we have LÉON KRIER: Many of you here at this eminent gathering are capable of getting a very large commission, maybe to build a city of fifty skyscrapers, each as high as the Empire State Building, but perhaps only two of the people at this table would choose to refuse that commission. Of course, after accepting it and coming up with your solution, you would say, "It is not our fault. We didn't make the zoning. We did not do our own plans." To you I say, you will burn in hell for what you are doing, because it is wrong and you know it's wrong!

ROCHE: Leo, you will probably burn in hell yourself for your arrogance in assuming that the role of the architect is that of dictator—that he dictates everything in our life, everything in our environment. The arrogance that Philip showed, the disregard for people, for use, is many times less than your arrogance, for you take on the whole city. The very idea that an architect will undertake a project like that without the participation of other people, without the involvement of people, is a madness that will ultimately destroy us all.

KRIER: I find it interesting that I should be accused of arrogance by Kevin Roche. I just write and draw and take responsibility for it. If you draw a plan of a city, if you make decisions about zoning, whether you like it or not, you decide how the people in that city are going to live and move around for the next fifty years.

ROCHE: You would do it without the involvement of people?

KRIER: Yes, absolutely, because the architect is supposed to be the one mind that plans and oversees all parts of the city.

ROCHE: What gives us the right to make those decisions?

KRIER: We take it . . .

Next, we have PETER EISENMAN describing a project for Berlin, a project, in fact, very close to the Berlin Wall. It's meant to be housing, and looking at the elevation you notice immediately a very curious thing: the top two floors are built at a diagonal, about fifteen degrees, to the rest of the façade, the bottom six stories. Eisenman says, in essence, that he had to do this as a kind of protest, because he didn't believe in the project. It is, in fact, the most willful of gestures, in my opinion a very foolish gesture. But listen to the architects:

CESAR PELLI: You state that for many reasons you don't believe in doing what you're doing.

EISENMAN: That's right.

PELLI: Then why do you do it?

EISENMAN: Why do I make a building on this site? I suppose that if I had the luxury, Cesar, of choosing another site in Berlin, I would. I am being as honest as I can.

PELLI: But you just said that you don't believe in building housing there. You don't believe in the type of housing that is being built. So why do you do it?

EISENMAN: Because I believe in doing my architecture.

PELLI: Then what is this architecture?

EISENMAN: It is not about housing.

PELLI: About what, then?

EISENMAN: It is about itself.

A bit later, we have CHARLES GWATHMEY, who presents a house.

PELLI: How many square feet are in the house? How many people is the house for? How much did it cost?

GWATHMEY: The house has 10,000 square feet. It is designed for a family of four. It cost two hundred dollars a square foot.

In other words it was a $2 million house. Finally, TADAO ANDO, a Japanese architect, presents a house he's building in downtown Osaka.

ANDO: I would like to find the true character of houses and an authentic way of life by overcoming physical limitations of size and by establishing—through complex spatial compositions—a close relationship between architecture and daily life, and between human beings, nature, and natural materials.

KRIER: Clap clap clap clap clap clap clap clap clap clap clap clap clap clap clap clap clap clap clap.

I should say that I have engaged here in highly selective quotation, and that many wise and beautiful things that I have not quoted were said at Charlottesville. But reading the proceedings I was amazed by several things, first of all the depth of feeling. It's immediately apparent that the architects involved cared very much about what they were doing and about the urban fabric. That they were as candid as they were indicates that they trusted each other, to a degree that is quite touching. The strongest impression, however, is that of confusion of purpose. In the largest sense, these experts are at sea in a sieve.

The synergy of which I wish to speak is that between architects, developers, the city's political institutions, and the general public. The question is, how does the city happen and how may the proportion of good things that happen be increased?

The first problem is that only a very small part of the built environment is the work of architects, and an even smaller the work of architects of the caliber of those quoted. Secondly, we have heard the architects talking but what we have not heard and will never hear is the discourse of the developers. But it is the developers who determine the future of our cities, not just this one but every American city. For every Gerald Hines who builds buildings that in general lend beauty and architectural interest to a city, for every Rouse Company pioneering imaginative new uses and re-uses for the cityscape, there are literally hundreds of honest but socio-aesthetically maladroit operators who think chiefly of maximizing profit. What stands over against these interests in almost all American cities is the political structure—very often, in dealing with the builders, a weak entity. In the worst case the city is in bed with the developers. In the best case it is severely circumscribed by citizen interest—by local zoning boards, as we have in New York, Landmarks Preservation Commissions and the like.

As to the average citizen, and I know no citizen more average than myself, he is, in relation to urban design, rather powerless. He doesn't have much to say about the city that surrounds him. This disenfranchisement is not the result of a plot or cabal. It's more or less the result of ceding power to the experts, whether they are experts in design, finance, or simply busy Deavers who "get things down." Is light rail better for Houston than heavy rail? I don't know; I could read all of Metro's surveys and still not know. The citizen is asked to decide things he is not in a position to decide. My instinct is that heavy rail is appropriate to New York, Moscow, Paris, London, and Tokyo, probably not Houston. The BART system in San Francisco is a pleasant ride; I've not tried Atlanta's. Planning is a risky business. Here is where the old cliché "I don't know about art but I know what I like" takes on fresh meaning. The citizen is almost by definition a non-expert; we are lucky if he knows what he likes.

This points to a considerable anomaly in the planning process. The planners don't want me to vote on light vs. heavy rail because I don't know enough—I haven't studied the question, I am an uninformed and thus unintelligent voter. Yet they are forced by law to submit these proposals to me, even though I go to the polls, if I go, wearing a dunce cap. Metro would argue that it has undertaken campaigns of education on the matter, but in the normal course these are campaigns not of education but of persuasion: the experts have already decided what is good for me and they want me to vote in such a way as to facilitate this predetermined end. If I were running Metro I would do the same thing. After all, I have studied the question, whereas you—the "I" of a moment ago—haven't. This is a theoretically unsatisfactory process that sometimes has excellent results. A study of the results of bond issues, in human and esthetic terms, in a particular place over a particular time, would be a fertile field for the sociologists.

What is normally done is to cede to a group of experts the design of the proposals, which are then ratified or not by the voters. The sticking point here is the quality of the experts. Are they good experts or lousy experts? We do the same thing in terms of the nation's business, which we cede to the congress, the executive, and the courts. The congress, expert in all manner of things, does much that I don't want it to do, including the creation of the $2.3 trillion deficit as of August of this year [1987] and a move to cut Social Security inflation adjustments for old people—neither of them things I want, both done in my name and endorsed by battalions of experts. But this is to say no more than that the system is imperfect, and if I don't like it, why don't I run for Congress? I don't have the skills to run for Congress, I have other concerns, but in a certain sense I have opted out of the progress that produces the results I'm complaining about. A paradox.

The other night I had the great pleasure of watching Senator Proxmire browbeating a three-star Air Force general during televised hearings having to do with the F-16, a General Dynamics plane that has had something like eighty crashes since it was declared operational. Senator Proxmire was having a great time, the general somewhat less so. In fact the general looked like he wished he'd never been born, aides whispering into his ear, sweat gathering on his brow. This man was so much an expert in the procurement line that the Air Force had sent him to testify. And the general was very good at it; he knew what an ECP was and what a DFA was and how many contract waivers were not too many. He knew what an acceptable rate of crashes per thousand sorties was, and I'm sure that, to him, everything he was saying was eminently reasonable, state of the art. Senator Proxmire, on the other hand, seemed to think that eighty crashes was rather a lot. What the general did not sound like was Philip Johnson saying "two million goddamn square feet that should not be built in this part of Boston." In other words, I like my experts confused, uncertain, even fearful.

In terms of the political establishment's contribution to the process, it's a little much to ask that the mayor and City Council of any very large city be estheticians as well as own all the other skills necessary to keeping the city functioning, prospering. This kind of problem is usually delegated to a City Planning Commission that is usually pretty well toothless—I don't mean just here, but everywhere. In the nineteenth century, Napoléon III famously gave Baron Haussmann all of Paris for his canvas, and the boulevards, parks, vistas that resulted are one of the glories of Western civilization. Great protest accompanied Haussmann's modernizations, but the results are there for all to see. Can you imagine a City Planning Commission that has the power of condemnation, as Haussmann had? Well, no, and perhaps it would be unwise to again give mere mortals such vast powers. If they'd been given to Corbusier in the 1930s, would his stuff have worked? I think not.

Where do you go to have a city planned for you? How much planning is healthy? Many theorists argue for leaving things alone. "The absence of a plan is itself a plan," said the Dadaist Tristan Tzara. My father, himself an architect of considerable distinction, felt size, scale was the root of the problem; he used to say that if man had been designed by architects he'd be sixty feet tall by now. Most city governments are not in power long enough to get much done in the way of placing a stamp on the built environment, and even when they are . . . You'll recall that Oscar Holcombe enjoyed eleven two-year terms as mayor of Houston, that is, four years longer than Napoléon III's reign as emperor, and no Paris flowered.

To the very fashionable argument that the best planning is no planning, I must enter a dissent—some planning, I think, is better than no planning. What is to be avoided is any sort of totalization, any sort of messianic dream. Albert Speer, Hitler's architect of choice, is what we don't want. Let the planners plan the left leg, the right shoulder, the pancreas, and possibly an ear—and forbid the rest of the civic corpus to them.

We get the word "synergy" from biology. It refers to the action of two or more substances or organisms to achieve results of which each is individually incapable. The painter Paul Klee put it this way: "One bone alone achieves nothing." More recently the term has been associated with the architect Buckminister Fuller, whose brilliant tensegrity structures, essentially cable and hollow tubes under tension, demonstrate the principle quite wonderfully. But what happens when the elements synergistically in play work to some extent against rather than for each other, as they do in the modern cityscape?

Let me cite ten areas of Houston that I think have been done well, a list by no means exhaustive, and consider which part of the four-part equation has been operative in each case:

(1) The Rice campus, including the area from the Museum of Fine Arts to Holcombe Boulevard

(2) The Village

(3) The so-called Museum area, including North and South Boulevards, the great oaks and generous medians making them probably the most successful residential streets in the city

(4) The Galleria, by which I mean the two main Galleria structures themselves; the surrounding area, less so

(5) Our own University of Houston campus, blessed with Texas shellstone and a certain architectural restraint

(6) Downtown, with its several notable big buildings and the grand civic enterprises such as the Wortham and the new convention center

(7) River Oaks, although visitors repeatedly ask, "Why did they put such big houses on such relatively small lots?"

(8) The Memorial area and, on a smaller scale, North and South MacGregor

(9) Elements of the Heights

(10) Westheimer, for its espousement of values that contradict all of the above.

You will note that five of the ten are identifiably the work of developers, two the work of institutions, and three—the Museum area, downtown, and Westheimer—more or less "just happened." The distinction is between an area that began with an overall plan, such as the Rice or to a lesser degree Houston campuses, and an area, such as downtown, that has the character of a battleground, as contesting commercial interests, princes of retailing and barons of banking, swept back and forth over a rather limited field in the years, say, 1900 to the present. The developers have their own ideas, not all of which are bad. It's a confusion of interests and a collision of interests, some fruitful, some not. What I ask you to bear in mind is the equation: so much ceded to the developers, so much to the planners, so much to happenstance, practically nothing to the individual.

To single out these areas is to ignore miles and miles of Houston that range from the ordered to the funky to the semi-slum, with semi-industrial mixed with residential and commercial mixed with residential. This mixed-use pattern (or absence of pattern) can provide its own pleasures. Very often I don't want to be planned for, I want to encounter the unexpected, which cannot be planned for, I even want "ugly"—"a little bit more ugly over here please, because I'm tired of looking at your noble spaces and fine proportions." The themes here are three: (1) Distrust the experts, (2) Hire better experts, (3) Hire better experts and then watch them very carefully, ready at any moment to leap into the air and say "No!" What would happen if we turned Buffalo Bayou over to the Rouse Company? I don't know. To many people the idea would be anathema. A strong cohort would vote for leaving the bayou alone. Another would opt for letting local designers handle what business there is, as Team Hou, young Houston architects, is doing the work on the bayou around Wortham Theater, the Sesquicentennial Park. Should the Rouse Company be invited in? I don't know. I am confused. I am at sea in a sieve. I don't much like what the Rouse Company has done in Baltimore, I haven't seen what they've done in Boston, but the South Street Seaport in New York seems to me quite successful—Lord knows people like it, on Friday evenings, after Wall Street closes down, it's the world's biggest cocktail party. I am a citizen, I can't make up my mind.

Or maybe I can. Let us construct an experimental model, as follows:

Let us say that I am a citizen and that I have a good idea or what I think is a good idea. I have noticed that the stretch of Main Street between Elgin and Binz is more or less dead—a dismal parade of small, faltering businesses, with only the big Sears store and a couple of handsome churches along its length still active. Let us also say that I have contemplated the vigor of the Westheimer strip running into Main, have relished its tackiness and have been acute enough to place some value thereupon. Let us say I take pleasure in the Museum district at Binz, and the vitality of Montrose from Binz to Westheimer. Synergistically putting all this together, I come up with a plan for making a pedestrian loop of these four streets—that is, closing them to cars, returning the streets to the people, creating an urban experience, a combination of Copenhagen's famous Stroget or "walk street," the *ramblas* of Barcelona, Paris's Boulevard Saint-Michel and Trafalgar Square in London. Seized by the beauty of my conception, I telephone the mayor, the governor, and the president to explain it to them. Unfortunately, each is occupied with other business. I am disappointed, but I persevere.

Meanwhile my idea is generating sub-ideas, some of which verge on practicality. I begin to worry about traffic flow, and decide that we will leave West Alabama and Richmond open to their customary east–west traffic—a great concession, given my dream of carlessness, but let no one say that I do not have the welfare of the city as a whole in mind. What about deliveries to the merchants in the area? If their businesses are to remain healthy, trucks must have access, at certain times, to the area. I recall that in Copenhagen the merchants are serviced between midnight and 9:00 A.M., and incorporate this in my plan. But then I must worry about overtime for the Teamsters and the folks who untruck the goods at the individual stores. My computer calculates that the overtime pay will be offset by greatly increased revenues in what will become the city's shopping core, an outdoor Galleria of superb economic strength. Should the city buy up in advance certain properties on the now-desolate stretch of Main that I am considering for the pedestrian loop? What are the ethics of the situation (since the city will know in advance what is to happen)? I telephone my Ethics Consultant, now out of jail and pursuing an intellectually rewarding ministry in Christian broadcasting. He assures me that the city, being the active arm of all the people, has a perfect right to make a profit on civic improvement of its own devising, and begins calculating city profits per front foot.

By now, the third assistant mayor has returned my several calls. I explain the situation to him, and he becomes very enthusiastic. He grasps the picture immediately. A way of putting excitement back into the city core, etc., etc. To make the pedestrian loop a reality, we will have to have a coherent design scheme—the kiosks, benches, and other street furniture, the barriers that demarcate the area, the landscaping, signage and so forth, should make a design statement, showing us, as a city, both sensitive to people and to worldwide design trends. We do not wish to appear retrograde vis-à-vis Vienna and São Paulo. What firm is big enough, or small enough, to be given serious consideration? Shall we award the contract to Michael Graves, at one end of the scale, or SOM, at the other? Or should there be, perhaps, an international competition? The third assistant mayor believes he can get Willie Nelson for the opening, because he has connections in Austin, maybe also Echo and the Bunnymen. His favorite colors, he tells me, are teal blue and more teal blue.

Very soon the project has grown so large that only Donald Trump, who flies in from New York, can handle it. Donald Trump immediately says some nasty things in the newspapers about our good mayor, because that's the way he's accustomed to doing business. The mayor, he says, lacks vision, and if the city will just give him the job he'll get it done in thirty days and well under budget. This gets the mayor's attention. Donald Trump, she says to the newspapers, is nothing but a damn Yankee, has lingered too long in the wicked, sinful cities of the east, and has about the esthetic sense of a tennis shoe, and her Mayor's Task Force on the Main-Binz-Montrose-Westheimer Pedestrian Experience has retained Walter

Gropius, Christopher Wren, Michelangelo, and Andrea Palladio for the project; their report will be in any day now, as soon as the annoying static between here and heaven is cleared up. In the meantime the schoolchildren are already out hustling the citizens for contributions toward the named paving bricks that will be used in the project, and the Mafia is wondering about the popcorn concession. The alarm bells have gone off at CRS-Sirrene and SOM is considering re-beefing its Houston office. And I look at all this and I say, yes, a citizen can make a difference.

1987

PRESIDENT NIXON'S ANNOUNCEMENT . . .

President Nixon's announcement that he is withdrawing seventy thousand troops from Vietnam over the next three months is both welcome and a little unfair. What is unfair is that in an election year the President alone can deliver this kind of good news. To achieve equity, the other major candidates should have the right to make troop withdrawals, too, if they wish. Senator Muskie, for example, might want to withdraw even more troops than President Nixon has withdrawn—say, between eighty-five thousand and a hundred thousand. Senator McGovern might want to withdraw them all. Governor Wallace, on the other hand, might want to put some back. Mayor Lindsay could conceivably withdraw between a hundred and fifty and two hundred thousand fat, prosperous taxpayers from the suburbs and bring *them* home to New York City. No end of possibilities. Real participatory democracy. The politics of rearrangement. We know a lot of ordinary citizens who'd like to be given a crack at it.

1972

MY TEN-YEAR-OLD DAUGHTER . . .

My ten-year-old daughter has just returned from a foreign country, where she lives for much of the year with that splendid lady, my former wife. As soon as she stepped off the plane, people began slapping red-white-and-blue Bicentennial stickers on her and she came under fire from three different platoons of Light Infantry, all in authentic period uniforms. She naturally inquired as to the meaning of all this, and the next day, when she'd unpacked and reacquainted herself with the neighborhood animal life, I tried to accommodate her. She is accustomed to adult conversations in which there are frequent generalizations such as "The Swedes are like this, but the Italians, on the other hand, are like that." Thus, she refers to her fellow-countrymen as "the Americans."

"The Bicentennial means that we have been a nation for two hundred years," I said.

"The Americans got loose from the evil English king," she said.

"Well, he wasn't so evil. Just not too bright. The point was that we got the feeling that the country should belong to the people who lived in it."

"What about the Indians?"

"You're right. I'm just telling you what happened."

"Tell me what's good about the Americans," she said.

"Well, we tried to design a government that would be better for the people than the old governments of Europe."

"Is it?"

"In some ways. There's still a lot wrong with it."

"Like what?"

"It doesn't take good enough care of the poor people, and it takes excessively good care of the rich people."

"Why is that?"

"It's mostly run by the rich people. You take a look at the Senate, the House of Representatives, the Supreme Court, and the candidates for President, and you won't find one genuine, one-hundred-per-cent, certified, raggedy poor person in the bunch. The wealth in this country is unevenly distributed."

"What's a sex scandal?" She'd been watching television.

"Oh, not so much. It's just something to keep the legislators busy, so they won't pass any especially dumb legislation." (I started to mention in this connection the notorious Mathias amendment, which would rob authors blind in regard to use of their work in public broadcasting, but decided not to burden her.)

"What else is *good* about the Americans?"

"They're helpful. In the beginning, a lot of people who were terrible bad off in their own countries came here to begin again. And they did well here. We were, by and large, hospitable."

"But what about the Indians?"

"I don't want to talk about the Indians," I said. "The Indians are all in the resort and casino business now and prospering, prospering. Except for the ones that are starving to death."

My daughter was trying to capture a moth in a Jefferson Market shopping bag.

"What else? What else is good about us?"

"We're sensible," I said. "We're sensible as an old shoe."

"If we're so sensible, how come we maintain the balance of terror?" (Her mother is an old-time ban-the-bomber and has spent many cold nights in sleeping bags at the gates of military installations in various parts of the world.)

"Very often we act on the basis of wrong information. We have this class of professional liars—" I pointed to the sizzling television screen, on which there was a political spot for Vlad the Impaler, and also to a magazine page that had an advertisement for a new type of dengue fever in an aerosol can. "The professional liars get paid to confuse people. If you're confused, you can't vote right and your worldly goods fall apart faster than necessary and you get persuaded to spend all your money on nuclear-powered catapults and microelectronic mousetraps to plant on the ocean floor and—"

My daughter whipped the cigarette out of my hand and smashed it into an ashtray—a little campaign she instituted within moments of her arrival.

"What is the great task?" she asked.

"The great task," I said, "is to make the word 'American' mean what it meant in the beginning—new hope."

"That's going to be a bitch," she said.

I don't know where she gets such language, but I didn't disagree.

1976

AS GRACE PALEY FACES JAIL WITH THREE OTHER WRITERS

In a number of well-run countries it is the custom to put writers in jail whenever the writers say something the government does not wish to hear, or to have heard by the citizens.

The P.E.N. American Center maintains a file on writers in prison all over the world, a file that is continually refreshed. Thus we know, for example, that the Kenyan writer Ngugi wa Thiong'o was released on Dec. 12 after almost a year in jail and is now enjoying the company of his five-month-old daughter, but also that the Bangladesh writer and editor Mazhar Ali Khan was picked up and put away on Dec. 3 and was subsequently released but is still facing charges of violating the Official Secrets Act. As of this writing, P.E.N. reports no American writers in prison for expressions of opinion.

On Feb. 13, this may change. On that date, the distinguished writer Grace Paley and ten associates, including three other writers, Karen Malpede, Glen Pontier, and Van Zwisohn, are to be sentenced in Washington on a misdemeanor conviction stemming from a nuclear-protest demonstration on the White House lawn.

Last Labor Day, Grace Paley and her colleagues left a White House tour, walked out on the lawn, and opened a banner that read: "No Nuclear Weapons—No Nuclear Power—U.S. or U.S.S.R." They also distributed leaflets offering the same message, and were quickly arrested and removed by White House guards.

Their conviction, after a jury trial in Washington in December, leaves them facing a maximum sentence of six months.

Our Government seems to be proceeding in a somewhat ham-handed fashion here. The demonstrators offered no threat whatsoever to the President, to the White House, to America as an idea, or even to the grass—they walked on it, says Grace Paley, "softly and carefully, armed only with paper."

The message on the banner was not inconsistent with some of President Carter's statements about the arms race and about nuclear power.

Further, the Administration's hyper-vigorous prosecution of this small breach of its hospitality is in embarrassing contrast to the behavior of the Russians in a parallel case.

At the same time that the Washington group was making its protest, seven other Americans opened a similar banner, written in Russian, in Moscow's Red Square. This group also distributed leaflets. They were arrested by the Soviet authorities, yelled at for a while, then let go.

The P.E.N. American Center has sent a message to President Carter, saying in part:

"We cannot stress too strongly the shock and dismay that will be manifest in the literary community, and in the larger world as well, if this very important American writer and her associates are sent to jail for a peaceful expression of opinion."

This seems a reasonable and true thing to say to the Government.

Certainly, the 1,600 writer-colleagues in P.E.N. and the four or five million reader-colleagues of these writers will, at the very least, seriously question the Government's good sense if they are dealt with over-harshly.

The authorities might also bear in mind that getting a message to the authorities is a difficult business, and sometimes *requires* walking on the grass.

President Carter has an opportunity here to use his good offices to prevent a considerable miscarriage of justice, and to avoid the shame of having the United States join Chile, Argentina, Iran, the Soviet Union, South Africa, and four dozen other nations on P.E.N.'s dismal roster.

1979

NOT LONG AGO . . .

Not long ago, I was in another part of the country—a warm, friendly part of the country, sort of over in the geographical middle—and I was suddenly seized with the desire to read again the wonderful first line of Hemingway's *A Farewell to Arms,* although I knew it by heart: "In the late summer of that year we lived in a house in a village that looked across the river and the plain to the mountains"—one of the great first lines in our literature. I wanted to read it again, although I already had it by heart, and I wanted to read, too, the lines immediately following: "In the bed of the river there were pebbles and boulders, dry and white in the sun, and the water was clear and swiftly moving and blue in the channels." As I say, I was in another part of the country, in a small, neat city, and I wanted to read this book again, that minute. So I went to the library and asked the librarian, a beautiful woman of about fifty (she had these little bifocal parts in the bottom of her glasses, as I have, a sign of maturity and wisdom), whether I could take a look at her library's copy of *A Farewell to Arms,* if it wouldn't be too much trouble. And she said no, I could not, because it had been banned.

I said, *Banned?*

She said, *Banned.*

I said, You're kidding me.

She said, No, I'm not. It's been banned. We can't have it on the shelf here. It's to protect the children.

Well, she blushed, and I blushed, and the building blushed, and I took her out to coffee after work and she told me what else had been banned—Mark Twain's *Huckleberry Finn,* Nathaniel Hawthorne's *Scarlet Letter,* Kurt Vonnegut's *Slaughterhouse-Five,* and a couple of dictionaries. Nothing of mine had as yet been banned, she told me, but a special subcommittee of the Banning Committee had been formed to consider my case, and I could have high hopes. It was all being done to protect the children, she said.

Well, I have spent a fair amount of time protecting children from things—mostly fundamental things like cold, hunger, automobiles, broken glass—and I understand the impulse. But I cannot understand protecting children from intelligence, protecting children from passion, protecting children from complexity, protecting children from lines like these, at the end of *Huckleberry Finn:* "And so there ain't nothing more to write about, and I am rotten glad of it, because if I'd a knowed what a trouble it was to make a book I wouldn't a tackled it, and ain't agoing to no more. But I reckon I got to light out for the Territory, ahead of the rest, because Aunt Sally she's going to adopt me and sivilize me and I can't stand it." Yes, what is being argued here is revolt, flaming revolution, but I think I would trust my fifteen-year-old with these sentiments. I think she could handle it. If she is not permitted to read *Huckleberry Finn,* she is not free.

1982

THERE'S ALLEGED . . .

There's alleged to be forty million dollars missing in the Iran-weapon-sale affair, and our government doesn't seem to be much worried about it. I don't see a great foofaraw in the newspapers. I don't see Administration spokesmen issuing terse bulletins on television about how close they are to the arrest of malefactors and the recovery of sums. I don't see Burberried government ratcatchers with little electronic devices in their ears fanning out in all directions. Nobody, to my knowledge, has asked the governor of Texas for the loan of a Texas Ranger, which is what a prudent executive branch would do in the circumstances. The misplacement of this uninteresting forty million, although it is probably a ho hum to many of the so-called big players of this world, I find—well, irritating.

Incidentally, I called the Department of Justice in Washington (202 633-2000, if you need the number) to check on the situation and get a progress report, and the phone rang sixteen times before I gave up. I guess they're pretty busy at Justice. I hear that a lot of "little guys" have been defacing the new, intellectually impregnable W-4 tax forms by pouring taxpayer blood on them, and that's probably a federal offense, and I guess that's what they're handling over at Justice right now, since they're so busy they can't even answer the damn phone.

What's more peculiar about this forty-million deal is that I don't get any sense of *embarrassment* coming from our President, Mr. Reagan. It's as if he hadn't noticed. In his State of the Union speech he didn't say, "By the way, folks, about the forty million dollars of your money that seems to have, uh, gotten away from us here, I want you to know that we're leaving no stone unturned and that I have today instructed the Attorney General and the General Services Administration and my housekeeper to turn every possible stone, great or small, in the pursuit of this lost money that we're just worried sick about, here in the White House." He didn't say that, or anything like it.

I remember years ago when I was working for a nonprofit institution and I couldn't find four hundred and fifty dollars. An associate and I went over and over all our bills and such, but we just couldn't find this four hundred and fifty dollars we were supposed to have. It was horrible. I lay awake nights for a week sweating about this four hundred and fifty dollars. We finally found it (we had paid an insurance premium and failed to enter the check in the checkbook), and my associate was so relieved that she hit me a sharp rap on the top of the head with her knuckles, as an old-time schoolteacher might. I understood what she was feeling. I don't propose this as an instance of an exemplary moral sense; it was just ordinary industrial-strength worry. That was a long time ago.

I know that the amount in question is only the lifetime earnings of a mere 58.7 citizens (figuring a hipshot average of thirty-five working years per citizen at an average yearly recompense of $19,460, on the basis of the *Statistical Abstract of the United States* that I sleep with under my pillow), and about the lifetime earnings of a mere 58.7 citizens who cares? We could lose that many citizens and their lifetime earnings in a light freeze and still have two hundred and forty-two million citizens and *their* lifetime earnings to play with. I don't want to run this thing up all out of proportion. I just want some slight governmental expression of dismay.

1987

ROME DIARY

Rome. The first day. I made the bed.

My second day in Rome. I peeled the onions. Roman onions, I find, are much like our own. The apartment has certain items of culinary ware. I used one of these to peel the onions.

The third day. I begin to worry about clean shirts. I have only fourteen left, and those in the shop windows seem oppressively dear. "Washing machine" in Italian is vongole al forno.

Wednesday. One would not have thought that four hundred pounds of baked clams could fit in so small a truck. But they are tasty in the extreme. I must watch my money more carefully. Remember: The 50,000 lire note has a portrait of Bernini, and the 100,000 a likeness of Caravaggio. Bernini's goatee falls a bit below the chin, while Caravaggio's is nicely rounded off along the jaw line.

The fifth day. One must attempt the language in the face of every possibility of humiliation. I said to a lady, "I love you un etto." An etto, I discovered, is not very much, about a quail's worth. This will be useful the next time I purchase clams but in the meantime I am out a movie and two bus tickets. I must watch my money more carefully as well as keep a tight rein on my emotions.

Twelve clean shirts remaining. Why does this make me anxious? Today I saw the Pope. He was most cordial, smiled and waved. I waved back, but I doubt he saw me, there were sixty thousand nuns between us. The nuns were pushing and shoving and exhibiting most un-nunlike behavior. The Pope raised his hand for the blessing and there was an explosion of light from sixty thousand Instamatics. I wonder who does their laundry?

Saturday. I washed a shirt and hung it on the line on the small terrace off my bedroom. Someone had left clothes pins on the line. The Roman clothes pin, viewed in section, is made up of two vertical masses held in tension, and is of somewhat greater width at the base than at the summit. The thrusts are nicely balanced. The inverted V formed by the two legs is pleasingly echoed by the wider V at the top of the structure. A series of skillfully conceived voids—a largish oblong, a rounded square, and two smaller rectangles—march from somewhat below the summit to the spring. The spring itself has an arm moving diagonally up and to the left on each facade, a refreshing bit of asymmetry which also hints at the steel's latent dynamism. At the sides, five parallel bands just above the terminus of each leg offer to the eye a sober horizontality, at the same time providing a grip when the object is wet. It rained just after I hung out the shirt.

I have neither television nor newspapers. I followed a whistling man down the street for several blocks, just for the music. He was whistling The Marine Corps Hymn and I thought he might be a fellow countryman, but he looked very barbarico, as we say here, and I hesitated to speak to him. I picked up the *Corriere della Serra* and it told me that BUSH INQUISITORE NON PESCARE. Our president menaced by fish, and me six thousand miles from home.

Bruto figura does not mean "fine figure of a man," as I had thought, but rather "bad impression."

1989

On Art

ARCHITECTURAL GRAPHICS: AN INTRODUCTION

(CATALOG FOR AN EXHIBITION, "ARCHITECTURAL GRAPHICS," CONTEMPORARY ARTS MUSEUM, HOUSTON, 1960)

In Japan the subtitles given American movies march bravely and inscrutably up the lefthand margin of the screen. Frequently the subtitles are ahead of the dialogue, or the dialogue leading the subtitles. Thus different portions of the audience find themselves laughing at different times—at the same jokes. The signs of the jungle are unintelligible to us, but readily available to the Bantu; in our own jungles, the Bantu find the signs mysterious, frustrating, even sinister.

C. Wright Mills has said that we live in secondhand worlds—that between the human consciousness and experience there is interposed a screen of communications, designs, patterns, and values which instruct us in what we are experiencing, and sometimes, have the experience for us. From an oversupply of information, we must constantly select that which is relevant, that which is true. This is a task for a sophisticated person. Some messages are contradictory; others are disguised. As Robert Benchley remarked of the headlines in French newspapers, not only do they not tell you anything, they ask you questions.

The city, then, may be seen as a texture of signs which must be correctly read if they are to yield their secrets. Many of these are necessary: we are all familiar with the anarchy which obtains when a traffic light breaks down. Others are gratuitous, a gift from the makers of, say, Wunda Cola, and hardly essential to survival. Both kinds of messages claim space in the visual landscape.

The mission of the designer who deals in architectural graphics is first to make his voice heard, his client's presence felt. He may accomplish this in ways which are obvious or subtle, tasteful or otherwise. Much of the time, there are additional missions to be performed, additional messages which the design must bear. The designer must for instance not only announce that here, before us, is the seat of the client's operations, but say something about what kind of operations these are. Sometimes he must present a highly edited version of the client's activities—as when a slaughterhouse chooses for its trademark the image of a contented cow. Frequently the packaging is intended, as the journal *Industrial Design* recently noted, to impart dignity to products that may not have any.

The general shift in emphasis from production to distribution which is one of the economic facts of our time has had ramifications in design, in message-sending. Many of the largest corporations are now paying a great deal of attention to the kind of image they present to the public. This is reflected in the increasing use of celebrated architects for factories and company headquarters, in the increasing homage paid to the idea of comprehensive design programs, embracing every facet of the corporation's endeavors. Along with the ostensible message—"This is baking soda"—other messages are designed into product, plant, trucks, letterheads, and perhaps even the salespeople: "This is modern, progressive, scientific, nuclear baking soda, made by people who are your friends."

The burden of carrying all these messages falls ultimately on the design and the designer. He must mediate between the character of the building his work adorns, the character of the client or the client's product, and the character of the situation in which his work will be placed, the already existing complex of messages with which his must compete. His job is not much less difficult when he is dealing with "neutral" or purely informational designs.

To say that contemporary typography reflects the machine is cliché, but it is also true. The sans serif types which dominate the field demonstrate, among other things, the extent to which the traditional alphabet is staggering under the tremendous variety of functions we are asking it to serve. Serifs are pared away, the romantic curves of another age replaced by more mechanical forms. Words are not suited to electronic computers, which utilize the language of mathematics, nor to such emerging phenomena as the post office's new letter-sorting devices, which reduce the old alphabet to clusters of horizontals and verticals. The inadequacy of our present system is also illustrated by the thousands of special symbols developed to handle special problems, those of printers, map makers, electrical engineers, chemists, biologists, and so on.

Thus the vocabulary of the designer is further strained. In this welter of competing interests, he must find a solution that is acceptable to all and is, if possible, beautiful. The problem suggested by Professor Mills, that our experience is structured by the very devices we use to clarify it, places a considerable responsibility on the man who is sending the message.

THE EMERGING FIGURE

(CATALOG ESSAY FOR AN EXHIBITION, "THE EMERGING FIGURE," CONTEMPORARY ARTS MUSEUM, HOUSTON, 1961)

Perhaps the most encouraging news to be gleaned from the art journals is found in those brief dispatches which nestle in the back pages, usually under some such rubric as "Thefts from Galleries Here and Abroad." We read: "In Cleveland, O., three bronzes by Twila Alber were taken . . . during the week before Christmas." These homely notes gladden the heart. The passion of the collector, it seems, knows no bounds. To steal is to proclaim the value of what is stolen, to add another kind of endorsement to those of experts and authorities. Among artists, the generations steal from one another whatever is useful, with an enthusiasm that can only be admired. It is not simply that the young appropriate what they need from their elders: the reverse is also true. This ongoing process makes thieves of all of us. We are all engaged in looting the past. (Only the greatest geniuses manage to steal from the future.) It is therefore not surprising to discover young painters concerned once more with "the figure" as an organizing principle. The sudden prominence, in the work of the children of the de Kooning generation, of the First Idea will inevitably be applauded as a sign that the revolutionary impulse of contemporary American painting has run its course. But as Thomas B. Hess has pointed out, "The 'new figurative painting,' which some have been expecting as a reaction against abstract-expressionism, was implicit in it from the start and is one of its most lineal continuities." Rather than a turning away from the lessons just learned, the current interest in the figure is an attempt to explore and consolidate the victory of the new style. The de

Kooning *Woman* series (an example is included here) can hardly be considered a counterrevolutionary gesture. James Weeks, a San Franciscan and friend of Richard Diebenkorn, like the latter proposes a kind of painting in which the organization of structural elements is not placed at the service of some kind of literary "meaning" but is, rather, enriched by anonymous human presences: people in the service of painting. Pamela Bianco and Robert Levers make paintings that seem to mean, but have recognized that the issue of figurative reference or the lack of it is not after all crucial. It is just as arbitrary to insist that a painting cannot own a reference to the human form as to insist, on ideological, theological, morphological, or other logical or extralogical grounds, that it contain one. "Meaning is beginning to date," writes the Rumanian novelist E. M. Cioran. "We do not spend much time before a canvas whose intentions are plain; music of a specific character, unquestionable contours, exhausts our patience; the over-explicit poem seems . . . incomprehensible." This is in fact our situation. The direct, unmistakable, and unclouded recapitulation of some aspect of human experience ("LOOK MA, I'M DANCING") is today self-defeating. We cannot rid ourselves of the feeling that such an account has been won too easily; we can place little faith in it. It is not that we prize difficulty for the sake of difficulty, only that we hope to know, as in the case of the collector who steals, that the experience is genuine.

ROBERT MORRIS: AN INTRODUCTION

(CATALOG FOR AN EXHIBITION AT THE WASHBURN GALLERY, NEW YORK, 1976)

Many of Robert Morris's new paintings are engaged with the idea of photography. The paintings are mostly eight by ten inches, the dimensions of the standard photographic print. As a black-and-white photograph reduces color to tones of gray, so with the paintings, with small patches of color introduced unexpectedly for small surprises. The occasions are, most often, the occasions of snapshots; a great deal of posing is going on. A sort of photographic realism prevails, not the Super-Realism which details the tiny organisms infesting our eyelashes but an immediate likeness of human, animal, mechanical presences. The "subject matter" is often taken from photographs, as in the several paintings after Brady and individual figures diverted from news pictures or hobbyists' magazines. (Even the paintings' frames are of a type originally designed for photographs.)

Much of what we think we know we know from photographs. The camera is an honest man, we are told, as truthful as a child's Washington or mad Alceste. Morris's not-photographs play against this notion in several ways. He manipulates a handful of images (doctors, patients, hunters, animal carcasses, jets, helicopters, Presidents) into reliable, straightforward untruths. Giving these paintings the same taken-for-granted credence we accord photographs (see! it's perfectly plain, there is Lincoln, there McClellan, there is the tent, and there, the helicopters) we suddenly feel the blast from the inexplicably present rotors.

Zones are crossed. The spatial (the jet planes are particularly intrusive, poking their noses into the eye doctor's office, into the ceremonies of birds), and the temporal: a Dürer head appears between two modern tongue depressers which are also fragments of landscape. There is "hidden noise" à la Duchamp. In one of the wooden boxes the following quotation, barely legible, runs around the inside: "It is a packer's axiom that any quantity of meat can be sold if the price is low enough, so in good times or bad the packer must force on the market the same mass of meat, if it does not move early in the week at a profit it will have to move late in the week at a loss." Sweet reason and pure noise. In one of the paintings a giant rocking chair is juxtaposed with a young volcano. One may or may not discover, by accident or investigation, that the chair is the one Lincoln was sitting in when he was shot.

Morris's people are wonderfully observed (or selected). The two silly bastards clinging to the fragile tail assembly of 591-A, strung out over New York harbor, are physically recognizable types: lean, shades-wearing, shabby, gasoline-in-the-blood. Their shirtsleeves are too short, they get paid by the hour, one didn't get around to shaving, his partner has a mechanic's ungainly body and a jailbird's hair (a mechanic's body is as identifiable as a dancer's). They are just the sort of folk to have gotten themselves into this terrible predicament, by lifelong inadvertence. In the painting of the two young boys pulling arrows from the target, it is possible not to notice that the boys themselves, like the target, are stitched with arrow holes. We fix at once on the two faces (quite clearly posing for somebody's Instamatic), the tucked-under, somewhat sullen head of the boy at left, the gap-toothed grin of the cute little devil at right. The degree of surrealist manipulation is very small: a few arrow holes. Morris seems to argue a reality already so surrealized that only the slightest underlining is necessary to make his point.

Great press photographers have an unbelievable gift for *being there,* instrument poised, when the vast dirigible bursts into flames. Similarly we have the painter's carefully detailed account of the (potentially) bloody encounter between the young woman, her head jammed into the clamps of an antiquated examining chair, and the light plane that is about to decapitate her. The plane's shadow is, oddly, a brightly colored, neatly plane-shaped rug—a precise pictorial statement of the psychological mechanism by which we hold off, preclude, full knowledge of disaster. Similarly, the painter captures the bowhunter's trimph (largest wild boar ever taken with bow-and-arrow in the continental U.S., or some such), at the same time deftly suggesting the ambiguities surrounding that triumph.

For we, the spectators, don't want the largest wild boar hung by the feet, prior to dismemberment for various suburban freezers; we want the wild boar to be crashing about in the underbrush still. The hunter's pipe is an insult to decency.

At times Morris gives us pure fancy. We are presented with an old Ford apparently made out of green Jell-O, and, quite helpfully, a mould of green Jell-O at approximately the same scale, so that we can verify this perception. The man painting the lush red tomato inside the blue-and-white U.S.A.F. insignia has spilled quite a lot of red paint—a playful demystification of our (unthinkable) armed might. "This is where I dined today"—an empty resort hotel dining room of an earlier time, its conscientiously aligned chairs, napkins, silver representing an exact quiddity of vanished certainty and ease. The transformations here are adroit, and also wise. Morris's work is a brilliant triple reverse—photograph, anti-photograph, painting—giving us finally, in Peter Handke's phrase, "the innerworld of the outerworld of the innerworld."

JIM LOVE UP TO NOW: AN INTRODUCTION

(CATALOG FOR AN EXHIBITION AT THE INSTITUTE FOR THE ARTS, RICE UNIVERSITY, 1980)

Not long ago Jim Love found himself telling a friend that he, Love, had "cried sheep once too often." He cites this to his own discredit, as a lapsus linguae. I take it to be, rather, a happy instance of the artist's transformational prowess. Any fool can cry wolf; to cry sheep is inspired, the work of a subtle, contradancing mind.

"Humor is the great alternative to psychosis," Gregory Bateson has remarked. It is clear that there was no comedy before the Fall, no one cracking jokes in Eden; there was no need. Holy books, Baudelaire points out, never laugh. The perfection they envision, should the Way be followed exquisitely and completely, robs humor of its necessity, its ground. In the earthly paradise, Baudelaire writes, "as no trouble afflicted him, man's countenance was simple and smooth, and the laughter that now shakes the nations never distorted the features of his face." Less perfect times are likely to produce a great many jokes, variously inflected; thus, the Twentieth Century staggers toward its close in a blizzard of one-liners.

The premier comic artist of the present century was certainly Picasso: one suspects that a goodly number of his jokes and meta-jokes have yet to be identified and deciphered. "Picasso was perhaps Love's point of departure, although he also mentions with admiration Gonzalez, Mondrian, Kline, Ernst, Magritte, Cornell, Calder, and a dozen other artists. In a letter to the writer, Love has said: "Magritte is the only one I have been consciously aware of as entering my work, but I have to be damned careful about Steinberg. . . ." He adds, generously: "Can't forget Schwitters, Victor Brauner,

Picabia, Matta, Hans Bellmer. . . ." Like all artists, Love has a multiplicity of fathers, including those fathers who nip in for a night and are never heard from again, leaving a half-remembered image with no name to put to it.

"Art is never chaste," Picasso told Antonina Vallentin. Love's eroticism is central to his work. Where directly expressed (as in *Double Dip,* 1964, *Portable Picnic,* 1967, and *Sugar and Spice,* 1976), it fondly presents the notion of sex as basic nourishment, recalling Blake's

> Abstinence sows sands all over
> The ruddy limbs and flaming hair,
> But desire gratified
> Plants fruits of life and beauty there.

The tasty-looking *Belly Button* is also a flower awaiting its Ferdinand, the ragged circumference particularly beautiful. Isolating aspects of crushing womanly beauty for close study, Love not only recapitulates preoccupations as old as man but also assures the constant availability of the subject matter, real breasts and bellies (the pieces are for the most part the result of direct casting). A sort of divine thirst is posited; the famous tag "There is no such thing as a large whiskey" springs to mind.

The portability of these objects insists upon the anxiety afflicting an unstable culture, one that, threatened by the Bomb or worse, anticipates the necessity of flight at any moment. Survivalists in California fill their garages with canned goods and shotgun shells; Love stocks up on tenderer provisions. But he is also able to furnish us with a variety of defenses and disguises, which have their own contradictions. The *Portable Bunker for Family Quarrels* assumes not only the inevitability of domestic strife but that such quarrels must be carried around with us forever, dismal baggage of the mind. *Aunt Nina's Bunker Bag,* with its floral-patterned sandbags, rehearses the various paradoxes involved in gentility (the prim, ultra-respectable patterning of the sandbags), threat (the bunker per se), and the possibility that even this haven must be transported to a safer place (the ornamented, lady-like handle).

The umbrellas and periscopes which reappear in Love's work restate the themes of defense and concealment. The *Self-Portrait for Nineteen Seventy-five* offers double protection: not only are the eyes of the subject concealed by shades but an actual window shade is present, ready to be slammed down over the whole (scant) scene.

The periscope in *Looking for Santa Claus and the Naked Lady* not only protects the unseen eye behind it but is itself protected by a steel umbrella, presumably from a metaphysical acid rain. In *Trouble Trouble Go Away* (1979) even the clouds, emblems of unease, require an umbrella against still more serious danger (the double-trouble of the title). Most threatening of all, perhaps, are the messages the sculptor might receive: one from Santa Claus saying with a terrible finality that WHAT YOU WANT IS NOT AVAILABLE (nor will it ever be), and the sinister *Postcard* (1977) and *A Day to Remember* (1977), messages so dire that they cannot be brought to consciousness but manifest themselves only as little puffs of cloud-script. By thus encoding the threat, Love saves us (and himself) from it—incidentally, a brilliant proving of Bateson's point.

Balancing the artist's efforts as a kind of psychic Department of Defense is his version of the Peaceable Kingdom, populated by idiosyncratic flowers, birds, dogs, bears. He sometimes "turns the pencil loose," sketching until something intrigues him. "Once," he writes, "I got fascinated by a strange bump in a line—which turned into how a shirt hangs out over your pants if you're a bit careless tucking the tail in. That turned into a goddamn dog, who had no business either standing up *or* wearing clothes. Then from somewhere came the Thurber line—'If you're a police dog, where's your badge?' So in about a moment that bump turned into a dog called out *finally* in an emergency to help direct traffic, barely time to get dressed. It's hardly a piece that will enter history, but . . . magic can happen this way. . . ."

The Kingdom is rich and various. The *Hundvogel* (dogbird or bird dog as you wish) of 1964 has the body of a dachshund and the head of a cockatoo, neatly marrying two of the artist's preferred images. Love's dogs share with his extremely large family of birds a perky alertness in confrontation with the non-dog, non-bird world. (I except the severely depressed *Bradley,* whose waggable tail is undercut by his hinged hindquarters, which imply collapse at any overture, including the pat friendly.) The wit of *S.O.B.* (1960) consists in the choice of the hammer head for the dog's head; one's acknowledgment of the rightness of this comes as swiftly as the parallel recognition of the beauty of the hoe blade, soft as steel, which forms the head and ears of *Little Elephant* (1959).

Picasso once more (from a conversation with Gyula Brassaï): "If it occurred to man to create his own images, it's because he discovered them all around him, almost formed, already within his grasp. He saw them in a bone, in the irregular surfaces of cavern walls, in a piece of wood. . . ." To be *able* to see is, of course, crucial. Love, an urban archeologist, makes his discoveries in the detritus of an industrial society; one bucket of odd parts from a Fort Worth junkyard yielded, he says, thirty objects. The prior history of these things blesses them with a special poignancy; their previous existence endures in the life of the new object. Mistakes, defeats, ruin itself are transmogrified into felicity, in masterly fashion. The suave *Park Avenue Doorbird* (1964) has for a tail a small, round collection plate for the accumulation of tips. The same tail appears in *No. 1 Shoeshine Bird,* in this case also resembling the step that lofts one into the shoeshine stand's seat. The *Crested Shavetail* (or just-born second lieutenant) has USA stamped on his tail, an indication that, temporarily at least, it belongs to the Government. The *Scarfaced Contract Bird* is a '30s movie gangster, with a pitted face in the shape of the legendary gat (or a kid's cap pistol made of pot metal). The *African Water Bird,* bowl on head, suggests a Masai woman, long of neck, supremely elegant of carriage. There are also references, in this Kingdom, not to life but to art: the polished *Partial Penguin* of 1978 has much to do with Brancusi.

In the early '70s Love began creating a personal bear garden, a series which provided some of his finest comic inventions—the bear as doorstop, floor mat, target, Wall Street operator, Trojan horse. Roughly at the same time came the jacks, ranging from large outdoor sculpture to desktop size. If the bears contain a colleaguely nod to the mice of Oldenburg, whom Love met in the early '60s, the jacks seem in part a satiric response to the minimalism of Judd, Andre, Serra, and Morris—the same use of off-the-rack industrial materials, the same high finish, the same call-up-the-plant-and-have-it-fabricated approach. The jacks belong to Love's group of Almost-Useful Objects: a sort of director's chair in steel, an extension cord destined never to be plugged in, a coat-hat-umbrella rack that verges on the practical, solid steel bow ties, a three-and-one-third-foot nail (slightly bent), a hammer whose claws curl like a Bighorn Sheep's horns, a significant tree for Godot not to show up at.

From the beginning of his career, the artist has placed in the field a small army of standing Figures, made up of (mostly) machine parts yearning to be human. It can be said of him that he either has a tribe or *is* a tribe; the figures havc a Benin-like consistency and vigor (Love first encountered Benin sculpture at the British Museum in 1960). A *Figure* of 1959, for example, gape-mouthed, with a spiked headdress, arms extended in supplication (and also truncated, there are no hands), might be a funerary object uncovered by an archeologist's trowel. A *Figure* of 1957, with ragmop hair, has a shocked tentative mouth, partially formed by hands thrown up in front of it in astonishment, and wide, staring eyes—the epitome of timor. *The Warrior* (1958) is surpassingly dumb—he wears a steel pot (standard-issue helmet) but his attenuated body implies that combat is the last thing he's fit for. *The Foot Soldier* (1959) is also a perverse war memorial; his most telling attribute is the large ring in his nose. *The Pedestrian* (1960) has clearly been caught in heavy traffic, with flailing arms and gyrating body. A 1961 *Figure* has a hand grenade for a torso and wirebrush hair—Don't Tread On Me written all over him. The *Surprised Lover* of 1963 seems caught from behind; there's a hint of a thirty-five-mm camera in the shape of the head, a whiff of blackmail in the air. The very unbuttoned *Figure without Brassiere* of the same year wonderfully parodies the erotic reliefs of Indian temple sculpture but also offers a real, palpable sexuality—the elaborate coiffure that authenticates this goddess (First in Fertility) is pure genius.

Love's work, amazingly diverse, consistently original, resolutely unfashionable, elicits a word not often associated with the comic spirit, whether the comedy be high or low: *nobility.*

NUDES: AN INTRODUCTION TO *EXQUISITE CREATURES*

In the contemplation of nudes, we congratulate ourselves upon the beauty of which human beings are capable. They reassure us about ourselves, about Being. We are a little lower than the angels, true, but notice that we can get along without that suspect radiance, equal parts paint and literature, on which the angels lean so heavily. The human body is, or can be, a sufficiency.

Seizing, that is, isolating, the beautiful has been an important part of photography's rationale since its beginnings, however much it has presented itself as a stern purveyor of unmediated reality. Thinking about women, Edward Weston found the formal beauty of peppers. Photographic seeing is a pointing toward a nomination. What is sought is the hitherto-unseen—Paris from the air, a fly's wing under a microscope, Weston's peppers.

Sir Kenneth Clark tells us that the nude is an art form invented by the Greeks in the fifth century. The human body is a vehicle, in the classical nudes, for conveying ideas or states of feeling. The "idea" might be homage to Gaea, the Earth Mother; the feeling, confidence in the supreme power of physical beauty. That the nude contains an erotic element can be sweetly affirmed, en route to other considerations.

The act of appropriation, first by the photographer and then by the spectator, provides psychological support for the human ego but can also be tinged with the most profound regret, "The ardor aroused in men by the beauty of women can only be satisfied by God," writes Valèry—that is, it will not be satisfied. Clark's book on the nude is subtitled *A Study in Ideal Form,* and one of the characteristics of the ideal is that it is always receding, slipping away from us, ungraspable.

In dealing with the nude, the photographer's problems (and the messages he manages to incorporate in the work) are not simple. The painter or sculptor can select a knee or an elbow from a vast repertoire of knees and elbows, possible and impossible; the photographer must confront *this* model, and having made the selection, deal with what is in front of him. Thus, to express rage, for example, as Picasso and de Kooning do in some of their shocking (or once-shocking) paintings of women, is rarely among the photographer's options, because the distortion of the body involved is simply not available from the model. On the other hand, the given has a way of asserting itself, becoming part of the message. Elaine's elbows are argumentative. Tatiana's breasts are wise, as wise as a federal judge. Claire's knee has been to Colorado, and went bankrupt there, kicking field goals for the Broncos . . .

The photographer places the model in a certain setting, which may be bare or replete. These choices are of moment. If he positions an apple in the foreground of his picture, a nude in the middle distance, and a giraffe cutting the horizon line, he is telling us something about the Garden, which is to be avoided, even if the apple is sexy, the Eve delicious, and the giraffe speaks German. It's difficult to find a pose that has not been used a thousand times or a decor that does not mean too much. The nude is a variety of still life, and in this genre delicacy of touch is everything, from Zurbarán to Morandi to the delicacy-within-grossness of Joseph Beuys. The best photographers seem to work with lessness (Deborah Turbeville, in this volume, is an exception). The simplest forms translate into and out of each other, emblems of basic images stamped forever on the mind. It could be argued that Morandi was really painting women, not bottles, and that Mapplethorpe is secretly photographing bottles, not women. We recall that Magritte deftly melded the two forms in his bottle-nude of 1943, *La Dame.*

The photographer, for the most part, has deliberately limited his means—a few draperies, the familiar wooden stool, plain as pine, light bouncing about, and the model. The hurly-burly of contemporary painting is absent (no broken crockery glued to the print). Color has been almost religiously renounced, as one might give up speaking aloud for Lent. Yet with Rubens and Renoir breathing down his neck, and with neither Cadmium Red nor Reddi Wip impasto available, the photographer must see the thin shivering white radish before him as all of female-kind, and persuade us that this is the case. His advantage is the curious authenticity of the medium—"a trace, something directly stenciled off the real, like a footprint or a death mask," as Susan Sontag puts it. Light has touched the nude, and here is the evidence.

The first thing to be noticed in the present collection is the level gaze and confident bearing of the subjects, a common denominator in almost all these pictures. The model has much to be confident about: She has been chosen (on the positive side) and she is temporarily liberated from any constraint other than the requirement *to be* (benison of the negative). "While the Greek nude began with the heroic body proudly displaying itself in the palaestra, the Christian nude began with the huddled body cowering in consciousness of sin," Clark writes. These nudes are hardly Christian; sin is not an issue. They are very much late-twentieth-century, as attested to by the consistent athleticism of the figure. And in the last moments of the twentieth century, these women seem, in the full sense of the term, self-possessed, if only for the duration of the shooting and within the special dispensation of the studio.

A considerable part of the photographer's gift consists in finding new ways to present "what the mind already knows" (the phrase is Jasper Johns's). Roy Volkmann takes a special interest in the tensed body, as in his photograph here of the Oriental woman balanced on one buttock on a polished black surface that mirrors the striking basalt of her hair. Her back is to us, her head turned to regard the camera out of a corner of an eye. The pose is strenuous but not cruel. It's made possible, in a sense, by the model's very long jawline (which the sharply turned head accentuates); this accords beautifully with the extremely long-waisted back. There's a hint of Henry Moore in the composition, as if it awaited a public space, courtyard or plaza, for exhibition. Another Volkmann subject is perched dangerously on a black-draped chair, a structurally dubious item with no rear legs. In profile, her body echoes the shape of the chair, suggesting a chair sitting on a chair, terrain of Magritte. Another, with easy insouciance, stands on one leg while executing a quite astonishing high kick. The feat is contradicted by the calmness of her face—I do this every day, she seems to be saying—and the demure way her hands are folded, fingers laced, in front of her right thigh. We are far from the classic nude, yet there is an odd kinship between the kick meant to emphasize the extension (and beauty) of the leg, and the back muscles of Hercules, carefully modeled, as he tears off a lion's jaw in many an ancient encounter: I do this every day.

Volkmann asks a certain physical strength from his models, and is amply rewarded. One, posing on the famous stool, again presents a richly handsome back. Her legs are extended to form a diamond shape. Above the waist the torso is thrust to the viewer's left and the hands are entangled in her hair to form a second, smaller diamond shape at the top of the frame. Here the pose partakes of the punitive. The effect is of an acrobatic moment that could only be caught in a photograph (no sculptor could hope to equal it), and the play of light across the ungentle surfaces is remarkable.

Throughout his work, Volkmann seeks contradictions, those which enable us to see, and there are a number of examples here of the body in more-or-less repose. A woman leans lightly against a stool and does nothing more than swing her left leg a few degrees to the right—it's sufficient. A wide-shouldered beauty, in another shot, does nothing at all but stand, legs slightly crossed, in the center of the frame, as if about to take a step toward us but hesitating. She lingers at the point of joining us outside the frame, but will not. One of the characteristics of the ideal is that it is not *here*.

Robert Mapplethorpe's vigorous investigations of several different sorts of subject matter—sexual, as in his photographs of black men, still lifes, as in his oddly powerful photographs of flowers, and portraits, children, celebrities, actors—have commanded wide attention, as has his recent book-length essay on the bodybuilder Lisa Lyon, *Lady*. An aesthetic Spartan, if not minimalist, informs his work, with emphasis on what can be drawn tonally from black and white, a freshness and verve in his selection of significant detail, and a sense of humor. The pairing of the woman whose upturned chin (the eyes are cropped) and breasts fill only the far left-hand section of the print and the dark-cowled observer, acolyte or seducer, on the facing page, is typically his: light and dark, two contrasting intensities—one, the intensity of the pose, the other, the intensity of the gaze.

It's the gaze, the *regard*, again, that distinguishes the woman in the white blouse with the embroidery on the outthrust shoulder;

she's got in abundance the sexual/spiritual confidence mentioned earlier, but owns as well an inviting reserve that recalls the first still shots of Lauren Bacall and other universal icons of the great days of the movie studios. The portrait of the woman in the robe with the white piping on the wide lapels is, on the other hand, carefully unglamorous but nevertheless a striking character study: The folded arms, mark of power the world over, speak volumes, and the knowing, slightly rueful expression underlines a comprehension of what that power means in practice. Mapplethorpe has the psychological insight of the revolutionary; that is, he seems consistently to seek the *other side* of any given question or situation (where the revolutionary's point of entry is to be found). Here it serves him well.

Gilles Larrains's images offer a contemplative view of the nude. The young woman with her hands folded between her legs is thinking, questioning the camera (as her interrogatory gaze makes clear). As in others of these pictures, there seems to be an uneasy truce between subject and photographer—almost-but-not-quite argument, contention, testing. The photographer achieves the image with some degree of mental effort. In another shot, three women epitomize not boldness but bravery. All are heavily laden with jewelry: necklaces, earrings, bracelets, pearls, bangles. There are ruffled skirts, a feather boa on the one at the left, rings, watches, petticoats, the whole armorium of allure is represented. The scene is one, finally, of a war party getting ready for a raid, bursting with intelligence, strength, and *joie de vivre.*

Larrain manages to locate, in all his photographs, bits of the subversive. In another shot the subject, in profile with her hands clasped on top of her head, has moved just as the shutter was released, giving a stroboscopic flutter to the hands, a slight shimmer around the head and arms. The white of the head, shoulders, and arms contrasts sharply with the black velvet of her dress (the pose is reminiscent of Sargent's famous *Madame X,* although the model is facing in the opposite direction). It's a strangely disquieting picture, its strong formal values set over against the irruption of accident, with estimable results.

Deborah Turbeville's work is often involved with the idea of lost time, as the frequent sepia coloring of her prints and her use of period decor emphasize. This distancing, added to the automatic distancing of photography itself, produces a particular pathos, there to be savored. These women will not be coming to tea, and, indeed, the very salon in which the tea might have been poured has long since become transmogrified into a useful K-Mart.

The four Turbeville women grouped around the large marble fireplace with its accompanying deco sconces slump attractively in twenties deb fashion in Bernice-Bobs-Her-Hair coiffures. We are permitted, for a moment, to see what was concealed by all those short white fringed and beaded dancin' fool dresses—an enchanting revelation. But the picture is loaded with other information. A naked baby is escaping from the picture plane at lower right, in a blur of baby-locomotion. There is an incompletely defined relationship hanging about the trio to the left—a troubled look on the face of the kneeling woman, a slight triumphantism on the face of the woman standing to her right, and the one at far left, pelvis pushed flat against the cold stone of the fireplace, is much too well informed about it all, whatever "it" is. It's impossible not to spin small dramas from the materials Turbeville provides.

She's a master at this sort of game, the Opera Potential, as her well-known pictures taken backstairs at Versailles, all shrouded statues and stacked canvases, the lumber rooms of Glory, convincingly demonstrated in another of the present works, a nude is stretched out belly down on a Corbu-style couch, staring at the spectator. Bracelets adorn her left wrist and her right hand is raised above her head in a sort of reverse question mark. Her left knee is on the floor, her right leg extended at full length; above her, a violently agitated painting almost as long as she is. At the center of the composition, the woman's upturned buttocks, in classic invitation. The seraglio awaits the abduction, which will probably be accomplished by flying machine, a 1928 Ford trimotor.

Turbeville manages the erotic better than almost anyone—she's not overwhelmed by it, neither does she scant it. An especially touching image presents a woman, ample of form, face slightly out of focus, eyes downcast, seated on a plush chair. The bow in her hair, in context, is almost vicious. The figure is placed just to the right of the center of the frame. The feet are placed primly together, the arms dangle submissively at her sides. A shadow on the wall to the left almost caricatures the pose. The picture is as frank and direct as Belloq's portraits of prostitutes in New Orleans's Storyville in the early part of the century. It's a drama of surrender, not quite unconditional, with an implied horizon of violence not far off—drama with no predictable dénouement.

1985

BEING BAD

(AN INTRODUCTORY CATALOG "APPRECIATION" OF "WORK FROM FOUR SERIES: A SESQUICENTENNIAL EXHIBITION" BY ROBERT RAUSCHENBERG, CONTEMPORARY ARTS MUSEUM, HOUSTON, 1985)

Rauschenberg's problem (one of Rauschenberg's problems) is how to be bad for thirty years or more. To sustain a high level of misbehavior over a third of a century is not the easiest of tasks. The German writer Heimeto von Doderer put it this way: "One begins by breaking windows. Then one becomes a window oneself."

Rauschenberg has tried as hard as anyone to be nonacceptable but early (and rather cheerfully) discovered that nothing is nonacceptable. Consider the variety and ingenuity of recent efforts in this direction. X whittles upon his penis, Y jumps out of windows, and Z, that dirty dog, paints East Hampton domestic interiors. MTV has severely compromised surrealism, perhaps ruined it forever, and Michael Graves is giving wretched excess a bad name. Beuys is in trouble; what's a boy to do when his fat melts? David Salle and Eric Fischl are looking more and more lamblike every day. And so on.

The difficulty here is not producing mere run-of-the-mill outrageousness, but the nature of the transformational process by which aspects of the world are made over into art. How to prevent the ugly (what we have agreed to call ugly) from becoming, in some sense, beautiful (what we now agree to call beautiful) over time, thus losing the electrical charge which made the artist choose it in the first place? You can't. But there are strategies of delay. Céline, with the aid of some truly revolting politics, managed to remain a monster almost to the end.

* * *

The transfiguration of the commonplace, in Arthur Danto's phrase, is both Rauschenberg's fundamental maneuver and his dilemma. He is particularly adept with that wonderful category, the messy, having studied same, no doubt, with de Kooning, who managed to be messier than Hans Hofmann, who now appears positively tidy. In 1962, visiting Rauschenberg's studio with the photographer Rudy Burkhardt, I noticed that the windows overlooking Broadway were dark gray with our good New York grime. Rauschenberg was then working on some of the earliest of his black-and-white silkscreen paintings, and the tonality of the paintings was very much that of the windows. We ran a shot of the windows alongside photographs of the paintings in the journal I was then laboring for—instant art history. New York is a great filthy gift, and its very filthiness has worked to the artist's advantage, has been tonic. Robert Hughes observes (quoting highly placed officials at the New York City dump) that Manhattan throws away more manufactured goods in a week than eighteenth-century France produced in a year, and the artist's use of these portable stigmata has been richly proportionate.

The photomechanical silkscreen, too, expands the bin of materials available to the collagist enormously. It provides access to anything that has ever been photographed, allows quotation at great length and at any scale. It permits superimposition of one image upon another in such a way that the first bleeds through the second, as physical collage does not—that is, it allows a heightened degree of messiness. The colors of the original image can be changed as the artist wishes. Parody is possible, even color-scandal à la Warhol. The process adapts to almost any surface; you can silk-screen onto veils or eggs or the mayor. No other artist has found so many brilliant uses for it, and in no other hands has its combination with orphaned objects been so potent.

There are constants within this welter of possibilities. Take for example his use of the familiar brown corrugated cardboard shipping carton, which presents itself again and again in his work. Flattened and torn, it invariably yields strong shapes (a fact not unknown to Schwitters). As *a thing* it is the very definition of mundanity, trash from birth—perhaps only the gray, hopeless shirt cardboard has less social status. To insist upon it is, metaphorically, to condemn the system of value in which its status is seen as abysmal. To say that other people have used the same or similar objects for the purposes of art or that the object is presented not ponderously but often with a deliberate gaiety misses the point, which is that the artist has chosen it repeatedly, that he is in some way committed to it. Rauschenberg will almost always pick the rough over the smooth, the flawed over the whole, the old over the new, but so, too, will many other artists. A procedure based on such choices requires that the ensemble be *bad enough*—that is, distinct enough from all other sights to allow itself to be seen, to take hold, even to prevail in a visual landscape that is already clamorous. Windows again: "The works had to look at least as interesting as anything that was going on outside the window," Rauschenberg says.

The artist seeks a construction that holds the viewer in a certain sort of tension, and it is in being able to pull this off, year after year, that major reputations are made and endure. One's own achievements become what must be circumvented. Rauschenberg excels, as he must, in getting to the left of his own history. He manages this by what can only be called acts of poetic intuition. If the basic principle of collage is the juxtaposition of unlike things within a visual field (in Rauschenberg's case, most often what Leo Steinberg has aptly termed the "work surface picture plane"), he need in theory only find stranger and stranger things and build not-quite-decipherable rebuses from them. The theory is straightforward enough but, of course, inadequate. It ignores the true source of this artist's power, which lies in the mystery of particular choices. Charles Mauron, writing of the reception of the early work of Mallarmé, notes that although readers felt rebuffed, excluded by the work, they nevertheless also knew it to be magnificently written. Seizure, as it were, is always prior to understanding. It is an essential aspect of the tension mentioned earlier, and it is where Rauschenberg's real genius lies—the tire wrestled over the goat's hind legs.

REIFICATIONS

(CATALOG INTRODUCTION FOR AN EXHIBITION OF WORK BY ELAINE LUSTIG COHEN AT EXIT ART GALLERY, NEW YORK, 1985)

To characterize the work of Elaine Lustig Cohen, one must begin by invoking distinguished names: Mondrian, Arp, Kupka, Robert and Sonia Delaunay, Rodchenko, Popova, Picabia, all precursors and sources of inspiration. Sundry other Cubists, Orphists, Neo-Plasticists, and Constructivists might be cited, along with a number of more contemporary figures. A half-dozen architects could be added to the list, as well as such biological sports as Schwitters and Cornell. But in the main, her roots are to be located in the great period from 1912 to 1936, and in Russia, France, and Germany.

What she has done is to bring, with unmatched vigor, invention, and verve, elements of these several rich traditions into the 1980s. Her selection of progenitors is thus of considerable interest—idiosyncratic and notably unfashionable. Every artist is the product of a (theoretically infinite) number of predecessors; reversing the usual fathering procedure, these are chosen by the artist, consciously or through the texture of the skin. The ground Elaine Lustig Cohen has occupied is not heavily populated with other artists; although not precisely neglected, it has nevertheless been somewhat obscured by the hectic rush of developments since 1939. In other words, hers has been a courageous as well as imaginative series of choices, perhaps inevitable.

Thus the formal virtues of *Obrero* (literally, "laborer") of 1979, shredded paper in brown, terra-cotta, black, and green, fragments of block sans-serif Spanish words ("Precio unico"), recall Rodchenko's *Poster for Trekhgomoe Beer* of 1923; the palette is similar, the disposition of energy across the surface of the work analogous. Rodchenko, eager to support his not-yet-compromised revolution in every possible way, urges consumption of good proletarian beer ("drink the beer with the double gold label"); our artist, not unmindful of the history of the intervening fifty-plus years, presents a much more troubled affiche. (I don't mean to argue that this particular Rodchenko is her point of departure, only that the affinities are perhaps not accidental.) Elaine Lustig Cohen's work is dominated by red pistonlike forms moving diagonally up the picture plane, a suggestion of mechanization, a suggestion of involuntary servitude. One of the pleasures of art is that it enables the mind to move in unanticipated directions, to make connections that may be in some sense errors but are fruitful nonetheless. Malevich: ". . . The visual phenomena of the objective world are, in themselves, meaningless; the significant thing is feeling, as such, quite apart from the environment in which it is called forth."

Obrero is collage on a scale that few artists have attempted, an instance of Cohen's extending and amplifying the tradition. Schwitters almost never worked this big (the Merzbau excepted), Cornell never. Ernst's collages seem, in regard to scale, almost timid, whatever their other considerable virtues may be. A related work, *Union de Centro* (1980) has many of the same elements and is an emblem that can be read in a number of ways (is it a Japanese war poem? a hommage to the Costa del Sol? a critique of Wyndham Lewis?). Picasso: "An idea is a beginning point and no more. If you contemplate, it, it becomes something else." What comes through above all is the strength and fecundity of Cohen's image, which earns contemplation, and the pure unmediated delight it gives the eye.

Among the paintings, *A Little Off the Ground* (1984) reminds me, oddly, of Gerald Murphy (especially, perhaps, the *Wasp and Pear*) and of Murphy's friend and teacher, Léger. Color is the mnemonic. Although the painting contains no figurative elements, the bold red-orange zigzag that electrifies its field stands in for all manner of meticulous depiction, and the "movement of color" so valued, indeed revered, by Delaunay and his disciples makes it a true feast. *Night Sky Lluch* (1984) is done with chilly colors, ice, black, cold reds, cross-hatching, the appearance of folded paper; there's a great deal of contestation going on, a struggle for space, a melee that echoes the pick-up-sticks clatter of Kandinsky. There have been, I think, no more convincing reifications of the Cubist-Neo-Plasticist-Constructivist ethic (allowing for the very great differences between these movements) in recent years than paintings like *The Croaked Moon* (1935), *World Backwards* (1984), and *Across the Sky* (1984). To be blunt, these works *look better* than most of the competition—a not-small claim, but defensible.

In other canvases, Mondrian is the issue. No contemporary artist has studied him more closely or drawn more nourishment from his insights. His stern right angles retained, his Calvinist blocks of primary color have been replaced, in Cohen's work, with more replete and charismatic hues (royal reds and purples). The subtraction practiced by such figures as Barnett Newman and, more recently, people like Brice Marden—emptying was the grand strategy of the 1960s and 1970s—is countered by Cohen's addition, complexity, and contradiction. A generosity of spirit manifests itself which parallels and tempers Mondrian's strict morality; Broadway Boogie-Woogie meets First Avenue Breakdance.

Hers is a daring enterprise, an art that is profoundly innovative yet historically acute, and wholly admirable.

ON THE LEVEL OF DESIRE

(CATALOG INTRODUCTION FOR AN EXHIBITION OF WORK BY SHERRIE LEVINE, MARY BOONE/MICHAEL WERNER GALLERY, NEW YORK, 1987)

Levine disposed early of a variety of ideas. Originality is the last refuge of a hero, and so on. The "theft" of images as a gesture having something to do with capitalism, and so on. Her early work could be described as a process of breaking windows.

♦

Art is a commodity, art criticism is a commodity, the apple is a commodity, the air is a commodity, the ground under our feet is a commodity. God is very much a commodity. My emotions are a commodity, my desires the very locus of commodification. My last illness is a commodity (twenty-two days at so much a day), my grave is a commodity (and not inexpensive). Perhaps it is time, Levine suggests, to stop worrying about art as commodity.

♦

Pierre Menard's *Quixote* excels that of Cervantes, although identical, because of the passage of time, which enriches (also impoverishes) our reading of the work.

♦

Every woman artist will tell you that she exists in a universe of discourse created by men, works with a language created by men, a language suffused, colored, drenched in male desire. That is, every woman artist is speaking a foreign language, like Beckett writing in

French. This should not be overstressed, because the languages involved have much in common—indeed, so much in common that they appear at times to be exactly congruent, like a photograph of a photograph.

♦

A picture on top of a picture. What happens in the space between the two.

♦

"Art must claw at the neck of the bourgeois as the lion does at the horse," says the German artist Dieter Hacker, reprising an old, old tune. Absolutely. Absolutely absolutely absolutely.

♦

The knots in the plywood are not real knots but, rather, plugs which the manufacturers, awash in nostalgia, structure in the shape of knots. But plywood, too, is a facture. Under the spreading plywood tree the village smithy does not stand. In gilding this lily, Levine pirates a part of its inauthenticity for her own purposes. That is, theft of a theft.

♦

Levine places herself in a special relation to the hero-artists of her choice. If this is a bit like sitting in the king's chair while the king is out having his prostate palpated, so be it. The guilty thrill of sneaking into the throne room is something she shares with us. She enters history while history is temporarily shut down.

♦

Where does desire go? Always a traveling salesperson, desire goes hounding off into the trees, frequently, without direction from its putative master or mistress. This is tragic and comic at the same time. I should, in a well-ordered world, marry the intellectual hero my wicked uncle has selected for me. Instead I run off with William of Ockham or Daffy Duck.

♦

Why the small scale? If one can offer the world "bleak little conceits" (to quote one of her critics), why not, as well, bleak big conceits? I suggest to the artist that she is reserving the pleasures of giant scale until later—postponing dessert. Touched by the shrewdness of this remark, the artist lowers her head and weeps.

♦

How many heroes can the art world accommodate at any one time? Two hundred heroes of the second water, thirty of the first water, and eight super-heroes. (Source: *Statistical Abstract of the U.S.*, Department of Commerce, Bureau of the Census, 1987)

♦

Or: The artist does not lower her head and weep, touched by the shrewdness of my remark. Instead she bangs me on the kneecap with a lead checkerboard. It's my move. I leave for Bahuvrihi.

♦

Something wrong, something off, something not right.

♦

What is the correct wear for a hero of art? It was said of a certain famous jazz pianist that he played very well, considering the lead gloves. Dali occasionally wore lobsters. Greek fishermen's caps were in favor with Constructivists of the Gabo Pevsner persuasion during the crucial 1936–43 period. I remember de Kooning in white overalls. "Bad" clothing is a mark of youthful intransigence and mettle but can also be a generational tic. Italian waiters' jackets from Banana Republic. Ordinary (markedly noneccentric) clothing provides an effective disguise.

Similarly, the discovery by artists of philosophers produces equivocal results. For a decade Sartre's squint was considered by many the one correct way of viewing the world. Locks of Wittgenstein's hair were part of every good Conceptualist's tool kit. Lacan provided a discourse so sticky that it could be used to patina anything, like Mop & Glo. Baudrillard is the man of the hour, as of Tuesday last. Art gets made despite these enthusiasms. Levine has been notably free of them, making her that most rococo of creatures, an Independent.

♦

Bahuvrihi is a term designating a compound noun (such as "bonehead") or compound adjective, that is, a word placed on top of another word. The first (the one on top) modifies, changes the second. Like a photograph of a photograph.

◆

Bad behavior: One thinks immediately of Duchamp, then, perhaps, of Picabia, then of Rauschenberg. The frontiers of bad behavior are ever-shifting. Someone you never thought would be capable of bad behavior, the least suspect of our several friends, is even now contemplating it. Who's the most bad Bad Behaviorist in town?

◆

Tearing at the neck of the bourgeois as the lion does at the horse, Levine presents the bourgeois (and everyone else) with the nexus of a fluxus (tie or binding of a flowing). She steps in the same river twice.

◆

And how does one know that one's badness is truly, essentially bad, and not, for example, not-bad-enough? Anxiety is everywhere, courage a necessity. Like a slogan for the Army: Be the Baddest You Can Be.

"Well, Sherrie, how are you feeling today? Pretty bleak?"

"The bleakest."

"Excellent."

◆

The loss of experience is a major twentieth-century theme. One makes love with *The Joy of Sex* hanging over one's head, and so on. To reclaim a sight from a museum (in Walker Percy's phrase) is a struggle because of the torrent of blague (of whatever quality) that surrounds even the most modest cultural manifestation. Unmediated experience is hard to come by, is probably reserved, in our time, to as yet undiscovered tribes sweltering in the jungles of Bahuvrihi. It's this that produces a need for "originality," essentially a desire to encounter something for the first time, before the experts have taken possession of it. Levine, having been original in negating originality, is now free to be original. The proposition is on the order of "Everything I say three times is true."

Enmeshed in political rhetoric (much of it others' political rhetoric, which comes to her unbidden), she must sometimes wonder if anybody gets the joke—that is, if anyone understands the subtly anarchistic humor that has characterized her work from the beginning. Scandal is, among other things, funny, which is why the word "delicious" so often attaches to it. Most real-world scandal is not created with comedic intent; the comedy proceeds, rather, from a door opened at the wrong moment, a photograph appearing in the wrong place (page one of the *National Enquirer*). Levine's scandal has comedy in mind from the outset.

♦

Art is always aimed (like a rifle, if you wish) at the middle class. The working class has its own culture and will have no truck with fanciness of any kind. The upper class owns the world and thus needs know no more about the world than is necessary for its orderly exploitation. The notion that art cuts across class boundaries to stir the hearts of hoe hand and Morgan alike is, at best, a fiction useful to the artist, his Hail Mary. It is the poor puzzled bourgeoisie that is sufficiently uncertain, sufficiently hopeful, to pay attention to art. It follows (as the night the day) that the bourgeoisie should get it in the neck.

♦

The four social classes under late capitalism are
Artists
Rich people
The middle class
Poor people
—this being the order of rank and precedence.

As the dominant class (morally/intellectually speaking), artists have a clear social responsibility to care for and nurture the three lower classes. This is not by any means their primary responsibility, which is of course to art, but neither is it a negligible one.

♦

Levine instructs us in the Kierkegaardian repetition, in which an action is repeated, with the substance of the maneuver, what is to be savored, being the distance between the first and second occasions. A humble example: I marry my wife again, ten years later. The second action is time-binding, and what is encompassed (represented) is everything that has happened between us in that placid or stormy ten years. The second marriage, clearly, has meanings that the first does not, and these, isolated, are what the maneuver is all about. The neck of the matter.

♦

Levine's stripe paintings have something off, wrong, *louche* about them, a deliberate provocation. She discards many possibilities—a pristine Barnett Newman look, the rainbow-play of Gene Davis, Brice Marden's balance—for something else. The stripe paintings create discomfort, a phenomenological sizzle of unease, as do the checkerboards. These are executed with an unclassifiable *élan*, in some sense dare you to fathom the secret project of which they are a part. They remain questions, resisting interpretation. They remind us of Johns' "things the mind already knows" while evoking the mind's night-side. By way of contrast, the knot paintings are relatively benign, omens of good fortune (finding gold nuggets in a stream of plywood), desire caught by the tail.

♦

Levine is an artist for a dreadfully confused time. (We are always congratulating ourselves on our madness.) Her work goes to the heart of our difficulties like the proportion five by thirteen, which, if you think about it—the golden section gone a bit berserko—is where we are.

Interviews with Donald Barthelme

INTERVIEW WITH JEROME KLINKOWITZ, 1971–72

Donald Barthelme once said that Joyce's *Finnegans Wake* should be taken as part of the landscape, around which the reader's life could be slowly appreciated, like one's home or neighborhood. The weekly *New Yorker* with its Barthelme fiction, on the coffee table or next to the easy chair, provides a similar landscape for the appreciation of ongoing American fiction.

The author of four story collections, the novel *Snow White,* and the National Book Award winner for children's literature, *The Slightly Irregular Fire Engine,* Barthelme is one of the most prolific story writers in recent times: of his one-hundred-odd pieces, more than half have not been collected, among them some of his funniest and most inventive fictions. Barthelme's work has become one of the great resources of contemporary American literature; he has, according to Philip Stevick, become "the most imitated fictionist in the United States today." Like waiting for the next Charlie Parker single of a generation or two ago, avid Barthelme readers have a consistent and progressive stream of Barthelme to anticipate and collect. When *The New Yorker* is a day late and the girl across the hall has your paperbacks of *Come Back, Dr. Caligari; Unspeakable Practices, Unnatural Acts; City Life;* and *Sadness,* you can always boogie on down to the library and with the *Reader's Guide* spend a solid afternoon reading the uncollected Barthelme.

Though he declined a personal or telephone interview because of his "paranoia in the face of microphones," Barthelme accepted a list of questions mailed to his West Eleventh Street apartment in the fall of 1971. We kept in touch by phone thereafter; more questions were sent the next summer, from which the following twenty evolved. The first was suggested by fellow fictionist Carl Krampf, and the last was posed by Barthelme himself.

JEROME KLINKOWITZ: When you improvise, do you think of the chord changes or the melody?

DONALD BARTHELME: Both. This is an interesting question which I'm unable to answer adequately. If the melody is the skeleton of the particular object, then the chord changes are its wardrobe, its changes of clothes. I tend to pay rather more attention to the latter than to the former. All I want is just a trace of skeleton—three bones from which the rest may be reasoned out.

KLINKOWITZ: As the son of an architect, are you conscious of any influences of that art and science on your own fictional work? "At the Tolstoy Museum" and "The Show" feature architectural drawings, but I wonder if it has had a broader influence?

BARTHELME: My father was a "modern" architect in the sense that he was an advocate of Mies and Corbu, et al. He was something of an anomaly in Texas in the thirties. The atmosphere of the house was peculiar in that there were very large architectural books around and the considerations were: What was Mies doing, what was Aalto doing, what was Neutra up to, what about Wright? My father's concerns, in other words, were to say the least somewhat different from those of the other people we knew. His mind was elsewhere. My mother had a degree in English from Penn, where they had met, and was a Northerner, a Philadelphian. There were five children. In the late thirties my father built a house for us, something not too dissimilar to Mies's Tugendhat house. It was wonderful to live in but strange to see on the Texas prairie. On Sundays people used to park their cars out on the street and stare. We had a routine, the family, on Sundays. We used to get up from Sunday dinner, if enough cars had parked, and run out in front of the house in a sort of chorus line, doing high kicks.

The backgrounds in the "Tolstoy" and "Show" pieces are not architectural drawings but early (1603) investigations of perspective.

KLINKOWITZ: In a story you mention that you once "wrote poppycock for the president of a university." I imagine this was about the same time you were editing the University of Houston *Forum*. Did any experiences from those days, or when you edited *Location*, have influences on your fictional form, style, or subject matter? Can you tell me some of the things you did with these journals?

BARTHELME: First remember that the "I" of the story is not necessarily the author. Then let me admit that I did, in fact, while working for the university, write some speeches for the then president. Editing the quarterly at the university and later working for Tom Hess and Harold Rosenberg on *Location* in New York were both happy experiences. I had to look around quite a bit for material and thus read quite a number of things I wouldn't have otherwise, not only fiction but also pieces in the fields of philosophy, psychology, anthropology, history. I read all the learned journals for a while. I first encountered Walker Percy in (I believe) the *Journal of Philosophy and Phenomenological Research.* We printed two or three speculative pieces of his before I ever knew he wrote fiction. Then he sent us part of *The Moviegoer* and we (with great joy) printed that. I first encountered William Gass's work in the *Journal of Philosophy.* Again, I didn't know at that time that he wrote fiction. Similarly, we ran in *Forum* pieces by people like Joseph Lyons, Roger Callois, Robbe-Grillet, Sartre, Hugh Kenner, Gregory Bateson, Leslie Fiedler. Some strange and beautiful pieces. Later with *Location* we did more or less the same kind of thing, only with much more emphasis on art. We ran pieces by Bellow, McLuhan (this was before he got so famous), Gass, Koch, Ashbery, etc. I enjoy editing and enjoy doing layout—problems of design. I could very cheerfully be a typographer.

KLINKOWITZ: Are academics still of interest to you as they must have been during the *Forum* period?

BARTHELME: Of course. But I'm not now reading the journals as I did then. George Steiner is interesting, Ernst Bloch is interesting, etc. But I read their work in books, mostly (in the case of Steiner, very often in *The New Yorker*). Probably I'm missing a great deal. There is a need for a cross-disciplinary journal that might provide a sampling of all the rest. Well-edited, such a journal could be very valuable. *Intellectual Digest* is not it.

KLINKOWITZ: Some of your earliest stories published in *The New Yorker* (and never collected) appear to be extended parodies of language and the forms it takes when used by newswriters ("Snap, Snap"), Italian directors ("L'lapse"), *Consumer Reports* ("Down the Line with the Annual"), and *TV Guide* ("Man's Face: A New Novel in Forty Coaxial Chapters"). Are such interests indeed the wellsprings of your art?

BARTHELME: These pieces were not stories but more or less standard *New Yorker* parodies. I enjoyed writing them because I've always admired the form at its best (for example, E. B. White's beautiful "Dusk in Fierce Pajamas"). Wellsprings, no.

KLINKOWITZ: Aside from the security and rewards of such a good market, is there any reason why you publish almost exclusively in *The New Yorker*? John Updike and John Cheever built their careers through such publication—do you have any sense that your own pieces are catching a new style of our society and becoming latter-day "*New Yorker* stories," as Updike's and Cheever's may have been for the decade before?

BARTHELME: Where else? I don't think there are, now, "*New Yorker* stories." Not with Borges and Singer and Nabokov and younger people like John Batki, as well as Updike and Cheever, publishing there. These people are all very different, as you know. And I trust the editors, especially Roger Angell, with whom I've worked for about ten years now, who has saved me from many a horrendous error.

KLINKOWITZ: Are there any consistent or coherent themes that you intend for your series of short stories? Of late, "Perpetua" and "Critique de la Vie Quotidienne" seem to suggest this.

BARTHELME: No. "Perpetua" and the other story were both once parts of a novel which failed. As were "Henrietta and Alexandra" and "Flying to America." They may be thought of as the neck, wings, and drumsticks of a turkey. ("Flying to America" has been twice cannibalized, since I have drastically cut it and combined it with another story to make "A Film.")

KLINKOWITZ: In addition to all the incredible things you write about, such as a balloon expanding "northward all one night" from Fourteenth Street to Central Park or "thousands and thousands of porcupines" descending upon a university, you often feature quite realistic—even topically current—items in your stories, such as "And Now Let's Hear It for the Ed Sullivan Show!" and "Robert Kennedy Saved from Drowning," in which the events you describe actually happened. How do you see these and other aspects of our culture fitting into the general premises of your art? On the surface, it seems like a pretty big jump from the porcupines to Robert Kennedy.

BARTHELME: The Ed Sullivan piece was not a story but an assignment for *Esquire.* And nothing in the Robert Kennedy story actually happened except the bit in which Kennedy comments adversely on the work of a geometric painter. I was in that particular gallery on a day when Kennedy came in and made the comment reported. The rest of the story is, like, made up. It's not that aspects of the culture "fit into" any premise of mine, rather that the work is to this or that degree shaped by the culture.

KLINKOWITZ: Do you have any theories about "the novel"—its life, death, or whatever? So many innovative writers have talked about it: John Barth in *The Literature of Exhaustion;* Jerzy Kosinski, who fears that television has killed off its readers; and Ronald Sukenick, who titled his novella *The Death of the Novel* and theorized about it as he wrote on. Any ideas?

BARTHELME: I think fewer people are reading. This has something to do with television and much to do, I think, with the fact that publishers are flooding the market with junk novels by what's-his-name and you-know-who and likewise—never mind. These odd productions make a lot of money, take up space both in the bookstores and in the minds of the readers, and effectively obscure the literary work. Gresham's Law. The situation does not, by the way, obtain in Europe, although the Europeans are learning. The question is, who is exhausted? Or what is exhausted? I invite you to notice that the new opium of the people is opium, or at least morphine. In a situation in which morphine contends with morpheme, the latter loses every time. There is also the problem of the allocation of the reader's time. To borrow a feather from Jules Renard—no matter how much care the writer has taken to write as few books as possible, there will still be people who don't know some of them.

KLINKOWITZ: What do you suppose are some of the new directions in fiction?

BARTHELME: The newest direction I've been able to perceive, given my American lack-of-languages, is John Ashbery's *Three Poems*, published this year (1972). These are three long prose pieces, quite amazing things. The German writer Jurgen Becker is doing something of the same sort, particularly in *Margins*, not yet published here except in excerpts. The German writer Peter Handke has opened some doors, for example in his sort-of-play *Self-Accusation*. The Viennese Oswald Wiener has written a half-novel, half-encyclopedia called *The Improvement of Central Europe: A Novel* (or something like that)—what I have seen of it suggests a new direction. We are having part of it translated for our newspaper, *Fiction*. In general the Germans seem to me more innovative, fresher, than the French at the moment.

KLINKOWITZ: Do you have any consciously formed notions about time and space that influence your work? Perception and imagination? Or, forgive me, "reality"?

BARTHELME: No.

KLINKOWITZ: In *Slaughterhouse-Five* Kurt Vonnegut, Jr., describes the Tralfamadorian "novel": "'each clump of symbols is a brief, urgent message—describing a situation, a scene. We Tralfamadorians read them all at once, not one after the other. There isn't any particular relationship between all the messages, except that the author has chosen them carefully, so that, when seen all at once, they produce an image of life that is beautiful and surprising and deep. There is no beginning, no middle, no end, no suspense, no moral, no causes, no effects. What we love in our books are the depths of many marvelous moments seen all at one time' " (p. 76). That sounds like a Donald Barthelme novel, or story, to me. What do you think?

BARTHELME: I wish I could write something that would adequately satisfy Kurt's definition. Kenneth Koch's as yet unpublished novel *The Red Robins* may be it. John Ashbery's wonderful *Three Poems,* although not a novel, may be it.

KLINKOWITZ: Do you have plans for, or are you working on, another novel? *Snow White* seemed to me a logical extension, both thematically and structurally, of your short story craft. Are there any different directions you would want to explore in a new novel?

BARTHELME: I am always working on a novel. But they always seem to fall apart in my hands. I still have hopes, however.

KLINKOWITZ: In Richard Schickel's *New York Times Magazine* piece last year, you were reported as saying that "The principle of collage is the central principle of all art in the twentieth century in all media." Would you care to expand and perhaps tell me how it specifically applies to fiction?

BARTHELME: I was probably wrong, or too general. I point out however that New York City is or can be regarded as a collage, as opposed to, say, a tribal village in which all of the huts (or yurts, or whatever) are the same hut, duplicated. The point of collage is that unlike things are stuck together to make, in the best case, a new reality. This new reality, in the best case, may be or imply a comment on the other reality from which it came, and may be also much else. It's an *itself,* if it's successful: Harold Rosenberg's "anxious object," which does not know whether it's a work of art or a pile of junk. (Maybe I should have said that anxiety is the central principal of all art in the etc., etc.?)

KLINKOWITZ: Schickel also reported that you are "easily bored" and in fact "fear boredom." Is this simply a personal idiosyncrasy, or do you think it reflects a larger truth about the role of fiction—maybe all art—in our times?

BARTHELME: I doubt that this is a condition peculiar to me. For example, I have trouble reading, in these days. I would rather drink, talk, or listen to music. The difficulties the painters are now having—the problem of keeping *themselves* interested—are I think instructive. Earthworks, conceptual art, etc., seem to me last resorts. Now there is a certain virtue in finding the absolutely last resort—being the Columbus of the last resort—but I don't think I'd enjoy the role. I do a lot of failing and that keeps me interested.

KLINKOWITZ: Are there any immediate popular sources for or influences on your art—TV, comic books, rock music, jazz? Or is there a common popular sensibility you might be aware of? Or any deeper cultural sources?

BARTHELME: As a raw youth, I was very interested in jazz. Similarly I now listen to rock constantly. In writing I pay a great deal of attention to rhythm, but I suppose everyone else does too. I'm very interested in awkwardness: sentences that are awkward in a particular way. As to "deeper cultural sources," I have taken a certain degree of nourishment (or stolen a lot) from the phenomenologists: Sartre, Erwin Straus, etc.

KLINKOWITZ: Do you have any favorite comedians, and reasons for liking them?

BARTHELME: The government.

KLINKOWITZ: Can you tell me about any of your favorite writers and reasons for liking them? Or artists in other media?

BARTHELME: Among writers of the past, I'd list Rabelais, Rimbaud, Kleist, Kafka, Stein, and Flann O'Brien.

Among living writers, Beckett, Gass, Percy, Marquez, Barth, Pynchon, Kenneth Koch, John Ashbery, Grace Paley.

Artists in other media: too many.

KLINKOWITZ: Did growing up in Texas warp you in any particular way? I only ask this because so many writers from Texas have proclaimed themselves Texas writers (whereas I have heard of few New Jersey writers). Or were you simply "born in Philadelphia"—and leave it at that?

BARTHELME: I don't think I'm a Texas writer in the sense that, say, Larry McMurtry is. I don't write about Texas. And "warp" I wouldn't say. I learned to read the signs of the dominant culture well enough, learned to impersonate a Texan well enough. It gave me something to place the rest of the world over against, as the philosophers say. That is, I could enjoy the difference. That I've lived in New York for the last ten years (except for a year in Europe) does not mean that I don't also enjoy Texas. I left with pleasure and return with pleasure.

KLINKOWITZ: In your story "See the Moon" one of the characters has the line, "Fragments are the only forms I trust." This has been quoted as a statement of your aesthetic. Is it?

BARTHELME: No. It's a statement by the character about what he is feeling at that particular moment. I hope that whatever I think about aesthetics would be a shade more complicated than that. Because that particular line has been richly misunderstood so often (most recently by my colleague J. C. Oates in the *Times*) I have thought of making a public recantation. I can see the story in, say, *Women's Wear Daily:*

WRITER CONFESSES
THAT HE NO LONGER
TRUSTS FRAGMENTS

TRUST "MISPLACED,"
AUTHOR DECLARES

DISCUSSED DECISION
WITH DAUGHTER, SIX

WILL SEEK "WHOLES"
IN FUTURE, HE SAYS

CLOSING TIME IN
GARDENS OF WEST
WILL BE EXTENDED,
SCRIVENER STATES

New York, June 24 (A&P)—Donald Barthelme, 41-year-old writer and well-known fragmatist, said today that he no longer trusted fragments. He added that although he had once been "very fond" of fragments, he had found them to be "finally untrustworthy."

The author, looking tense and drawn after what was described as "considerable thought," made his dramatic late-night announcement at a Sixth Avenue laundromat press conference, from which the press was excluded.

Sources close to the soap machine said, however, that the agonizing reappraisal, which took place before their eyes, required only four minutes.

"Fragments fall apart a lot," Barthelme said. Use of antelope blood as a bonding agent had not proved . . .

INTERVIEW WITH CHARLES RUAS AND JUDITH SHERMAN, 1975

(PACIFICA RADIO, BROADCAST 1976)

FIRST PROGRAM

DONALD BARTHELME: You know, we say of a certain writer, "He has a great deal to say," or we say—negatively—"He has nothing to say." The problem has to do with what can be said. If I want to say to the world "eating people is wrong," and *that's* what I have to say—that's Flanders and Swann, that line—I might as well not say it. I might as well go home and start manufacturing earth shoes or something of this kind.

INTRODUCTION BY JUDITH SHERMAN

BARTHELME READS "I BOUGHT A LITTLE CITY"

BARTHELME: My grandfather was, early in his career, a semi-pro ballplayer and he did a lot of barnstorming. He traveled around and played for the Atlanta Seagulls, or whatever the devil it's called, and ended up in Galveston where he settled down and went into the lumber business and became a lumberman, and he had two children. One of them was my father. My grandmother decided that my father should be an architect, thinking some connection with the lumber business, so he went to the University of Pennsylvania, which at that time had an extremely good School of Architecture, and he studied with a man named Paul Cret who was a well-known teacher at that time, and met my mother there. They both went to Penn. I think he worked for Cret in Philadelphia for a couple of years, and then went back to Texas to set up his own practice. And so I was raised in Texas, and spent up to 1960 in Texas.

CHARLES RUAS: Did you go to the University at Austin?

BARTHELME: No, I went to the University of Houston, but I never got a degree of any kind. I got a job on a newspaper down there [the Houston *Post*] and newspaper work was more interesting than going to college, so I did that for three years. Then I went in the army for two years and so on.

RUAS: The reason I ask is that in your stories there are so many references, erudite references, such as Helvetius's wife being seduced by Franklin and certain problems that concerned Aquinas—such as the fullness of nothing.

BARTHELME: I studied philosophy and had the advantage . . . You know, you go through college, or go to college, and if you run through one or two or three very good teachers you're extremely lucky, and I had a philosophy teacher whose name is Maurice Natanson. He is now in the Philosophy Department at the University of California at Santa Cruz, and he's just a wonderful guy, an excellent teacher, and I took everything. Semester after semester I took everything he offered, pretty well. Not that I was such an excellent student, but he was a marvelous teacher. He won the National Book Award in Philosophy and Religion, I think last year, for a book on Husserl. Excellent book. We're still friends and so on. So what I mostly did, at school, was study philosophy, which explains that.

RUAS: What about all the references to literature?

BARTHELME: I wanted to be a writer since I was ten, and therefore read a lot.

RUAS: Was that from your father? Or your mother?

BARTHELME: Well, my father had himself wanted to be a writer, I think, although he doesn't discuss it that much. He was editor of his university paper—he went to Rice University before he went to Penn—and was himself a good writer. But he was sort of on a track and became very interested in architecture and made his career in architecture. So I don't know precisely whose influence that was. My mother has a degree in English from Penn. She had originally thought she'd be an English teacher and she may have actually taught in Philadelphia—I tend to think not—but she had five children, of which I'm the oldest, which precluded her from a teaching career.

RUAS: Does she remain extremely literary? Even with five children—

BARTHELME: Oh yeah, they had a lot of books in the house and so on.

RUAS: I'm wondering if there was an immediate or direct influence. Especially when you have a large family.

BARTHELME: No, I was not told to be this or to be that or anything of that kind. I do believe this was my idea, I can't blame anybody else for it. I think the military references obviously stem from the fact that I was in the army for a couple of years. Luckily I got to Korea just as they signed the truce, so I didn't have to do any fighting, for which I'm profoundly grateful. But I did spend sixteen months there on the side of a hill and I still have—as many people have—this dream where I'm back in the army again, and I keep saying to the people, "Look, I've already done this, I don't have to do this again." But I'm still back in the army. I finally wrote a story about it ["The Sergeant"] but it didn't prevent the dream from coming back. It's not one of your pleasanter dreams.

RUAS: You'll have to rewrite it or write it out.

BARTHELME: I don't know what to do about that, but . . .

RUAS: You do believe in the concept of writing things out? That they leave you?

BARTHELME: I don't know, I think you keep returning to the same themes, even though you try not to do the same thing again and again and again, or try to disguise the fact that you're doing the same thing again. I don't know if anybody's fooled, but you yourself are possibly fooled enough to enable yourself to keep writing.

JUDITH SHERMAN: It seems that you also know quite a bit about, or at least use the languages of, the art world, the music world, sometimes even the medical world. Where do those come from?

BARTHELME: Well, I'm extremely interested in contemporary art, and I spent two years as a director of a small museum in Texas—it's called the Contemporary Arts Museum, in Houston—more or less by accident. What had happened was that I was on the board, and the then-director left, and they had to find a new one. While we were looking for a new director somebody had to run the place, so they asked me to be acting director, which I did for six months, and I was very interested in it and so they said, "Why don't you just keep on?" which I did until I came to New York. That was in '62, so in '60 and '61, part of '62, I was running this museum, which is not a very big museum, it's just sort of a small one, but it dealt exclusively with contemporary arts.

SHERMAN: It had its own collection then?

BARTHELME: It had a meager collection. What we did was we assembled shows, contemporary exhibitions, but always in the field of contemporary art, and—

SHERMAN: —Did you assemble those shows?

BARTHELME: Yes, I put on the shows.

RUAS: Donald, since that was '60 to '62, was the crucial turning point—

BARTHELME: —I'm not absolutely sure of the dates, but I know I came to New York in '62.

RUAS: Who were the visual artists that you brought in from that period, do you recall?

BARTHELME: We put on shows, for example, and it's not so much that we brought, physically, the artist down there and showed the artist, they were theme shows very often. For instance, that was the period when there was sort of a boomlet in figure painting, so we did an exhibition of contemporary painting using people who were interested in the figure, and we showed people like Leon Golub, the Chicago fellow, and a number of West Coast people, and Lester Johnson, the New York artist, who deals—still—in the figure, and so that was the thread that the show was hung on.

RUAS: I mean, it's an interesting period, because somewhere toward the end of the '50s and around the '60s the abstract expressionists finally lost their hold on the art scene and there was a flurry of figurative painting which announced, then, pop art, which of course became superfigurative. And you arrived in New York. And did you become involved in the art world?

BARTHELME: I knew some people because as part of the museum program we had visiting lecturers. Harold Rosenberg came down to lecture, for example, and Elaine de Kooning came down to teach a short course, and Kenneth Koch came down to read, and we had [Buckminster] Fuller down to speak.

RUAS: All these people demystified.

BARTHELME: I don't know whether you've ever heard Kenneth read, but he's an absolutely terrific reader and he just knocked the people out. They loved him. I believe he read on a double bill with Robert Bly.

RUAS: It's amusing to me because at that time the three poets were O'Hara, Koch, and Ashbery.

BARTHELME: There were four. Schuyler, Jimmy Schuyler; you're leaving him out. The poets feel that the so-called first generation of the New York School was O'Hara, Koch, Ashbery, and Schuyler.

Schuyler is a full member. This at least is the way the poets I know feel about that. And then they can tell you who's the second generation, usually Ted Berrigan and Ron Padgett and so on, and then there's a third generation.

RUAS: The interesting thing is at that time Ashbery was editing an art journal, so that the link—

BARTHELME: —No, he was in Paris when I got here, he was working for Tom Hess, who was then editor of *Art News.* John was in Paris, I believe, then he came back over here and became a managing editor or something.

RUAS: But he had worked with *Art News,* then, just before?

BARTHELME: Tom Hess, when he was editor of *Art News,* made it a practice to hire poets to do the short reviews and also from time to time longer pieces, so there was a liaison between the New York school of poets and *Art News* when Tom was editor. As a matter of fact, I came up here to be managing editor of a journal that Tom Hess and Harold Rosenberg were publishing through the Longview Foundation, called *Location.* It was to be an art-literary review, and Harold and Tom said come on up and put this thing out for us, which I did because I was ready to move.

SHERMAN: Were you writing while you were in Texas?

BARTHELME: Yeah, yeah, oh yeah. But not particularly well. I couldn't figure out how to do it for a long time. And then, finally, I sort of began writing things which I thought weren't too terrible, and that really happened at the time I was working for the museum.

SHERMAN: You said that you were just figuring out how to do this writing. How does one go about figuring out how to do it?

BARTHELME: Well, I certainly can't speak for everyone.

SHERMAN: All right, how did *you*?

BARTHELME: I think you do it by selecting fathers. In the beginning, you know, I thought Hemingway was just as far as writing could go, and so because Hemingway had been a newspaperman, I sought and got a newspaper job with the idea that this had something to do with writing—as indeed it does—and eventually what happened was that the newspaper work didn't teach me all that much about writing, but it taught me a lot of other things. It taught me what a union was, for example, which I had known only in the abstract.

RUAS: Why did Hemingway's beginning as a newspaperman attract you so much when Faulkner, whose style is the exact opposite of Hemingway's, also started writing in a small-town paper? And many, many others as well.

BARTHELME: I sort of began with Hemingway.

RUAS: Did you move on?

BARTHELME: Yes, of course, obviously, as I got more and more fathers accumulated—

RUAS: —That's what I'm curious about.

BARTHELME: For example, Kleist. I was not in a position to read Kleist in the '40s. I didn't even know there was a Heinrich von Kleist. Now I give my students Kleist to read. Kleist is another way of doing things. I didn't know anything about Kafka at that point, and how can you write without at least knowing that Kafka exists? It was simple ignorance. I just didn't know enough. And then as one reads more and more and more you get more fathers in your hierarchy of fathers. And then, after summoning twenty or thirty fathers, perhaps *you* are born, or perhaps you are *not* born.

BARTHELME READS CHAPTER 12 OF *THE DEAD FATHER*

SHERMAN: I feel like every time I'm about to put my foot down, because I know it's going to happen, the ground moves.

BARTHELME: One tries to bore the people as little as possible, and that's probably what accounts for that.

SHERMAN: In *The Dead Father* I felt that. After the first two chapters I went back and started over again because I—

BARTHELME: —Why, were you at sea after the first two chapters?

SHERMAN: If you read a science-fiction novel, for instance, there's a whole other world that you're in, but the author says, "In this world such and such happens, and these are the rules that govern this world," whereas *you* just plunge right in—

RUAS: What you want is the unpredictable within a framework, so that in this world gravity works in reverse, and matter is anti-matter.

SHERMAN: See, I immediately try to grab onto allegory or something, and then—

BARTHELME: —That's not what I want—

SHERMAN: —it's hard to let it go and say, "Let go now."

RUAS: Yeah, but to a certain extent you can't avoid allegory. For example, in *The Dead Father*—

BARTHELME: —Well, you bring the allegory in, you see. Someone asked just the other day, and I assume seriously, if this had to do with the fall of President Nixon. It made me . . . you know, shocking . . . and how can it possibly be read that way? . . . It has nothing . . . not even close . . . It's a guy I don't know that well, but I assume he's not a bad reader.

RUAS: No, I mean the elements of allegory are there in terms of technique. That is, whether the reader falls into the trap of interpreting the work allegorically is his problem.

SHERMAN: It's hard to let go, though.

BARTHELME: But I regard this book as being very plainly written, and I assume it is extremely accessible.

RUAS: But you're saying "plainly written" in terms of sentence structure, aren't you? And sequence? And also construction of paragraphs and so on. But you do not mean that in terms of content.

BARTHELME: I certainly don't write to exclude anyone.

RUAS: I know you don't write to exclude anyone and, as you said earlier, *The Dead Father* was, as you called it, much more elaborately written than in its final draft and in its published form. And I see that you continuously edit, even your published works—

BARTHELME: —Oh yeah—

RUAS: —so that there's a constant honing—

BARTHELME: —Yes, yes.

RUAS: I'm wondering, since the honing is a process of elimination and simplification and strengthening the structure, is that determined to some extent by some other media? For example, the fact that the tempo of writing and of prose is extremely influenced by the visual tempo of television and other media.

BARTHELME: Not television so much as films, I would say. Films have had their very well-documented effect on painting, just as photography has had its very well-known effect on painting, and its less well-known effect on literature. For instance, John Ashbery, in some of his poems—more so in the earlier poems—uses what can only be called a "jump cut," and uses it marvelously, very effectively. But that's a film technique. You won't find it in Wallace Stevens. You do very much find it in John's work. And there are other influences from film. One is, at least I feel it is, that you have to move faster. People are not going to sit still.

RUAS: You have to move faster and be visual.

BARTHELME: I don't think you have to "be visual." I think it's more a matter of pace. Certain of our best writers still write enormously long books, Tom Pynchon for example, but these long books are not like the long books of the past. Within *Gravity's Rainbow,* which is quite a long work, over 700 pages, everything is moving. It's an enormously crowded book and the pace is very, very swift.

BARTHELME READS "THE GREAT HUG"

BARTHELME: I think that the effort is to reach a realm of meaning that is not quite sayable. You stay away from what can be said and you try to reach what can't quite be said. Yet it is nevertheless meaningful. And there is such a realm and it is very difficult to talk about. It's not quite nonverbal, but that comes fairly close.

SHERMAN: Either a word has to sort of reverberate at a point and do double or triple duty, or the combination of the words has to evoke something.

BARTHELME: It's a phenomenon the classic example of which is [Sergei] Eisenstein's discussion of montage, where he juxtaposed different pictures, or the same pictures in different ways, and got different responses from the viewers. One of the beautiful things about words is that you can put words together which in isolation mean nothing, or mean only what the dictionary says they mean, and you put them together and you get extraordinary effects. Ashbery does this all the time. Kenneth [Koch] does it beautifully, and many writers can do it.

RUAS: But there are two forms of exploration. You mention Eisenstein's discussion of montage. In Joyce it led to an investigation of language, and exploration of the nature of language. And yet, in other writers, you have the language transformed because the writer is investigating the realms of experience that have not traditionally been part of the mainstream of literature.

BARTHELME: You grab something outside of literature and drag it into literature and renew the writing thereby.

SHERMAN: The problem seems to me one of dredging up something that's inside that seems untouchable and maybe antiverbal—in many cases something visual or even as nebulous as something musical—and in some way creating that experience on the page with words. And words tend to slip around a lot because you're working with other people's heads and what those words will do in their heads. And, okay, you start out with a blank piece of paper and now you're trying to get from there to here in some not necessarily predictable sense. For instance, you have a way you want *The Dead Father* to be read and you have to ensure that. And so where do you start?

BARTHELME: In terms of ensuring how the thing will be read, obviously it is a function of what you put down. Let me tell you how one story was written, which might give you an idea of the procedure.

I'm not suggesting that all stories of mine were written this way, but I was walking down West Eleventh Street one day and this gigantic dog began barking fiercely at me from a third-story window. And so I immediately fantasized that the damn dog was going to jump out the window and jump on top of me, and that's the way the story of "The Falling Dog" began. So then I went from the dog to what kind of person was it the dog might fall upon and I obviously came up with a blocked sculptor. There was a time in art, and there's probably still a time in art, where the artist was sort of expected by the art world—I don't mean the world of other artists, but the gallery world—to produce a new sensation each season. It was just morally wrong almost to do the same thing this season that you had done last season. That's an exaggeration, but there's enough truth in it to make the story work. So he had been doing . . . what had he been doing before?

SHERMAN: Yawning.

BARTHELME: "Yawning Man." And this is sort of a joking nod in the direction of Ernest Trova, the Chicago sculptor, whose very beautiful works had to do with . . . What did he call them?

RUAS: He began with what, *The Plastic Man*?

BARTHELME: I think he had done a *Falling Man* series. The dog jumps on him, he's pinned to the sidewalk by the dog, and the whole space of the story is what he thinks about while the dog is on top of him. Finally, he gets the idea of the falling dog, and he goes through a whole row of changes on the idea of falling dogs and various materials and so on, and then at the end of the story he grabs the dog and rushes happily off to the studio. So that's how the story came to be. It began with an actual non-event. A dog barked at me. And it ends up as being about the way a particular world functions—that is, the art world—or was functioning at the time. Does that help at all?

SHERMAN: Yes. The whole idea of an image . . . Often when I was rereading and taking notes, what would frequently end up happening is I would say, "Oh yeah, this is the story ["The Indian Uprising"] that has the hollow door, the hollow door—

BARTHELME: —Hollow-core door—

SHERMAN: —hollow-core door tables. And these images that keep floating in and out, sometimes, as far as I can tell, have no reason for being there at all.

BARTHELME: I would hope they all have reason for being there. There was a time, and probably it still obtains, that . . . The story is people all over America have made such tables, and that taking a hollow-core door, making a table out of it, or using it for a bed, so forth and so on, is sort of a thing that people did when they were very young, and usually when they first got married and got their first place—because it's cheap, you know, and you can make furniture out of it. It should evoke a kind of man-woman-youth complex.

SHERMAN: Yes, in the story, every new relationship had another hollow-core door table—

BARTHELME: —Right. You go to the hardware store and you buy your wrought-iron legs and then you take them home and you screw them into the corners of your hollow-core door and there's the principle piece of furniture in your house aside from the bed, which is another hollow-core door with a piece of foam rubber on top of it. And that's what that alludes to.

SHERMAN: Sometimes I feel that an image occurs to you and you can't resist the temptation to do it. Going out and shooting peccadillos ["Views of My Father Weeping"], which then becomes a cross between a peccary and an armadillo or something like that. Do you sometimes resist temptation, and maybe not resisting it makes everything a lot richer, to do just those things that—

BARTHELME: —Well, do you object to the peccadillo?

SHERMAN: No, oh no. In fact, I remember where it was I read that and cracked up and everybody looked at me. I was waiting for a bus. There were a whole bunch of people at the bus stop.

BARTHELME: But why is it a question of resisting temptation?

RUAS: Because you're playing with two . . . The word peccadillo becomes a play on two tangible images, the peccary and the armadillo, and the concept of the peccadillo has this dual image behind it.

BARTHELME: Writing should be playing, you know.

RUAS: Definitely. I'm really interested in the whole concept of how the concrete image then—through your interplay—becomes, eventually, a concept. For example, the peccadillo becomes almost an oxymoron that you're playing with.

BARTHELME: Yes. Well, eventually what I'm trying to do is to get to the point where the guy and his father are shooting at each other. You go out aimlessly with rifles, and say, in such a situation, you take the rifle off the wall and go out and walk around. This is ranch country. Say no game appears, and then you have this goddamn thing in your hand. Its entelechy is to shoot, so you begin shooting at tin cans and so forth and then there's a vermin—the armadillo is more or less classified as vermin. And what I really wanted to end up with, but didn't end up with, is the guy and his father shooting at each other, which, as you know, should be a shock to you as you get to that point in the story.

RUAS: But the shock is based on the reversal. That is, if "peccadillo" means gratuitous whim, then obviously—

BARTHELME: —It means misbehavior of a kind.

RUAS: Unmotivated misbehavior.

BARTHELME: Well, it is a kind of lightly viewed misbehavior. I mean, it is not so serious as misdemeanor, but still . . . I see what you mean, there is a sort of casual or, you know, accidental quality to a peccadillo.

RUAS: To a peccadillo, which then you are reversing by having the father and son the target of the peccadillo, and—

BARTHELME: —But I wanted it to be very casual.

SHERMAN: Yes, that lended some excitement to it.

RUAS: Except when you have the father and son shooting, using each other as targets, then that's no longer conceptually within the same framework as shooting at a rodent.

BARTHELME: Or a tin can on a fence post.

RUAS: Yes, whether animate or inanimate, that is an object—

BARTHELME: —Yeah, what I wanted was a sense of casually drifting into it, and then, at a certain point, fundamental issues present themselves and this guy and his father are taking potshots at each other. You get from the casual to the fundamental issue, which is quite something.

RUAS: Which in retrospect, of course, necessarily transforms the whole concept of "peccadillo." That is, if the father and son are shooting at each other and consciously using each other as targets, then obviously, in retrospect, the tin can, the rodents, and the pests become substitutes for what eventually is a climactic revelation. So that by the time you've reversed the definition of "peccadillo," the reader—seeing the antagonism between father and son—then has to reinterpret everything that's gone before and can only interpret it, it seems to me, as disguised motivation.

BARTHELME: I think it's rather more setting the reader up for surprise. If you wrote a story, two guys of different ages standing on a street, and one guy suddenly—or they both suddenly—pull out knives and go after each other, that's a rather dumb way to suggest that there's a latent, violent final relationship between them. But by putting in the tin cans—I think there was an abandoned car there, too—the peccadillo, which is meant to be a bit disarming . . . And okay, we'll sit here for a moment and chuckle over "peccadillo" and we move on. It's sort of setting the scene. It's, one would hope, a more subtle way of getting to that moment where they've been shooting at each other.

RUAS: But then your construction, Donald, it seems to me, parallels very closely certain techniques used in the art world. That is, conceptual art and minimal art.

BARTHELME: Well, I'm not so sure about minimal or conceptual art.

SHERMAN: Certainly it parallels musical constructions.

BARTHELME: Conceptual art is not something I'm overly fond of. It seems to me entirely too easy.

RUAS: Why would you say it's easy?

BARTHELME: Well, because it *is* easy.

RUAS: To be able to delineate concepts and have people understand the concept?

BARTHELME: Yes. I think *as art* it is entirely too easy.

RUAS: Is it that you want an object produced that would continuously say the same thing to you?

BARTHELME: No, no, I want an object produced that's going to say very different things to me at different times of the day.

RUAS: But the object has to stay there unchanging?

BARTHELME: Had I decided to go into the conceptual-art business I could turn out railroad cars full of that stuff every day. My younger brother, who is a writer, Frederick Barthelme, was very interested in conceptual art at one time, and was as a matter of fact in a Museum of Modern Art conceptual art show, and he was very friendly with Joseph Kosuth, who is sort of the papa of conceptual art. So I've listened to endless conversations about conceptual art, more than I wanted to hear about it, until my brother—who did it very well—finally stopped doing it and turned to prose on the grounds that there was not enough intellectual excitement in conceptual art.

RUAS: There's a constant debate that conceptual art inevitably leads to a narrative. That the viewer who understands what he sees and constantly has to define it does eventually create a narrative, and that he comes away with a narrative rather than with an image, which is the way we traditionally think of a work of art.

BARTHELME: There obviously is narrative painting, gigantic French battle paintings, Delacroix and so on. There is also in art a mysterious object, or what Harold Rosenberg calls "the anxious object." The mysterious object does not declare a narrative necessarily. Very often, as Harold points out, it asks questions. He says, quite beautifully, its first question is of itself. Harold phrases it, I believe, "Am I a masterpiece, or am I a pile of junk?" The mysterious object can also ask other questions.

BARTHELME READS "THE AGREEMENT"

RUAS: "The Agreement" is built around constantly recurring questions, and yet the elements in the interrogative form a cast of characters so that the construction is extremely formalistic. For example, the reference to the protagonist's daughter, the bypassing of the lover and the focusing in on the lover's lover, the imagined vision of the visitor and its many transformations—old woman, old man, lover's lover, mailman, photograph of the daughter—which tie all of these elements together very, very neatly, so that one can see how completely structured it is. And yet the repetition in the sequence creates the illusion for the reader of accidental, obsessive, recurring thoughts, so that the effect of the story on the reader, and the actual writing, occur at poles apart. The question then becomes the nature of investigating, of the investigation in the story.

BARTHELME: I can tell you how that story germinated. I am, in fact, separated from a wife—

RUAS: —You have a daughter—

BARTHELME: —We have a daughter.

RUAS: I have a son, so I can identify with that clearly.

BARTHELME: Okay. My wife is a Dane—

RUAS: —Mine is Swedish. I identify perfectly—

BARTHELME: —who lives in Copenhagen—

RUAS: —Mine in Stockholm.

BARTHELME: My daughter spends about eight months of the year with her mother, the school part of the year, and spends a month at Christmas, and the summers, with me—

RUAS: —My son does that also—

BARTHELME: —Okay, therefore we have a situation where my daughter is not present for much of my life, and one wonders what the hell is going on with her during the time she's absent. There is a phrase, standard I believe to all legal separations: "From the beginning of the world, to the execution of this agreement." It's legalese. Upon inspecting my copy of this document I was struck by that phrase, especially the "From the beginning of the world" part, which gives a vaguely biblical air to this jargon-filled document.

RUAS: But the biblical air refers back to the vows, marriage vows.

BARTHELME: Yes, it does indeed. However, it is a kind of borrowing of authority on the lawyer's part, or whoever first drafted this kind of document. It's borrowing the moral authority of religion, the Bible or whatever, for a strictly temporal division of property, stipulation of alimony, child support, all of these grim matters. The lawyers are reaching outside their own realm for words to give their temporal doings a stamp that comes from another realm. So I was struck by that phrase, and that—together with my anxiety—is quite adequately represented in the piece. It's the genesis of the story.

RUAS: I recognized certain details of what must have been autobiographical, such as sending postcards, stamps for the stamp collection, which are details that refer specifically to a child who's known and identified.

BARTHELME: Yes. You make these hopeful little maneuvers—

RUAS: —To keep in touch—

BARTHELME: —with the idea they somehow allow you to keep in touch. And of course they don't. They are a very poor substitute to having the child on the premises, standing on your shoes, and in general being there. And of course in this kind of situation a lot of things become threatening that maybe otherwise wouldn't be. The telephone becomes threatening. I sometimes get telephone calls at nine o'clock in the morning—this is to leave out entirely the three o-clock-in-the-morning telephone call from some drunken friend in Nebraska—but if the phone rings at nine o'clock . . . Usually no one calls me at this hour except my former wife from Copenhagen, and of course—

RUAS: —Because of the time difference—

BARTHELME: —in every case, we're on very good terms, and she wants to discuss some rather ordinary matter, but it's still threatening because she might be announcing that some terrible thing has happened, and it's somehow more threatening because of the distance. You know, you could have a child at school and get a telephone call and be worried about that, but the intensity is increased by the distance. And it is this sort of emotion, fear mostly, that the story attempts to deal with. It also folds in some other anxieties, until you get a pretty complete blanket of anxiety hanging over this poor fellow. And those fears are not usually expressed in such concentrated form.

RUAS: I identified so readily with the anxiety over your daughter because they're so similar to the thoughts that flit through my mind about my boy, such as riding a bicycle—he's learning to ride a bicycle—and that's very worrying when you're six hours and several thousand miles away.

BARTHELME: True.

RUAS: But, however, in other images, the interrogative does bypass the emotion that creates the anxiety. So, for example, the lover's lover bypasses the complex of emotion from . . . whatever. I needn't specify.

BARTHELME: Yeah, but another kind of anxiety, at any rate.

RUAS: Exactly.

BARTHELME: But by bypassing, you are able to present it in a much stronger way than if you confronted it directly. I mean there are some things that have to be done by backing into them, and by moving sort of straight ahead through that question of, "Does my lover have another lover or not?" I mean it's stated, but you don't examine it. It seems to me the intention was to make it much sharper than would've been the case had one confronted it directly.

RUAS: So that we're going from a very concrete emotional relationship to the anxiety itself.

BARTHELME: Well, a good example is the title of Joseph Heller's novel, which is *Something Happened.* Now, to any contemporary American the phrase "something happened" is terrifying. "Good God, don't tell me about it. What was it?" It's that sort of feeling—brilliant choice of title on Heller's part—and because it's not explicit it is freighted with menace in the way that it wouldn't be if the title of the book were *My Kid Got Smothered When I Embraced Him,* or something like that—

RUAS: —Or, *I Killed My Kid*—

BARTHELME: —Or *I Killed My Kid.* So the indirection is a way of presenting the thing that somehow works more strongly than in direct statement, in this case.

RUAS: Then the third technique of the visitor, creating anxiety. That is, if we begin with the mailman and the telephone operator and continue through the imaginary visitors, then—

BARTHELME: —All impingements on his space, right?

RUAS: Yes. Then we're at the third level of abstraction in the construction of this story. And then there's a deliberate interweaving of the images, such as the mailman played against the old man spitting blood over his red dress, which is a play on the old lady streaming blood over her red dress that echoes the truck, the child, the bicycle.

BARTHELME: You have a situation that may be peculiar to New

York, but is probably not so, where there's a certain anxiety about answering the bloody doorbell. You don't know what's going to be standing there when you answer the bell. I think that might be a special New York paranoia, but it's increasingly nationwide.

RUAS: And also, it's for very good reasons.

BARTHELME: Yeah, there are very good reasons for that. But, you know, man ought not to live this way. We should not be in a state or condition where you can't answer the phone, or answer the door, without this small or large amount of anxiety attached to that rather simple act.

SHERMAN: What was interesting was that the anxiety was not about violence, but about responsibility. If you answer the door and there's someone there spitting blood—

BARTHELME: —Well, that's right, that's akin to walking down the street and suddenly someone collapses, and immediately you are responsible. What are you going to do? Are you going to handle yourself well? Are you going to do the right thing? Are you going to keep walking, as many people do, mostly out of the fear of not being able to perform adequately in this emergency? And again, in New York very often because it happens so often.

RUAS: The refrain, it works almost as formally as a refrain in a poem. Is the impossibility of meeting responsibilities—

BARTHELME: —The task beyond feasibilities—

RUAS: —a task beyond feasibility and the speculation on either simplifying the task or changing strategy? And I'm extremely curious about the word "strategy," since that's a New York concept.

BARTHELME: Well, it comes from the theory of games, I suppose. That's the place where it has its original home.

RUAS: But it's applied in an area which—

SHERMAN: —Actually, it's a military word.

RUAS: As well.

BARTHELME: What is brought on here, what I'm attempting to deal with in a glancing way, is the redefining of the problem in such a way as to make it solvable, which often is a situation in which you are deceiving yourself. But it's one of the strategies of psychoanalysis, for example. You look at situations in such a way as to make them dealable with or livable with and the real issues leak out, leak away, are cosmeticized, or ignored, and it does have the virtue of making you able to proceed and live some sort of life. But you're still ignoring fundamental issues, and it's that kind of consideration that's being talked about here. There is not necessarily a specific task that is beyond his abilities—the whole goddamn thing is beyond his abilities. The Project Life is in some sense beyond his abilities. And he's not going to win this game. If the game is called life, he's going to lose. We know that, and I expect our denial of death is all about this question. How do we perform when we're playing a game, when we know we can't possibly get out alive? And so on and so on and so on. It's this range of questions that is being addressed. That's not really very helpful.

RUAS: It's helpful in the sense that, so far in our discussion, you've kept referring to a "him," so that essentially the construction of the story seems to be stream of consciousness. There is a protagonist, except I'm extremely uneasy with the term "protagonist" because you've brought in the concept of psychoanalysis, etc. etc. But your story remains a construction where there's an avoidance of the definition of self, which, of course, is an aspect of anxiety.

BARTHELME: These problems are not really dealable with—that's the root of the matter—yet one has to attempt to deal with them, and if this story says anything, it is a reminder that these problems are beyond us. And yet we deal with them, usually rather poorly.

BARTHELME READS "NOTHING: A PRELIMINARY ACCOUNT"

ENVOI BY JUDITH SHERMAN

SECOND PROGRAM

DONALD BARTHELME: Strange things happen in the book-review sections of many newspapers out of the country. Really odd things are said. I quoted that line, did I not, "He is like Mark Twain, only not as good." It turned up somewhere, I forget where. I wanted to put it on a book jacket but they wouldn't let me.

INTRODUCTION BY JUDITH SHERMAN

BARTHELME READS A SHORTENED VERSION OF "CRITIQUE DE LA VIE QUOTIDIENNE"

BARTHELME: Writing a novel gives me great difficulties. The short story is easier for me, but I also enjoy—perhaps enjoy is not quite the word—I also feel that I ought to write novels.

CHARLES RUAS: Are you working on a novel now?

BARTHELME: Yes. Interestingly, interesting to me anyhow, writing *The Dead Father*—and this has never happened to me before—told me, if not what, at least how to begin writing the next one.

JUDITH SHERMAN: Which is how?

BARTHELME: I'm not going to tell you, because it's a secret.

SHERMAN: From whom?

BARTHELME: From youm.

RUAS: Is there a relationship between your work on the novel and the shorter pieces?

BARTHELME: There is this relationship, at least: while I am failing at writing a novel I can also write short stories. So I can sort of psychologically reinforce myself, because writing a novel is an extended effort and it consists of failing, for me, for a long time. And then something begins to come together, and it's very good to be able to write short stories during that period because it reduces the anxiety somewhat.

RUAS: I was wondering, in terms of content, if there was also a relationship in the sense that in the shorter works of fiction you tried out either subject, or material, or forms that would not go into the longer work.

BARTHELME: Some of the stories are little plucked chickens from aborted novels. They are parts of novels that did not go well. Not too many, but some of them. What would be an example? Well, the "Critique" story was once part of a considerably longer manuscript.

SHERMAN: What about the "Edward and Pia" stories?

BARTHELME: No, no, they were just two stories.

RUAS: Or "Perpetua"?

BARTHELME: "Perpetua" was again part of a different attempt—

RUAS: —A different novel?

BARTHELME: Yes, which did not succeed either. One difficulty in a novel is keeping yourself interested, or keeping the critical part of your head from destroying what is there—or from despairing.

SHERMAN: I'm still interested in the secret. Is it a secret because you think if you talk about it it will sort of disappear?

BARTHELME: Yeah, it's a strictly magical procedure to protect this notion. That's why it's a secret.

SHERMAN: Okay.

BARTHELME: It's just personal magic, like throwing salt over your shoulder. Like all magic, it has to be closely attended to.

RUAS: Some of the pieces, you said, came from novels that you never completed. Would that be correct, or am I misunderstanding? Novels you never released?

BARTHELME: Oh, they were never completed. You get so much down on paper and you look at it and you say, "This is not going anywhere, this is no good, but maybe I can salvage some of it." There are only maybe three or four cases of that, though.

RUAS: I was wondering if the concept of the novel as a genre was for you essentially attached to the idea of realism?

BARTHELME: No. I mean the question of form in the novel is central. The problem for me is I'm interested in pushing the form, if not forward, at least in some direction, and that's kind of hard to do. For example, the problem is critically posed very often in some such terms as, "What is post-Beckettian fiction going to look like?" I didn't make that up, that's a real term—"post-Beckettian fiction." In other words, Beckett is seen as someone who has taken the form about as far as it can go. But of course that's ridiculous, as there is no closure, ever. But there is still certain fiction which is classified as "post-Beckettian," which always gives me a chuckle. The problem is real for the writer in the sense that he has to do something that's credible after Beckett, as Beckett had to do something that was credible after Joyce. I'm pretty sure Joyce was Beckett's problem, and Beckett now himself becomes the problem for all the rest of us.

RUAS: It's a curious statement, Donald, because it seems to indicate you place yourself in terms of a larger perspective of the experimental novel, rather than being an American novelist following the tradition of Fitzgerald, etc.

BARTHELME: Very much so. One chooses one's problem. Other people might identify the high points of the twentieth-century novel differently. They might choose to exclude Joyce, exclude Beckett, and deal instead with other writers. So those people have chosen a different problem. I'm not imposing my problem on everybody else. What you observe, Charles, is quite correct. I mean, Hemingway and Fitzgerald are not problems for me. I learned, as I believe I've said, immensely from Hemingway. Hemingway was everybody's problem at one time.

BARTHELME READS "PARAGUAY"

RUAS: Which takes us back to Beckett.

BARTHELME: Right, right, right.

SHERMAN: I just don't see it.

BARTHELME: What don't you see? How Beckett is a problem?

SHERMAN: I just don't see, having read *The Dead Father*, what the connection between Beckett—

BARTHELME: —You mean it's not like Beckett, in any sense?

SHERMAN: Right.

BARTHELME: That's the achievement.

RUAS: That's the accomplishment.

BARTHELME: If there is an achievement.

SHERMAN: Why is what someone else has done become a problem?

BARTHELME: Well, let's put it back in terms of Beckett's relationship to Joyce, which we know was quite close. Therefore, looking at what Joyce had done, Beckett must have felt, "Good lord, this enormous achievement here that I myself have to do something"—I'm speculating about what Beckett might have thought—"that is as monumental and totally different. How in the world am I going to do that?" And he found a way.

SHERMAN: Okay, but his relationship was very close and very personal, and obviously he was a great admirer of Joyce and all that—he wouldn't have hung around that long otherwise—so I can see why Joyce was a problem for Beckett. I don't see why Beckett is a problem for you.

BARTHELME: I suppose it's because that I'm enormously impressed by Beckett. I'm just overwhelmed by Beckett, as Beckett was, I speculate, by Joyce.

RUAS: But this is the problem, the artistic problem of the lion in the path. It's a problem I would imagine many writers have had to face.

BARTHELME: Yes, there are always lions in the path. And we also discussed choosing your fathers, and, of course, there's a problem there.

RUAS: It seemed to me that *The Dead Father* was such a direct allusion to *As I Lay Dying* that I thought the American tradition was stronger in your bloodstream, so to speak.

BARTHELME: But it would have been long ago, it would have been twenty years since I'd read any Faulkner, I blush to confess. In his very intelligent review of *The Dead Father*, a gentleman in *The*

Washington Post, Joseph McLellan, made a reference to that Sylvia Plath poem, "Daddy": "I have had to kill you/ . . . There's a stake in your fat black heart . . ." which I have also read, but hadn't consciously thought of. [*Ed. note:* The review appeared in *The Washington Post* on November 11, 1975.] It would've been a good number of years ago. So there are doubtless other parallels lurking around in the subconscious.

RUAS: Donald, this leads us back to the relationship of your shorter fiction to the novels, because in Beckett not only do the novels seem to form a continuous flow even in the titles—*Murphy, Molloy*—but his short fictions also seem to to be continuations or part of the novels, in the sense that the same momentum, the same characters, reappear in them.

BARTHELME: In Beckett's case the shorter pieces, especially those three long pieces—what's the title of that? I don't remember myself, I would have to check—but they struck me, and I may be entirely wrong, as parts of novels that Beckett did not choose to continue with. That's a guess. Perhaps a Beckett scholar could identify them as such or not such.

RUAS: But if Beckett is the lion in your path, in his work there is a continuum from the novels to the plays to the short stories. In fact, despite the fact that he works in so many genres—drama, novel, short stories, poetry—there is a continuous style, a unity, that is the same whether he writes in French or English.

BARTHELME: By the way, let me make clear that I am not proposing myself as successor or heir to Mr. Beckett, in any sense. I'm just telling you that he is a problem for me because of the enormous pull of his style. I am certainly not the only writer who has been enormously influenced by Beckett and thus wants to stay at arm's length.

RUAS: Well, when you accept the definition of lion in the path—

BARTHELME: —There are other lions in the path as well.

RUAS: The implication, I assume, was—

BARTHELME: —Shouldn't be, it's just that Beckett is the largest problem for me. This is by the by, but you have noted that Beckett's own work is getting shorter and shorter and shorter—seemingly so—and, of course, as with any artist, he may turn around tomorrow and surprise us by producing a work of immense length that we know nothing about, so not too much significance should be attached to this.

BARTHELME READS "ON ANGELS"

SHERMAN: Before, you almost implied that you tried to work in longer forms, in novel forms, and that's always an attempt, and then—

BARTHELME: —It's an ongoing project.

SHERMAN: Why?

BARTHELME: Why? Because both the short form and the novel form are extremely interesting and problematic. When I retire I'm going to try and write poetry.

RUAS: When you retire from what?

BARTHELME: Writers don't retire, they just have heart attacks and so on.

RUAS: Why are you waiting until some future date?

BARTHELME: Because poetry is the most difficult of all, and I want to put off facing it as long as I can.

RUAS: You're not doing a Thomas Hardy on us, are you?

BARTHELME: What do you mean by "doing a Thomas Hardy"?

RUAS: Having poetry as your true love and writing novels and shorter fictions until you can renounce fiction for the higher realms of poetry.

BARTHELME: I was sort of half joking, but I am pointing to the status of the different genres as problematic.

SHERMAN: Do you attempt poetry now?

BARTHELME: No. I did. When I was very young I wrote poetry like everyone else does. But I don't try now.

RUAS: And yet, given the way you construct some of your stories, and with your concern for form, there is an element that's extremely poetic, in the sense of your use of imagery, the elliptical construction that you tend toward in the stories, so that I'm wondering whether your wanting to write poetry also means that you're reserving a special part of your imagination or feelings, which you think poetry would best express.

BARTHELME: No, no, no. There's another factor, too, which is there's no necessity for me to write poetry—since John Ashbery is doing it so well.

RUAS: Actually, it seems to me that this is one of the most fertile, one of the most creative, periods of American culture in terms of poetry, and the amount of good poetry being written and the number of poets—

BARTHELME: —Quite so.

RUAS: On the other hand, there seem to be many fewer—

BARTHELME: —I could have said that about Kenneth Koch, for example—

RUAS: —But there are fewer novelists and short-story writers of stature in America today.

BARTHELME: I think there are a great many.

RUAS: Who are your favorites?

BARTHELME: I don't make lists like that anymore, because—

RUAS: —It makes enemies?

BARTHELME: Well, it doesn't make enemies, it's just that I've come to believe it's a bad thing to do. It is divisive, in that if I gave you a list of my five favorite writers, it would imply that many other writers, whose work I greatly admire, were somehow in the opposite camp, or something of that sort. It's a nonsensical division and doesn't need to be made. I think catholicity should be emphasized. The *New York Times* used to love to make up teams of one sort or the other, as you recall, and the implication was—I always felt—what they'd really like is for us to get down in the arena equipped with standard gladiatorial equipment—such as the mace, the sword, and very bright armor—and slaughter each other.

RUAS: Yes, and someone such as Norman Mailer took it seriously and really is living it out, in terms of that role.

BARTHELME: Oh, I don't think so. Why do you think that?

RUAS: You know, his concept of being "The Champ."

BARTHELME: I think maybe he just does that to tease interviewers. That particular stance is, of course, the Hemingway stance. You know, "I'm never going to get into the ring with Mr. Tolstoy," and so on. I don't think Mr. Mailer is all that serious about it. He's certainly serious about his writing and he certainly conceives of his writing at the highest level of ambition—and I'm not using "ambition" pejoratively at all. I mean he thinks in quite large terms. All that business about being "The Champ" and so on, I think it's more playful than anything else.

SHERMAN: Do you think you have to keep up with and read everything that's coming out?

BARTHELME: Not at all, not at all. I sort of look over what's being done. But I can tell very quickly whether I'm going to read a book or not.

SHERMAN: Do you ever read your own work for recreation?

BARTHELME: For recreation?

SHERMAN: Well, you know—
BARTHELME: —No, no, no, no, no. No, no. No.
SHERMAN: It's always work?
BARTHELME: Yeah. For recreation, I get a nice glass of vodka and beef bouillon and listen to music. That's what I do for recreation.
SHERMAN: Now *that's* work.
BARTHELME: Healthy vodka, healthy beef bouillon . . .

BARTHELME READS "THE PRESIDENT"

SHERMAN: In "Paraguay" there are two altered quotes.

BARTHELME: Yes. It's very difficult to include them while reading, because the introduction to the first paragraph of the story is quoted wholly and attributed to a book about an Englishwoman's journey through Tibet. It was published by Collins in 1906, I believe, and that's the entire first paragraph of the story. I'd have to look it up to make sure. The second paragraph is a quote by Corbusier, and while both are attributed and footnoted in the story itself, it's difficult to include the footnotes while reading. [*Ed. note:* The quotes are from Jane E. Duncan, *A Summer Ride Through Western Tibet*, Collins, London, 1906; and Le Corbusier, *The Modular*, M.I.T. Press, Cambridge, 1954. Both are slightly altered.] I'm glad you raised the question. See, it's found material, it's analogous to a found object in sculpture.

SHERMAN: But those stories and the Robert Kennedy story, to me, raise the question of how do you know where the found object part of it leaves off? For instance, much of the Robert Kennedy story actually sounds like Robert Kennedy or sounds like something that is real.

BARTHELME: There are no found objects, there's nothing real in the Robert Kennedy story whatsoever, with one single exception—the part in the Kennedy story where Robert Kennedy comes into a gallery and looks at a painting and makes some joke about, "Well, we know he had a ruler," or something of that kind. That actually took place, because I was in the gallery, and I believe it was a Kenneth Noland show, when Kennedy came in and did make the remark attributed to him. But everything else is imagined. None of the rest of it is a found object.

RUAS: Judy's question raises the question of the found subject of the story. For example, in the Robert Kennedy story, did the incident eventually make you recreate the story?

BARTHELME: Do you mean was that the genesis of the story?

RUAS: Yes.

BARTHELME: No. It was a story I wrote in Copenhagen. It was written about a year before he was assassinated, I believe. I always want to put a date on that story when it's reprinted so that people won't think it was written after he was assassinated. But the incident was in no way the genesis of the story. I could not tell you what the genesis of the story was. Actually, I don't remember.

RUAS: You've spoken about being more at ease, or finding it easier to write shorter fiction, and I was wondering whether the subject matter and the form appeared complete in your imagination?

BARTHELME: Oh no, no, no, no, rarely, if ever. For example, when I wrote "Sentence," I suddenly had the idea of an interminable sentence, and in that sense the form did come, but mostly what God sends to me is perhaps a line, or beginnings of a situation. Then I explore either the line or the beginnings of the situation and see what comes of it. Receiving the gift of an entire form of a piece all at once is quite rare for me.

SHERMAN: You said once before, when we were choosing what stories were to be read, that "The Indian Uprising" is a key story to you. Why is that?

BARTHELME: I think that it's emotionally important. It was in part, obviously, a response to the Vietnam war. It was in response to certain things that were going on in my personal life at the time, and a whole lot of other things came together in that story. I couldn't really sort it out for you more clearly than that.

SHERMAN: Having recognized a couple of quotes in that story I wonder whether one should take the time to go through the story. Are there a lot of pullings-in from—

BARTHELME: —You're referring to the—

SHERMAN: —the "silence" quotes—

BARTHELME: —the Eliot references, for example—

SHERMAN: —Gilbert and Sullivan—

BARTHELME: —and Gilbert and Sullivan and so on. I suppose these could be isolated identified parallels, but I would think that they are all perfectly clear. For example, I had no trouble with the Gilbert and Sullivan quotes, and I assume with the Eliot—

SHERMAN: —Shakespeare—

BARTHELME: —Yeah, paraphrases and so on. I don't see what the question is.

SHERMAN: Well, it's a whole problem of quotes in a work. In fact what started happening, because I did recognize those . . . Then someone comes through a door with a loaf of bread and all that stuff, and then there's a whole thing about his coat, and I started connecting it with *La Bohème*—

BARTHELME: —That was not necessarily intended, but you're perfectly free to, if you like.

SHERMAN: That's what happens when I begin to recognize that there are quotes from other people, I immediately begin looking for the other pathways.

BARTHELME: Well, sometimes the quotes are just there for fun, as in, for example, Miles Davis, in a '61 Carnegie Hall concert, does a very beautiful thing called "So What?" and somewhere on there—I'm not sure whether it's Miles or one of the other people on that track—he quotes "I Found a New Baby," and it's just very funny and refreshing somehow.

SHERMAN: So, on one hand it makes a game on another level out of the story, which is nice, and of course the reader is free to find whatever is there, but do you realize you're doing that, what you do to the reader when you're writing that?

BARTHELME: Do you suggest I'm doing something bad to the reader?

SHERMAN: No! Oh, no. No, not at all.

RUAS: You don't think it's perpetrating unspeakable and unnatural acts upon the reader?

BARTHELME: If it sends the reader off in a direction that he cannot profit from, then the reader is perhaps not relaxing enough, and he's symbol-hunting where he shouldn't be. He is refusing to allow the thing to stay on the surface and be what it is. And in that sense, that is not my problem really.

RUAS: But the problem of the intertext and all of its suggestiveness really takes us to the construction of your stories. One does want to translate the Comanches, if it ["The Indian Uprising"] was about the Vietnamese war, into—

BARTHELME: —It is not "about" the Vietnamese war. It is in part a reaction to the Vietnamese war. And there's also a mention of heroin, the Eliot quotation replaces "hyacinth" with "heroin." The heroin is really—political dimension sounds a little pompous—a political comment on the fact that we allow the heroin traffic in our country to exist. If we wanted to get rid of it, I suspect we could get rid of it. Somebody wants it to continue. In a way, the heroin traffic is paralleled by the Vietnamese war, so it's a kind of political comment in the story.

RUAS: Given the collage technique used in the story, one tends to interpret continuously.

BARTHELME: One is allowed to, yes. It's a possibility of the story.

RUAS: Such as the time jumps in the personal, very personal, relationship, and the jump of scenes and places. So that to continue to grasp the whole, the reader's forced to impose or create a structure.

BARTHELME: Yes, in this story particularly, the reader is being asked to work pretty hard. I don't think it's in any sense at the limit of what a reader can do, but he is asked to do a lot of work. So that the reader's participation is very great, which is a thing I want, and invite.

BARTHELME READS "THE INDIAN UPRISING"

RUAS: I asked you about the collage technique because I was wondering if the pacing of your prose style and the pacing of the images is related to the technique of splicing in television—

BARTHELME: —Well, jump cuts, in that particular story. What would in film be called "jump cuts." For example, that might be something I learned from the films.

RUAS: Then I would ask about the pacing of your prose style, your rhythm. To translate prose into a visual technique isn't very helpful. But in watching the news on television, the visual information is spliced so quickly, and the sequence is so rapid, that you're given full visual information without being able to really articulate or define exactly what it is that you've understood by the image presented before. You jump to the next one and the next one and the next one.

BARTHELME: Complicated by the introduction of wildly dissimilar material, like commercials—

RUAS: —Yes, and also completely irrational language which does not want to clarify or give further information about what they consider self-sufficient information, visual information.

BARTHELME: And further complicated by whatever is going on around you in your home while you're theoretically watching the news. There are four or five levels there of noise or information, or combinations of noise and information.

RUAS: I was wondering whether in writing you were—

BARTHELME: —Trying to be a television set? No, I wouldn't think so. Trying to destroy a television set? Might be a little closer.

SHERMAN: But at least what the television has taught us is that human beings can keep many things going on at the same time.

BARTHELME: Well, I think we knew that before television. I mean, the radio taught us that. You're listening to the radio, talking on the telephone, and making love—all at the same time. This is at least theoretically possible. It's pre-television, really. I don't say that's desirable, but I just say that it's possible.

SHERMAN: Something that occurred to me is that in many of the quotes in "The Indian Uprising" and in "Paraguay" there is much made of the whole idea of silence and space, which seem to be two things that are lacking in present-day life—especially in Manhattan. I'm wondering, are you concerned with the contemporary human being's lack of focus, lack of ability to find silence and space?

BARTHELME: It's not an inability on the part of the person. It is something that is imposed on the person from outside. Of course I'm concerned about it. First, there's the question of whether or not we all go mad, and when will it happen. In February? Or will it not happen at all? The behavioral sink idea. "Paraguay" is in some way dealing with that, or attempting to deal with that question.

SHERMAN: You can't read on the subway without getting very strange looks.

BARTHELME: I've been told. *Sadness* was a different sort of title and I—

RUAS: —It's ironic, isn't it?—

BARTHELME: —thought a long while before using it. And somebody, I think it was Rust Hills of *Esquire*, inquired how the devil I ever got the publishers to accept it, how I got away with it. I'm not sure I did get away with it in the sense of having it work as a book title, but it's not embarrassing to look at. Of course, it's ironic, as well as being what it is. It's both things. Whereas *The Dead Father* is a nonparody—it's not a parody of anything, it's a simple announcement of what the thing is, and I was very happy with that title because it was so plain. It is well to be simple once in awhile.

SHERMAN: You are the type of author that one must work at reading. It's not distraction. It's fun, but it's not distraction. So I see in things like "The Indian Uprising" that if one takes seriously the political statements, and aims for them, it would allow a world—or a type of reader—that would therefore have the energy to read this type of work. And in making literature difficult you're doing two things here: you're demanding that attention, while at the same time you're making a call for some sort of silence and focus and all that sort of stuff.

BARTHELME: I would say, first, that one does not make literature difficult for the sake of difficulty, at all. One does it any way possible. Difficulty is not something that I seek or try to impose on anything that is written. It is sometimes, not always, a characteristic of what I write, a certain order of difficulty. I don't think it's so damn difficult, but I am told over and over again that it's difficult, which sort of surprises me.

SHERMAN: Difficulty was not what I meant.

BARTHELME: Complexity, possibly?

SHERMAN: It requires something of the reader rather than sitting back and letting it wash over you, the way Mahler does.

RUAS: But that brings up a problem. If, for example, complexity—which in part selects your reading audience—is an aspect of your work, and yet at the same time simplicity is a criterion for you, I was wondering in some work—

BARTHELME: —Then I have a certain amount of mental difficulty in constructing the work—

RUAS: —Yes.

BARTHELME: Yes, I do. It is a difficulty to get both things.

RUAS: But in the spirit of parody, are you also cautious, in the sense that—

BARTHELME: —Immensely—

RUAS: —unspeakable practices and unnatural acts can take you into preciosity. Is that a danger in terms of your work?

BARTHELME: It is, but I don't worry about it. Again, any particular line has been scanned a number of times, and if it still looks meaningful to me after having been inspected by the quality control department for these qualities, if it can survive my rigorous quality control program, then it's probably all right. And even if it's a mistake, I choose to make that mistake. I mean, *I* don't think it's a mistake. You know what I mean. People always say "precious," "facile," this sort of thing. It comes up over and over again—

RUAS: —Why, do you think?

BARTHELME: —usually in reviews and provincial newspapers. Why? Because the surface is so agitated it might lead an inadequately prepared critic into this kind of notion. Inadequately prepared critics are what we mostly have.

RUAS: And you think that therefore they tend to think of you as an amusement? Entertainment?

BARTHELME: Oh, I think they want me to go away and stop doing what I'm doing. Remove myself from the scene. I think they are probably tired of dealing with me.

RUAS: Critics generally have a problem classifying your work because of the diversity of it, and the way you play with your role as a writer.

BARTHELME: We have to distinguish between reviewers and critics, on the one hand, and once we've made that distinction, we also have to distinguish between critics and idiots masquerading as critics.

SHERMAN: You said that there are less well prepared, or poorly prepared, critics. What is it that makes a well-prepared critic?

BARTHELME: I don't know. I imagine him to be an extremely thoughtful man. Period. Are you asking me how one goes about preparing oneself to be a critic? I don't know, I'm not a critic. I do know that there are such. Remember that the only effective criticism of a work of art is that made by another work of art. But I am also endlessly interested in what Harold Rosenberg, for example, has to say, or Tom Hess, about a work of art—or what Richard Gilman has to say about a book. Or what Dick Poirier has to say about a book, and so on.

SHERMAN: What about those lists that get going now and again? How do you generate them?

BARTHELME: The lists are sort of self-generating. They are fun to do. I see them as somehow incantatory, and they perform that function for me.

SHERMAN: They just come?

BARTHELME: No, they are constructed, as with everything else.

SHERMAN: Sometimes it's the combination of an adjective and a noun, and I wonder how that happened, or—

BARTHELME: —Well, for example, there's a list of animals that the Dead Father slays in that book. There it was simply a case of picking out animals whose names appeared to me from the entire animal kingdom—which is, as you know, quite large. That's how that particular list was made. And also, some of the animals were chosen for reasons of the story. He slays animals not normally considered game animals—household cats, for example.

SHERMAN: And animals that are not normally found in the same place at the same time.

BARTHELME: Oh yeah, it's all jumbled. A jumbled jungle. For example, the house cat is in there to display a little bit of an aspect of the Dead Father's character. It's sort of a mean thing to do to slay a house cat, isn't it?

SHERMAN: Well, it wasn't any less mean to slay the rest of them.

BARTHELME: I think it strikes at our susceptibilities a little more. That, in any case, was the intent.

BARTHELME READS "BRAIN DAMAGE"

ENVOI BY JUDITH SHERMAN

THIRD PROGRAM

BARTHELME READS THE BEGINNING OF HIS INTRODUCTION TO *GUILTY PLEASURES*

INTRODUCTION BY JUDITH SHERMAN

BARTHELME READS THE REMAINDER OF THE INTRODUCTION TO *GUILTY PLEASURES*

BARTHELME READS "SWALLOWING"

JUDITH SHERMAN: It seems to me that in many of what you would call stories there are selections that are parody, are what you'd call nonfiction. Where do you draw the line?

DONALD BARTHELME: Well, it's a somewhat difficult line to draw, but I went to some trouble to label this item [*Guilty Pleasures*] nonfiction to distinguish it from the stories. I think of it as journalism. A certain part of it was written out of anger, obviously a very creative emotion, at the government. I just feel that they ought to be thought of as distinct from the fiction. There is one link. The piece called "Nothing" could have gone into a book of fiction, but it would have been slipped in as a change of pace, and I think it really belongs here.

SHERMAN: Why?

BARTHELME: It's an odd ox, it's an odd piece. It's really a whatchamacallit.

CHARLES RUAS: It's really a mind trip on "nothing."

BARTHELME: Well, it's a meditation.

RUAS: Zero degree of writing, or a content drama.

BARTHELME: It's a meditation rather than a fiction.

SHERMAN: Except for the beginning and the end, why do you see "Swallowing" as being a nonfiction piece, in any way different from "Robert Kennedy Saved from Drowning"?

BARTHELME: It was different in intent. It was meant to express a general sense of outrage at the way the government was behaving in 1972 and prior to 1972, and of course in 1972 we didn't know as much about the government as we know now. The degree of outrage would of course have been higher had we known what we know now.

SHERMAN: Yes, but other than that first paragraph, when you talk about how the president tells us something and we swallow that, then you go into the cheese being argued about, or maybe I just don't get the analogy there.

BARTHELME: Well, let me see how to say it. I was probably figuring that I could damage the government most severely by making fun of it, because it takes itself so seriously and behaves, very often, so badly. Now I know damn well that the government is not really damaged by anything I might write about it, but it's missionary work. It's a way of trying to persuade people that this government is behaving badly and suggesting to them that there are remedies, there are things they can do about it—like vote the bastards out.

RUAS: Can you remember in '72 what triggered off the story? The whole Watergate scandal?

BARTHELME: Well, I took pen to paper about it on four or five different occasions. All of those things in that section are attacks on the Nixon administration. They were obviously lying, and they seemed at that point to be getting away with it. It's like saying, "Here, wait a minute, this guy here is a bad guy, and let's do something about it." And then, of course, the thing went on and on and on and on and up to this morning's newspaper, where the Gulf Oil Corporation is found to be doing various peculiar things with its money, its surplus of money. The unraveling is still going on, as you know. And I recently set pen to paper on a number of things. I wrote a piece for *The New Yorker,* it ran in the front of the magazine, triggered by this business—the assassinations, the planned assassinations—and it was meant to be a funny piece about the super dart gun they had developed to deliver to foreign leaders. [*Ed. note:* This piece was first published in the "Notes and Comment" section of *The New Yorker,* September 29, 1975, and was later incorporated into *Here in the Village.* It is reprinted in this book as "A fable . . ."] But it wasn't called a dart gun, you see, they called it a Microbioinoculator as I remember. And last Sunday I read in the paper that the C.I.A. had at one time considered dusting Mr. Castro's shoes with a certain chemical that would cause his beard to fall out, and I wondered who in the world was the idiot responsible for this masterstroke. Had it been stronger I would have written a piece about that. And then the whole business of the F.B.I. and Martin Luther King, which is absolutely sickening. There's just no way to deal with it really. That's beyond humor, you can't do anything with it.

RUAS: But, Donald, I gather now, just from what you've said, that it's actually the particular actions of individuals that trigger off your satirical vein.

BARTHELME: Against an ongoing background of chicanery.

RUAS: In the vernacular, swallowing something does mean being gullible, so that when you transform it to this gigantic cheese at the World's Fair, with a poet living in it—

BARTHELME: It's really the enormity of what we have swallowed. That's the point. We have swallowed endless amounts of prevarication.

RUAS: But the person who does the swallowing, as you point out, is a poet, and I'm wondering if—

BARTHELME: His line is, the advertising I think is an Alka-Seltzer commercial, "I can't believe I ate the whole thing." Alka-Seltzer says there are remedies for this. Well, similarly there are remedies for what we've swallowed.

SHERMAN: Is the steel voice of the poet the same as the barbed wit of a certain writer in this room?

BARTHELME: No, the poet was meant to be all of us together, standing up and doing something about this rat's nest. It is, in a way, a call to action, or it was so intended. It was published on the *Times* Op-Ed page [November 4, 1972], and very deliberately written for that. They asked me to do something, or maybe I suggested it to them, I don't remember. But it was published on thc Op-Ed page because I thought that was where it would reach the most people.

BARTHELME READS "THE ROYAL TREATMENT"

RUAS: Donald, how many pseudonyms have you?

BARTHELME: Just the one.

RUAS: Which one?

BARTHELME: Lily McNeil.

RUAS: And?

BARTHELME: That's all.

RUAS: Is that the only one? I thought you had three or four.

BARTHELME: No. When I was a starving young writer I published a couple of pieces under pseudonyms because they were trash.

RUAS: You're not turning against trash now?

BARTHELME: No, no, no, in literary terms they were trash and they were just written to make money, so I didn't want to sign my name to them. But there were only a couple of those.

RUAS: Okay, and this may sound very academic, but let's clear it up once and for all: is Lily McNeil a play on Rrose Selavy [*Ed. note:* A pseudonym used by Marcel Duchamp]?

BARTHELME: No.

RUAS: A transformation of Lily to—

BARTHELME: To what?

RUAS: Into Donald, and vice versa.

BARTHELME: No. It was just chosen because I originally thought I wanted to write the *Cosmopolitan* Girl piece ["That *Cosmopolitan* Girl"] and I thought it would be funnier if it was signed with a woman's name. It caused some amount of commotion. *Esquire* called up and wanted to know if Lily would be interested in writing a monthly column for them, giving the women's view on things. And I said I'd ask her, and Lily said she didn't feel up to it. That also appeared on the *Times* Op-Ed page under the by-line Lily McNeil, and I thought there it would be funny to have a Queen instead of a King and so that's why Lily was useful in that case. But again, this ["The Royal Treatment"] was written somewhat later—I don't recall what year it was published [*Ed. note:* July 1973]—but the internal evidence demonstrates that a lot more chicanery had been unveiled by that time. And in those pieces in the political section—the George Washington crossing the Delaware ["An Hesitation on the Bank of Delaware"] and so on—there is an escalating series of events culminating in "Mr. Foolfarm's Journal." Mr. Foolfarm is characterized as an advisor to the government.

BARTHELME READS "MR. FOOLFARM'S JOURNAL"

RUAS: The funny thing about this sort of unintelligible language is that it's wreaked its vengeance on us, as if it hadn't been bad enough in the first place.

BARTHELME: And on the perpetrators.

RUAS: And on the perpetrators. But it sort of entered the language very generally, didn't it? In the culture? That is, in jargonese.

BARTHELME: "Synecdoche" they're calling it now. In other words, when the C.I.A. is talking about killing people they use language that is ambiguous, which might mean "knock him off," for example; might mean—literally—"kill him;" or it might mean "depose him," speaking of Castro. So this is apparently an art which is developed to a very high level in Langley, Virginia. And, of course, it will to some degree enter the language, unless we guard ourselves very carefully.

SHERMAN: How do we do that?

BARTHELME: You say, "What do you mean, 'Knock him off'? What do you mean when you say that?" When you find language that is ambiguous and potentially dangerous, say "What do you mean? In plain words, what do you mean?" Then he's got to say we either mean deposing him through legitimate political means if there are any, or we mean killing. Don't let people get away with it.

RUAS: But that presupposes that they will give you definitions that are not ambiguous.

BARTHELME: "What do you mean?" is a question that can be repeated indefinitely, until you finally locate the meaning—if there is a meaning to be located.

RUAS: But the problem becomes aggravated in the media, which purports to actually do the job of translation. In making all the information accessible to everyone there is that same tendency to use jargonese or to be ambiguous.

BARTHELME: No, I think there the problem is because of the pressure of time. Both in gathering the news and in presenting it, you get a very thin, rather than a rich, version of events. The six o'clock news or the seven o'clock news is a marvel of removing the context from events, so you get a very thin version of events on television. You get a somewhat fuller version in a newspaper—a good newspaper like the *Times*—and, finally, when you get to the land of scholarship, in the best case you get a more meaty version. But it's a long time lapse between the seven o'clock news and the scholarly works which will much, much later be written about the particular event.

RUAS: Isn't that thinning out of information exactly where political opinions and slants are inserted so that the listener is unaware that this is biased, information is being deleted, withheld for a specific purpose?

SHERMAN: Sins of omission, rather than commission?

BARTHELME: Well, I don't think this is deliberate on the part of the media. The media do try very hard to tell the truth, I believe. It's that the form does not permit, in many cases, a fleshed-out version that would permit the consumer of the news to understand the particular event adequately.

SHERMAN: I think there is a problem, especially now, when the news almost requires a knowledge of economics and all sorts of other arcane fields. There's no time in a network newscast to go into what the repercussions of what such-and-such a move would be. You have to look to other places for that, and most people aren't willing to do that work.

BARTHELME: There are two things involved: what happened, and what does what happened mean. And the best newspapers have been moving in the direction of trying to explain—not only tell you what happened, but to give you the implications. But television, unless it does a special or something on a particular event, has great trouble doing that because of compactness.

RUAS: but on the other hand, for a writer who wants to actually get a point across satirically by sort of etching in acid the problem that's confronting the population—such as Lily representing the silent majority and proclaiming a monarchy, which is a pretty good takeoff on Nixon's attitude toward the populace—then you're using the language, you're playing with an existing set of ideas, and simply pointing out the absurdity of it.

BARTHELME: Yes. For example, in the George Washington crossing the Delaware piece. One suspected that Nixon had too many houses and that some amount of this—the improvements and so on—was being paid for with public money. Perhaps this may have been strictly legal. But perhaps this was not such a good idea, and so I posited the situation where George Washington refused to cross the Delaware until Congress provided him with, I believe, £2000 to build a house for his horse. I was hoping to make this small point in that way.

SHERMAN: Okay, I have a series of questions that all go together, but all going in a different direction. There's been much talk lately, Edwin Newman and the gang, of the danger that the American or English language is in. [*Ed. note:* Television commentator Edwin Newman's *Strictly Speaking: Will America Be the Death of English?* had been a bestseller in 1974.] Do you think that the English language is in danger? Is there anything writers can do about that? Or other people who care about language? Should they try to do anything about it? Because we've seen now the political repercussions of a reduction in the efficacy of language. It seems as if there's going to be an imminent reduction in the literacy of particular folk in the United States.

BARTHELME: First thing, what writers can do is write well, use the language well. We have a really wonderful language that provides us with a hundred million ways of saying anything we want, and the writer's task is to write well. As to the second part of your question: very often people say that the lower level of literacy is caused by television in some pernicious way. I don't think that's true at all. I think it is a function of a degenerating school system, especially the secondary schools. I noticed in the paper this morning, Christopher Jencks came out with a report that seemed to say that whether a child was in a good school or a bad school made no significant difference to his progress—unless I'm misquoting him, I hope I have it right—the crucial factor seemed to be what the child got at home, and education was not going to be the social equalizer that we had hoped it was going to be, and that income redistribution was the answer. I shouldn't attribute that to him because I'm not absolutely sure that's the way his argument runs, but if I understand it, that seems to be the tendency.

SHERMAN: I think the whole urge toward literacy is much more cultural. I don't think we can lay all the blame at the feet of the school system, particularly secondary schools. After all, children should learn to read well before secondary school, and that's mainly what I'm worried about. If one is to be fed all one's information through the electronic media, that's a very selective bunch of information.

RUAS: Not only selective, but it's also completely alinear information that's being fed in, so that it doesn't encourage any sort of analysis, the need for analysis, or any in-depth structuring of one's knowledge.

BARTHELME: Grace Paley suggests that it is not television but the telephone that has reduced the level of literacy in the country.

People don't write letters any more, they pick up the phone and talk to each other that way. There very well may be something in that.

RUAS: I'm really startled because it seems to me that the general trend is not only to put children into schools. Most parents think their cultural obligation is putting the child in a good school rather than a public school. More than that, parents now have to resort to daycare centers, etc., which are also neutralizing institutions, according to that analysis.

BARTHELME: I think also that recent educational theory places extraordinary importance on the first five years of life, and there is apparently a lot more we could do to prepare the child for its long voyage through life at that point than we are now doing—than I did for my child, for example.

SHERMAN: If we try to deal with all the problems of raising a child now we'd be here forever. Just the problem of learning how to read! I don't care how good a school the child is in if when the child goes home there are no magazines, there are no books, and the child never sees an adult reading, then it becomes something to maybe learn and quickly outgrow, that only children have to read.

BARTHELME: Here television does come into play. I recall with my daughter Anne—our house was full of books and we were constantly reading, and she was constantly watching television—I asked her one time what her mother was doing and she told me that her mother was watching a book.

RUAS: Which reminds me of another curious anecdote: Alexander was about two years old when *Sesame Street* came on—and *Sesame Street* was geared for four-year-olds, five-year-olds—he was watching it at two and quite able to follow it and pick up all of the vocabulary and counting in those programs, those early elementary programs, so that at two he had a larger vocabulary than the older children toward whom *Sesame Street* was directed.

BARTHELME: Similarly, Anne's vocabulary is quite good, but her motivation to read is not as strong as I would like it to be.

RUAS: Well, that's what I was going to point out to Judy. That a child in a house full of books may really learn to dislike them.

SHERMAN: Yes, there's no telling is there?

RUAS: My solution was to start collecting illustrated books.

SHERMAN: What made you decide to do a children's book?

BARTHELME: Oh, I just felt like doing a children's book.

SHERMAN: I guess that's the world's best answer.

BARTHELME READS *THE SLIGHTLY IRREGULAR FIRE ENGINE,* DESCRIBING THE ILLUSTRATIONS AND RELATING THEM TO THE CAPTIONS

SHERMAN: In the children's book there's one of those lists again. I'd like to go through one and figure out how these things occur to you.

BARTHELME: If I can tell you.

SHERMAN: Yes, it's the page opposite the knitting pirate. "We have Chinese acrobats. I think that the cat-seller will be around before lunch. We have an elephant that falls downhill"—not just an elephant, an elephant that falls downhill, head over heels. "We have some flying machines, although they're somewhat primitive. We have Chicken Chow Mein. And we have a pirate." That's—

BARTHELME:—Well, that list was dictated by the pictures I had picked out for the book. Everything, I think, except the flying machines, does appear later on in the book, and that's where the list came from.

SHERMAN: Okay, so the pictures came first and—

BARTHELME:—I gathered together the pictures I thought I could use. That book was dictated by the pictures. The text was written to fit the pictures.

RUAS: Which raises the next question, that along with all of the pictures you have captions that sometimes are directly related to the picture, such as this wonderful sort of stout, knitting pirate with holes in his stockings and so on. And above it, it says, "BURIED JEWELS/ Oceanic Dredging Company." Sometimes you use words very much as you use the illustrations.

BARTHELME: Those legends, as I call them in the children's book, come from a nineteenth-century printer's type-specimen book. It's a catalog from which printers can order type, samples of type specimens, and whoever set the specimens was wonderfully funny and imaginative. So I didn't write those words, I just took them out of the catalog and used them both as a design element to make the pages more interesting and also because what was said was very often quite appropriate and funny in itself.

SHERMAN: Including "GARDENS WATERED/ CARRIAGE-WAYS SPRINKLED/ DESERTS DRENCHED."

BARTHELME: My favorite is "Laughed at by Plain Folks."

RUAS: But I love "MODERN ENTERTAINMENT/ Barnumian Charioteering/ Trapeze daredevilism . . ."

BARTHELME: Yeah, the printers were wonderfully literate in the nineteenth century.

RUAS: So it functions as almost calligraphic in the sense that it's illustrative and yet very, very amusing in meaning.

BARTHELME: Right, right.

SHERMAN: I remember what happened to [Samuel] Richardson when he started printing his letter forms into stories. The pirate, you didn't put him together? He was really like that?

BARTHELME: No. The pirate comes from a rather well-known children's book of the period, which had an entirely different story. I don't remember the title.

RUAS: American or English?

BARTHELME: I would assume American. This is something I've been told. I only had the two pirate pictures, the one standing in front of the mirror with the djinn peering over the shoulder, and the one of him sitting there knitting. But there is apparently a whole book, which I've never seen, dealing with this pirate. If I knew how to go about getting it, I would go get it and find him in his original home.

SHERMAN: When you were talking about the pictures dictating the story, sort of hanging a new story on old pictures—

BARTHELME:—On very diverse materials, really—

SHERMAN:—sort of reconstructing *Eugénie Grandet*—

RUAS:—Follows the same technique?

SHERMAN: Well, to me it's similar. You take what this could be, this could describe anything, if—

BARTHELME:—Yeah, the Balzac piece [Barthelme's story "Eugénie grandet"] is sometimes taken to be, you know, a very smart-ass dismissal of Balzac, whereas I think it is a tiny little *hommage* to Balzac.

SHERMAN: I thought of it as a dismissal to the little catalog.

BARTHELME: To the little headnote there? Yeah.

RUAS: Yeah, the digest of great books.

BARTHELME: Yes.

RUAS: Donald, when you bring together visual material and writing, and also you select whether it's pictures or typography, the curious thing seems to me that, although this is a children's book, all the material is extremely elusive for an adult. The bust of the police chief, that's Plato, isn't it?

BARTHELME: I think it's Socrates, I'm not sure.

RUAS: There's the same sort of parodic and fantasy element which for an adult, by association, has so many more implications.

SHERMAN: When I first read this I thought, "That's not a children's book." Now, when I heard you read it, I thought it was.

BARTHELME: Well, it has been accused of being not a children's book. However, a number of reviewers tried it out on children and reported very positive responses. I tried it out on my own daughter, who was then six, and she was kind enough to say that she liked it very much. Now, there probably wasn't much else she could say.

BARTHELME READS "THE TEACHINGS OF DON B."

RUAS: In "The Teachings of Don B."—Donald Barthelme—what is the "Yankee Way of Knowledge" that you are posing to the Yaquis?

BARTHELME: Well, my feeling is that the whole thing is a bit absurd, and I was trying to make that point. If you read those books, which you may or may not have done, you suddenly realize that a certain amount of credulity is a necessary apparatus to read the books with.

RUAS: Why would you say credulity instead of a suspension of disbelief, which is a thoroughly respectable function of reading?

BARTHELME: Well, that's why I say it in the piece itself. I use both, but originally "suspension of disbelief."

RUAS: And yet the strange thing is that Casteneda is one of the few people who was a cultural force of the sixties who has actually continued to hold his audience.

BARTHELME: Well, he offers them a certain promise. I suppose people buy his books because they get something out of them. Whether what they get out of them is spurious or not is another matter.

SHERMAN: There was something else I wanted to ask about and maybe this is the time to deal with it. It's the teaching of writing. I'm really curious as to how you do that.

BARTHELME: Well, okay. The first thing one has to bear in mind when you say you are teaching creative writing is that it's a kind of misnomer. I cannot speak for my fellow teachers, but I can tell them what I do. I act as an editor in regard to their manuscripts, and we work on them and try to improve them. In other words, I don't go in there and make lengthy pronouncements about the art of writing. I function as an editor.

SHERMAN: What does an editor do? I'm not going to assume that most people in the world know what an editor does.

BARTHELME: An editor takes a manuscript and reads it, and if he sees ways in which it might be improved—and most pieces of prose, especially student work, can stand quite a bit of improvement—he does his best to develop the potential of that particular piece. He might say something like, "Well, George, the phrase you have here, 'Passionate rush of upsurging desire,' is perhaps a little purple for the purchase of a new pocketknife." And then the student says, "Yes, that's right, I have got that somewhat out of proportion. I will tone it down." Of course you do very much more complex things than that, but that's essentially how I go about it.

RUAS: What about investigating the content of the writing?

BARTHELME: I can sit down and say to a student, "What is this about, really?" And very often, when asked the question, the man or woman realizes that he's left out what the piece is about, and then we go looking for what the piece is about, and very often find it, and he puts it back in and so on and so on and so on. I give them assignments, just little exercises. One of them is to go out and interview a child under twelve, not a member of their own family, and find out what the kid is really thinking about. That's usually a fruitful assignment. Or I give them a more abstract assignment. I say, "John loves Mary. Prove it, in two pages." And you don't prove that John loves Mary by having John give Mary a mink coat or whatever, and so they have to struggle with the problem of having to prove that John loves Mary in some way that is truly touching and valuable, that conveys the required emotion. About the only thing I give them in the way of general pronouncements is that I forbid them absolutely to use weather in any form. This, with student writers, ties their hands behind their backs—

SHERMAN:—Weather, outdoor weather?

BARTHELME: Weather weather. Thunderstorms, rain. I say, "This is entirely an artificial prohibition and as soon as you leave my class you can use all the weather you want. But for this space of time, weather is *verboten.*" That immediately gets rid of a lot of really bad writing.

RUAS: Why, because—

BARTHELME:—Because it's so easy to use weather as the equivalent of an emotion, and you know—

SHERMAN:—And Shakespeare's already done it better than anyone else can.

BARTHELME: Yes, and one very good student, at the start of this semester, said, "What, no weather? What would *Lear* be without weather?" And I said, "The exception to this rule is if you write *Lear.*"

RUAS: That's curious, because I was having a discussion with a friend about Turgenev and my friend pointed out to me that, in contrast to the other Russian writers, he really has very few descriptions of emotion; he uses the weather or nature description whenever a character is about to react to someone else, and actually bypasses emotion altogether.

BARTHELME: It's far too easy to do.

RUAS: For a student.

BARTHELME: Yes, student writers tend to use it as a crutch. So we get rid of that from the word go. Then I do other things. At a certain point during a semester I will have some sense of my students' individual personalities, and I pair them off with each other and they meet outside of class and go over each other's manuscripts and work as each other's editors. I pair them for good reasons, and usually they like it. It extends the teaching process, they're teaching each other. Or another thing I might do is say, "Today, I'm not going to say a word, and I will decide which stories we'll discuss in class and one of you, Tom, Dick, or Harriet, will lead the discussion." And I sit there and don't say a word and this usually produces quite a good class, because they like that. The thing to do is to get them involved, and to have the students talk and teach each other. And, as Grace [Paley] says, if you can get them to fighting with each other you've really achieved something.

RUAS: In contrast to the paring-down process, do you also make them write a three-page sentence?

BARTHELME: No, I try to "make" them do as little as possible. I don't mean work. I try to create an atmosphere in which they work like the devil, but I try not to impose things on them. What I'm trying to do is to get them to do what they want to do and to get them to do it as well as is possible.

RUAS: Do you also recommend certain writers to read?

BARTHELME: Oh yeah, sure, sure.

RUAS: Such as?

BARTHELME: My colleague Mark Mirsky has a reading list of about a hundred writers, which I think is very good. I usually give them about six books a semester. Kleist, for example, Rabelais—I've completely forgotten—Rimbaud. And of the newer books, I might give them Márquez, I might give them Beckett, I might give them William Gass—more recent work—all chosen to show them the different possibilities.

SHERMAN: It's strange that so many of them are not written originally in English.

BARTHELME: The older ones.

SHERMAN: They must be good translations, then.

BARTHELME: The standard translations. Louise Vèrese in the case of Rimbaud. There are several translations, I forget who did the Penguin translation. Do you remember, Charles?

RUAS: Of Rabelais? No, I don't.

BARTHELME: It's somewhat livelier than the Putnam translation. Most of the students have not read the three older writers on their own, and so they do represent different kinds of problems and possibilities. You know, Kleist is not terribly well known. He is a famous writer but I don't believe he's much taught to undergraduates, unless they're German students. What I assign is assigned for certain technical reasons: Kleist to show them how to do things at Kleist-pace, Rabelais for other reasons, Rimbaud for still other reasons.

SHERMAN: That's the question I'm asking. What are they reading for?

BARTHELME: The virtues that these writers display in English are sufficiently grand to impress the students with possibilities and it's their own possibility that I'm interested in teaching them. I want them to know that it's possible to do things this way, or that way, or another way.

BARTHELME READS "THE PHOTOGRAPHS"

ENVOI BY JUDITH SHERMAN

FOURTH PROGRAM

BARTHELME READS EXCERPTS FROM *SNOW WHITE*

JUDITH SHERMAN: The first time I read this [*Snow White*], the first time I'd ever heard of you, as a matter of fact, I had a rough time getting through it. There were too many things in the way. I couldn't get at it—notably the cover of the Bantam edition. Since I had no idea who you were, I thought, "Oh, this is going to be a sort of intellectual porno novel." That's the way I was viewing it, I was having trouble reading it. It was only in rereading it—I'm not going to say

I found it easier—that I found it interesting, delightful, and I was having a good time reading it—

DONALD BARTHELME: —And I hope nonporno.

SHERMAN: Nonporno, nonsexist, non-all those other things that I was expecting it to be.

CHARLES RUAS: You were thinking of *The Story of O* or one of those? A parody of that?

SHERMAN: No.

BARTHELME: You were probably thinking of those pornographic renderings of the Disney version that were floating around at one time.

RUAS: Is that what you were thinking, in terms of the title?

BARTHELME: No, no, no. As a matter of fact, when I began this book I didn't even know that Snow White was Snow White. I did have the situation of the seven men living with the single woman. I did know that Snow White was Snow White, but I didn't call her Snow White. And then, as I went along, of course it became obvious that the correct thing to do was to call her Snow White.

SHERMAN: At any rate, I would not suggest that someone, if they're going to read works by Donald Barthelme, read this book first.

BARTHELME: Why?

SHERMAN: Well, in our first interview I said that often a reader brings to a book a certain set of prejudices, and it takes a while to get around them. With both this and *The Dead Father,* I find that it's easier to let the prejudices get in the way. Again, there's this feeling: if I put my foot down here, is it going to land on solid earth or is it not? And often it doesn't and you've got to be able to let go and go with it more than you do with the shorter pieces, where it's not quite as scary.

BARTHELME: Yes. If I understand what you mean by "solid earth," I would say that maybe solid earth is not always desirable.

SHERMAN: That's what I mean. Solid earth is definitely not desirable.

BARTHELME: It's a very solid and reassuring sound, the very solid earth. But maybe some of it is on top of you. Your grave.

SHERMAN: If one is listening to a piece of music and the music goes in a direction that you weren't expecting it to go, it should be a source of delight rather than—

BARTHELME: —Yes, sure, sure. In any kind of art, surprise is one of the artist's strongest moves.

SHERMAN: Right. This and *The Dead Father,* when one first

approaches it, demand that the reader immediately let go and go with it. Where the shorter pieces—

BARTHELME: —Are shorter.

SHERMAN: Are shorter. Right, yes, you're committing yourself for a shorter time and you're willing to do it. Whereas, when you're starting a novel, you want to get it all.

RUAS: The thing that interested me was your picking up this idea of the commune and using it as your basic structure, in terms of your experimentation with the narrative form.

BARTHELME: I think when this was written—it was written in '65, '66, published in '67—

RUAS: —No, '65.

BARTHELME: Was it published in '65?

RUAS: Yes, it appeared in *The New Yorker* in '65 and then—I was double-checking—in '67.

BARTHELME: Oh, I know. The first copyright date is '65, and it refers to a part of the book—

RUAS: —In *The New Yorker*?

BARTHELME: No, not in *The New Yorker.* I think it was in *Harper's Bazaar,* the part that has to do with Snow White writing the poem. It appeared in considerably different form in *Harper's Bazaar,* I think it was. [*Ed. note:* The section of *Snow White* under discussion first appeared in *Harper's Bazaar,* November 1965, as "The Affront."] But the book itself, the original copyright date was '67, so it was finished in '65 and '66. I don't know why it was important to establish that.

RUAS: No, it is, because unlike in some of the shorter pieces, you're actually using a current social phenomenon.

BARTHELME: That's what I was getting to, that communes were all around us at that time, and furnished an obvious ground for this little number here.

RUAS: But in your narrative, you go from character to character and deal with different psychological moods. You play the character's psychological mood as if it were a scale.

BARTHELME: It's a sort of floating narrator. You never know which of the men is speaking and very often he says "we," so as to define a collective attitude toward what is going on. But the narrator is never precisely named as being Hubert or being Dan or being Clem or whatever, although each of these characters is given soliloquies from time to time, but the overall narrator is assumed to be one of the men with whom Snow White is living. But you never know precisely which one is telling the story.

RUAS: And this is juxtaposed with the portrait where each of the men is described very satirically and objectively. Are the two compatible?

BARTHELME: The assumption is that one of his fellow commune members is speaking about him. The "we" narrative position is a very fruitful one. I don't mean necessarily here, but in general.

RUAS: So that the narration reflects the collective situation?

BARTHELME: Yes.

RUAS: And you're trying to recreate that consciousness where it's all intermingled and at the same time schizy enough so that one can wonder if the narrative voice is not also observing himself as well as others.

BARTHELME: What's nice about the "we" narration is that "we" could be a couple or an army, and there's lots of opportunity for play there. And in a commune there's ample opportunity for conflict, as accounts of real communes have amply demonstrated. It would be almost a forcing atmosphere that tended to produce conflict. You've both read accounts of this or that commune and the way it fell apart, or a different kind of narrative of the way in which the early days of the commune were very hectic, but now we have everything and so on and so on. It's a thing I don't much credit, but I've read it that way, too.

RUAS: Is this based on personal experience?

BARTHELME: Oh no, no, no, no, no.

RUAS: Which means yes, so many noes—

BARTHELME: No, no. Well, I did live in a commune in the army, in the sense that there were twelve of us living in a tent on the side of a hill for what seemed like decades. But outside of that, the largest communal experience I've had is a three-person commune consisting of husband, wife, and child.

RUAS: So this phenomenon of the '60s wasn't part of your personal exploration? You were doing it simply as a literary experiment?

BARTHELME: Right. I'm not concealing from you some dark communality.

RUAS: But Don, in your style, that means that you are.

BARTHELME: No, no. Sometimes things are what they seem.

SHERMAN: What I connect up with is that genre often used in B-movies, in which you get a group of people together who are not connected in—

BARTHELME: —*Lifeboat.*

SHERMAN: Yes, *Lifeboat, Airport,* all those. It's a way of getting it together in a '60s sense. But then the book is not about the problems they're going to have. The problems are mentioned. Bill is either suffering from or not suffering from anxiety, and they are obviously concerned about it and discussing it, but the book doesn't center on—

BARTHELME: —Well, the men in *Snow White* are not that randomly selected. They have various personalities, but it's implied, you'll recall, they had a common father.

SHERMAN: Oh, right.

BARTHELME: Because remember, there was the business, a very little bit of business, about their father, who is said not to be very interesting—a canned good is more interesting and so on.

RUAS: For you that was an important element?

BARTHELME: It wasn't an important element because very little space is given to it. They had a common father just as they are business partners, because making the baby food is one of their businesses, and it's implied that some form of real estate speculation is their other business because they're always going out to wash the buildings and keep them clean. So they're joined together in several ways: the common father, the business partnership, and the cohabitation with Snow White would be the three joinings.

SHERMAN: And the father, by being made not very interesting, is gotten out of the way.

BARTHELME: Yeah, right, because I didn't want to make too much of the common fatherhood. I just wanted to state it and walk away from it.

RUAS: But you didn't walk away from it if your last novel is called *The Dead Father.*

BARTHELME: No, but within *Snow White* I walked away from it. No, I'm not sure that fatherhood is a major theme, latent in *Snow White.*

RUAS: But motherhood is a theme in the whole Snow White story.

BARTHELME: In that she mothers the men. Her attitude toward them is much more motherly than sexual. That's true, and she's always looking elsewhere and scanning the horizon for the arrival of the prince she feels is owed her, which suggests a father, or the possibility of further children, or that these men are essentially children. The implications go in several directions.

RUAS: But at the same time, perhaps I was also influenced by that book jacket, the cover, which sort of forces a certain element, a visualization, on you that's not wanted.

BARTHELME: Yes.

RUAS: I was thinking that I perceived her very much as a teenybopper.

BARTHELME: I didn't intend that.

RUAS: I realize that, but in the reading, since there's so much play, I felt a complete back-and-forth ambiguity between the mothering aspect and the totally nondefined individual.

BARTHELME: I think it would probably be wrong to try and locate, say, the character of Snow White. She is a pretext for being able to write, to use certain kinds of language. She also has other aspects, but all of these people in this book are pretexts for being able to encounter certain kinds of language, and less to speak about the character of any one of them. Although some threads of character may adhere to them, it's probably the wrong way to enter the book.

RUAS: And yet the book is fixed, though, in time and place, it seems to me.

BARTHELME: Well, the story of Snow White and the Seven Dwarfs is known to all, and therefore a wonderful thing to use in a novel because you can play against expectations, you can go with expectations, you can contradict the story, you can affirm the story. You have lots of choices, and the ground for the story is common mythic property.

SHERMAN: Which is something I'd like to talk about. Once upon a time, a writer in society was there to set down or conglomerate the legends and myths of the culture—Homer, etc.—up until maybe Cervantes. He was the one who started going off on his own. And today it is required of an author—almost required—that the plot, the setting, the whatever, be new, that it be made of whole cloth out of one's head—if that can be done at all. John Barth obviously is using the myths much more than anyone else I can think of—

BARTHELME: —And John Gardner, also.

SHERMAN: John Gardner, right, of course.

BARTHELME: I don't think you can make up anything out of whole cloth. Anything you write is already determined to a great degree by the whole history of the culture or the the civilization, or what you know of it, or have encountered of it. I would not want to say that there was any one way to proceed, or that any particular thing is required of a writer at this particular moment. There are many ways to proceed, and some people do very well by ignoring myth entirely. Some people do very well by consciously embracing it. I don't think that's an adequate answer to your question.

RUAS: Do you consciously, in your work, search out the mythic aspects? Either to debunk or play with?

BARTHELME: Clearly, I'm constantly engaged with them. They probably seek me out. I mean the myths that mean the most to me are probably the ones that I have to deal with.

RUAS: As in *Snow White.*

BARTHELME: Yes, right. It just occurred to me that as a member of a large family—in other words, a number of men competing for the attention of a single woman—the Snow White myth, if you want to call it a myth, would naturally be more meaningful to me than it would have been if I'd been an only child.

RUAS: I wouldn't call it a myth. I'd call it a tale, a folktale.

BARTHELME: Fairy tale, yes.

RUAS: The myth is, what, the Oedipus story?

BARTHELME: But there is a sense in which fairy tales can contain mythic elements.

SHERMAN: I feel great resonance from those myths that are about someone having to accomplish something and having every imaginable kind of problem thrown in his way before he gets to the—

BARTHELME: —The journey of the hero, right? To bring back the boon. You are given no boons until you've turned over many stones.

RUAS: But then there's a dual aspect, and perhaps this is my reading, but I did read the novel as being particularly of the mid-'60s and, more specifically—and perhaps this is of our own experience—I located it in New York, and downtown, do you know? In the cultural atmosphere of the East Side, where all this fervor, all this activity, occurred.

BARTHELME: Well, the thing is loaded with cultural baggage, probably too much so.

RUAS: Why do you say that? That amazes me.

BARTHELME: Because I think that if I had to do it over again I would do it somewhat differently.

RUAS: We can see the constant interest of what you call "cultural baggage."

BARTHELME: Yes, in the best case. Still, it's possible that this is overdone here.

RUAS: Because, you know, I would want to pit you against historical actualities.

BARTHELME: I'm already pitted against historical actualities, and I need no more pitting from you, Charles.

RUAS: No, I was speaking of your reaction, for example, when you actually read about the Manson case and so on, where this collective thinking, which is suggested in the narrative technique, was in actual practice with a center of consciousness. I mean, obviously, the genders were reversed, but there was a center of consciousness.

BARTHELME: First, I was appalled by the Manson case. There's no other way to be. Walker Percy has a novel, I believe it's *Love in the Ruins,* wherein the principle character is holed up in a hotel with a rifle and "they" are coming. And then the whole thing happened subsequently, after the book was published—a guy, a sniper on top of a New Orleans hotel, shooting at people in the streets. And everybody said, "Walker, how did you know that was going to happen?" And, of course, he didn't know it was going to happen. It was a possibility in the culture that he had located ahead of time, I guess by osmosis.

RUAS: Would you apply that to *Snow White*?

BARTHELME: I would not say that *Snow White* predicts the Manson case. I couldn't imagine anything predicting the Manson case, or Charlie Starkweather, or any of that kind of thing, except that the tradition of people running amok is not a new thing in the world. People do it. The Manson case had its own special features, in that usually the guy that runs amok is an individual like Starkweather. Wasn't it Starkweather who had the girlfriend who traveled with him and he had her under his thumb to the point where—

RUAS: —Yes.

BARTHELME: As that very good film, Terry Malick's *Badlands,* shows. But the Manson case is remarkable in that he had so many people hypnotized or mesmerized.

RUAS: The analogous element would be that when you have a collective consciousness of that sort, then all barriers break.

BARTHELME: You do have the precedent for the Manson case in Nazi Germany. And you could probably go back in history and find many other examples of mass hysteria.

RUAS: Curiously enough, I was thinking about what you had said about Beckett. In Beckett's novels, especially the later works, there is, it seems, an ahistorical tone to the setting and the characters. I don't know whether he deliberately seeks to eliminate all specific historical references or whether that's simply fundamental to the way he perceives the characters and their situations.

BARTHELME: There have been some critical suggestions that some part of Beckett's work does specifically represent, or have to do, with France—occupied France—especially the business of working on the farm as Beckett did, and the behavior of the French peasantry among which he found himself. I would suspect that Beckett is trying to leave as few hawsers as possible running from his work to historical actuality.

RUAS: Is that also an aspect you want in your novels as opposed to your shorter pieces, where there is a very direct pitting against historical actuality?

BARTHELME: Well, I think that can be answered by reference to the new novel [*The Dead Father*], which is much less rooted in historical actuality than *Snow White* is, so the direction is toward less of that, it would seem to me.

SHERMAN: Yes, the new one is much more mythic, in feel rather than in specific reference to a myth.

BARTHELME: Yes, it contains almost none of the direct time references that, perhaps, *Snow White* has too many of.

SHERMAN: I assume that, and this is a feeling only, that you did not begin writing *Snow White* at the beginning and it went forward that way. I suspect that there were parts that existed.

BARTHELME: You're right. It is not a book that could have been written from page one until the end. But I think that's true of most writers. They don't write Chapter One, then Chapter Two. They try things out, and that doesn't work so they abandon that line of exploration and do something new, and these things are finally assembled into a more or less orderly machine.

SHERMAN: You said something before about this being a vehicle for certain things you wanted to do with language. Such as?

BARTHELME: Mostly play with it. Make certain kinds of sentences. That's all.

BARTHELME READS "A SHOWER OF GOLD"

BARTHELME: The piece is clearly inspired by all this fake existential language that was around at the time. Existential language was very popular in those days and so it's a reaction to its spurious appeal. Although it's philosophically based on very solid matter—not the piece, the existential language—it is also a very cheap means of self-dramatization. And that's more or less what this piece is about. This piece happens to be *about* something.

RUAS: But there's still a vogue for anguish, isn't there? But now it's called "depression." We've gone from existential to psychoanalytical terms.

BARTHELME: Discovered depression, sort of legitimized depression. Well, depression is real. The terms in which it's talked about are very often rather peculiar.

SHERMAN: I see his final speech as saying, "Okay, everything is absurd," but he's trying to get around having to play that game.

BARTHELME: Well, the key line is "How can you be alienated without first having been connected? Think back and remember how it was." The logic there, I think, is sound. The whole business of alienation, which is based on Sartre's work, was at that time being bandied about by people who had never come near *Being and Nothingness* or the people that Sartre built upon—Husserl, and so on, Heidegger.

SHERMAN: Buber.

BARTHELME: Yes, right.

SHERMAN: I-Thou relationship with the president.

RUAS: That ["A Shower of Gold"] was one of your earlier published pieces.

BARTHELME: Yes.

RUAS: How long had you been writing in New York when that appeared?

BARTHELME: As I recall, it appeared in '62 or '63 [*Ed. note:* It first appeared in *The New Yorker,* December 28, 1963], just about the time that I moved here.

SHERMAN: In what did it appear?

BARTHELME: In *The New Yorker* originally.

SHERMAN: The problem with a story like this is that here again there's a walking-the-thin-line between fiction and the nonfiction forms, the parodies.

BARTHELME: Yes, this is more parody than anything else. It's not in the form of parody. In other words, it does not parody a specific work, it deals with a whole class of things. I'm very fond of the barber [in "A Shower of Gold"] having authored four books called *The Decision to Be,* as if he had any choice.

SHERMAN: Often I feel, especially when I first started reading your stories, and again when I started reading this book [*Come Back, Dr. Caligari*], as though I'm reading somebody's dreams—especially the first couple of stories in here, several stories in here—characters change identity, or the people you thought were around at the beginning of the story turn out to be different people by the end. I just wonder how much of that is a conscious technique?

BARTHELME: Well, I would hope all of it was a conscious technique. Many writers use dream material in their work in one way or another, and I am certainly no exception. There is some of it in *The Dead Father.* I don't know whether you recall it, but the business where he's sort of shoved into a bullring sort of space. Thomas is bound and there are a lot of people, both men and women, walking around, gripping between their teeth pieces of paper on which things are written. That is pure dream material.

SHERMAN: Oh, right, the "murderinging" and all that.

BARTHELME: No, not the "murderinging." The Great Father Serpent has the "murderinging" message on his piece of tin, his thundersheet. But the business of being tied up, walking around with a lot of other people, gripping a piece of paper between your teeth, which has a message on it which is about you but which you are not allowed to read, but you try—all of that is straight dream material.

SHERMAN: And try to keep your message from other people, at the same time trying to see theirs.

BARTHELME: Yes, right.

RUAS: The satire always has this underpinning of Pascal and Nietzsche and Sartre, which is not in turn satirized.

BARTHELME: Well, no. It is not Sartre that is being satirized here. It is—to call them commentators would be too courteous—exploiters.

RUAS: Which seems to indicate that the satire has a definite sort of commitment.

BARTHELME: It would be to Sartre if it could be located anywhere. The story is about the process with which real ideas are weakened, cheapened, wholesaled, diluted, so on and so on. I don't know if you recall, but there was an awful lot of that going around in weak solutions at the time.

BARTHELME READS "THE BIG BROADCAST OF 1938"

FINAL ENVOI BY JUDITH SHERMAN

INTERVIEW WITH LARRY MCCAFFERY, 1980

LARRY MCCAFFERY: You've published two novels but most of your work has been in short fiction. Do you have an explanation for this tendency?

DONALD BARTHELME: Novels take me a long time; short fiction provides a kind of immediate gratification—the relationship of sketches to battle paintings.

MCCAFFERY: Didn't I see somewhere your claim that you're always working on novels?

BARTHELME: Over a period of years I can have a dozen bad ideas for novels, some of which I actually invest a certain amount of time in. Some of these false starts yield short pieces; most don't. The first story in *Sadness*—"La Critique de la Vie Quotidienne"—is salvage.

MCCAFFERY: Do you have a routine in your work habits, a daily schedule?

BARTHELME: I get up very early, read the *Times*, and then work until lunchtime, sometimes a bit after. If I'm particularly involved in something, I work at night.

MCCAFFERY: Do stories typically begin for you by landing on you, like the dog in "Falling Dog"?

BARTHELME: Well, for about four days I've been writing what amounts to nonsense. And then suddenly I came across an interesting sentence—or at least interesting to me: "It is not clear that Arthur Byte was wearing his black corduroy suit when he set fire to the Yale Art and Architecture Building in the spring of 1968." I don't know what follows from this sentence; I'm hoping it may develop into something.

MCCAFFERY: Do most of your stories begin in this way—from the sound or texture of a sentence, rather than from a plot idea or a character?

BARTHELME: In different ways. I did know someone who was at Yale teaching in the architecture department at the time of that notorious fire; I'm not sure if the date was 1968, I'd have to check. I don't believe they ever found out who set it. I certainly have no idea. But I'm positing a someone and hoping that tragic additional material may accumulate around that sentence.

MCCAFFERY: At the end of your story "Sentence," your narrator says that the sentence is "a structure to be treasured for its weaknesses, as opposed to the strength of stones." Am I right in assuming that one of the things that interests you the most about the sentence as an object is precisely its "treasured weaknesses"?

BARTHELME: I look for a particular kind of sentence, perhaps more often the awkward than the beautiful. A back-broke sentence is interesting. Any sentence that begins with the phase, "It is not clear that . . ." is clearly clumsy but preparing itself for greatness of a kind. A way of backing into a story—of getting past the reader's hardwon armor.

MCCAFFERY: Can you describe what's happening once you've found this initial impulse? Obviously you aren't aiming at developing characters or furthering the plot or whatever else it would be that most writers would say.

BARTHELME: A process of accretion. Barnacles growing on a wreck or a rock. I'd rather have a wreck than a ship that sails. Things attach themselves to wrecks. Strange fish find your wreck or rock to be a good feeding ground; after a while you've got a situation with possibilities.

MCCAFFERY: Have you ever studied philosophy of language in any kind of systematic way? Critics are always suggesting that your stories read like "glosses on Wittgenstein" and so forth . . .

BARTHELME: No, I spent two years in the army in the middle of my undergraduate days at Houston. When I came back to the university, which must have been about 1955, there was a new man—Maurice Natanson—teaching a course entitled "Sociology and Literature" that sounded good. I enrolled and he was talking about Kafka and Kleist and George Herbert Mead. I wasn't a particularly acute or productive student of philosophy, but in that and subsequent classes I got acquainted with people Mauri was interested in: Husserl, Heidegger, Kierkegaard, Sartre, and company.

MCCAFFERY: You were originally interested in journalism, weren't you?

BARTHELME: It seemed clear that the way to become a writer was to go to work for a newspaper, as Hemingway had done—then, if you were lucky, you might write fiction. I don't think anybody believes that anymore. But I went to work for a newspaper while I was still a sophomore and went back to the newspaper when I got out of the army. I was really very happy there, thought I was in high cotton.

MCCAFFERY: By the late '50s, when you became editor of the *Forum,* you were obviously already interested a great deal in parody and satire as literary forms. What so attracted you to this type of writing, as opposed, say, to the standard, realistic narrative forms?

BARTHELME: People like S. J. Perelman and E. B. White—people who could do certain amazing things in prose. Perelman was the first true American surrealist—of a rank in the world surrealist movement with the best—and Nathanael West was another. Wolcott Gibbs—all those *New Yorker* writers. Hemingway as parodist, *The Torrents of Spring.*

MCCAFFERY: And you've already mentioned Kafka and Kleist . . .

BARTHELME: Kleist was important to Kafka, something I didn't find out for a while.

MCCAFFERY: Somewhere in here you got involved as a director of an art museum. What was the background of that?

BARTHELME: A peculiar happenstance. I was entrusted with a small museum for a couple of years—the Contemporary Arts Museum in Houston. They had just lost the director, didn't have a prospect. I'd been on the board. They asked me to fill in temporarily, which I did for a while, and then they made me director—probably more fun than anything I've done before or since. For two years I mounted shows and developed programs in music, theater, and film. In consequence I met Harold Rosenberg in 1962. At that time Harold had in mind starting a new magazine which he and Thomas B. Hess would edit. They needed someone to be the managing editor—that is, someone to put out the magazine—and they hired me.

MCCAFFERY: This was the now-legendary magazine *Location*?

BARTHELME: Yes. It was meant to be not just an art magazine but an art-literary magazine. We were able to publish some wonderful material—some early Gass, some of John Ashbery's work, Kenneth

Koch's stuff. It was supposed to be a quarterly, but in fact we published only two issues. Tom and Harold were not worried about putting the magazine out on time and certainly never put any pressure on me. We waited until we had enough decent stuff for a good issue. That experience was a great pleasure—listening to Tom and Harold talk.

MCCAFFERY: This must have been about the time you first started selling pieces to *The New Yorker.*

BARTHELME: Yes. Also, once in a while when I was low on cash I'd write something for certain strange magazines—the names I don't even remember. Names like *Dasher* and *Thug.* I do remember picking up five hundred bucks or something per piece. I did that a few times. Kind of gory, or even Gorey, fiction.

MCCAFFERY: Have any of these things ever resurfaced?

BARTHELME: No. Nor shall they ever.

MCCAFFERY: I've always suspected that your experience in working for the museum must have had at least as much impact on your sensibility as any literary influences.

BARTHELME: It was a very small place. My responsibility was to put some good shows together, mildly didactic, modestly informative. So I had to study quite a lot very fast to be able to do this—to make intelligent or useful shows. Luckily I've always gotten along quite well with painters and sculptors, mostly by virtue of not asking the wrong questions of them. There's a style of conversation . . .

MCCAFFERY: It's been my experience that it's always in bad taste to ask a painter what his work "means." Now that I think of it, this seems to hold true for writers as well.

BARTHELME: It's a separate study, "How to manifest intelligent sympathy while not saying very much." The early '60s were, as you know, an explosive period in American art, and I learned on the job, nervously. Just being in the studio teaches you something. I'll give you an example: when we were doing *Location* I went over to Rauschenberg's studio on lower Broadway with Rudy Burkhardt, the photographer, to take some pictures. Rauschenberg was doing silk-screen pieces and the tonality of these things was gray—very, very gray. I looked out the windows and they were dirty, very much the tonality of the pictures. So I asked Rudy to get some shots of the windows and we ran one of them with the paintings. They were very much New York Lower Broadway windows. A footnote.

MCCAFFERY: Your narrator in "See the Moon?" comments enviously at one point about the "fantastic metaphysical advantage" possessed by painters. What was he referring to?

BARTHELME: The physicality of the medium—there's a physicality of color, of an object present before the spectator, which painters don't have to project by means of words. I can peel the label off that bottle of beer you're drinking and glue it to the canvas and it's there.

MCCAFFERY: Like a lot of painters in this century, you seem to enjoy lifting things out of the world, in this case words or phrases, and then . . .

BARTHELME: And then, sung to and Simonized, they're thrown into the mesh.

MCCAFFERY: But what you're doing—this rearrangement of these "real" elements into your own personal constructions—is related to collage, seems to partake of some of that metaphysical advantage you're describing.

BARTHELME: This sort of thing is of course what Dos Passos did in the Newsreels, what Joyce did in various ways. I suppose the theater has the possibility of doing this in the most immediate way. I'm on the stage and I suddenly climb down into the pit and kick you in the knee. That's not like writing about kicking you in the knee, it's not like painting you being kicked in the knee, because you have a pain in the knee. This sounds a bit aggressive. Forgive me.

MCCAFFERY: Another aspect of painting that seems relevant to your fiction is the surrealist practice of juxtaposing two elements for certain kinds of effects—in fiction or poetry, different sorts of language.

BARTHELME: It's a principle of construction. This can be terribly easy—can become cheapo surrealism, mechanically linking contradictions. Take Duchamp's phrase, in reference to *The Bride and the Bachelors,* that the Bride "warmly refuses" her suitors. The phrase is very nice, but you can see how it could become a formula.

MCCAFFERY: How do you avoid falling into this trap in your own work? Is there a formula for avoiding the formula?

BARTHELME: I think you stare at the sentence for a long time. The better elements are retained and the worse fall out of the manuscript.

MCCAFFERY: One last aspect of painting that I'd like you to comment upon in relation to your own work is the tendency of painting in this century to explore itself, its own medium—the nature of paint, colors, shapes, and lines—rather than attempting to reproduce or comment upon something outside itself. This tendency seems relevant not only to your work but also to that of several other important writers of the past fifteen years. Is this a fair analogy?

BARTHELME: It is. I also think that painting—in the '60s but especially in the '70s—really pioneered for us all the things that it is not necessary to do. Under the aegis of exploring itself, exploring its own means or the medium, painting really did a lot of dumb things that showed poets and prose writers what might usefully not be done.

MCCAFFERY: What sorts of things are you thinking of?

BARTHELME: I'm thinking mostly of conceptual art, which seems to me a bit sterile. Concrete poetry is an example of something that is, for me, not very nourishing, though it can be said to be exploratory in the way that a lot of conceptual art is exploratory. I can see why in some sense it had to be done. But perhaps not twice.

MCCAFFERY: What about some of the "New-New-Novelists" in France—Pinget, Sollers, Baudry, LeClézio? They seem to be trying to push fiction to the same limits of abstraction that conceptual artists have been searching for.

BARTHELME: A work like Butor's *Mobile*—after a time there's nothing more you can say of this than "I like it" or "I don't like it"—the stupidest of comments. A more refined version is "I know this is good but I still don't like it." And I think this is a fair comment. There are more *recherché* examples of this kind of thing. *Tri-Quarterly* did an issue a while back entitled "In the Wake of the Wake"—published several gallant Frenchmen whose work I'd seen in scattered places. The emphasis was toward "pure abstraction." For me this is a problem, since they get further and further away from the common reader. I understand the impulse—toward the condition of music—but as a common reader I demand this to be done in masterly fashion or not at all. Mallarmé is perhaps the extreme, along with Gertrude Stein. I admire them both.

MCCAFFERY: Don't we find this kind of metafictional self-inquiry about language and fiction-making surfacing quite often in your works? I'm thinking about stories like "Daumier" and "See the Moon?" or *Snow White*, which even has a questionnaire for the reader appearing in the middle of it.

BARTHELME: Wouldn't "metafiction" bc "fiction-about-fiction"?

MCCAFFERY: Yes, although I personally like to use the word "fiction" in a fairly broad sense.

BARTHELME: I don't have any great enthusiasm for fiction-about-fiction. It's true that in 1965 I put that questionnaire in the middle of *Snow White.* But I haven't done that much in that direction since. I think I've actually been fairly restrained on that front. Critics, of course, have been searching for a term that would describe fiction after the great period of modernism—"postmodernism," "metafiction," "surfiction," and "superfiction." The last two are terrible; I suppose "postmodernism" is the least ugly, most descriptive.

MCCAFFERY: What do you think about Philip Roth's famous suggestion back in the early '60s that reality was outstripping fiction's ability to amaze us?

BARTHELME: I do think something happened in fiction about that time, but I'd locate it differently—I think writers got past being intimidated by Joyce. Maybe the reality that Roth was talking about was instrumental in this recognition, but I think people realized that one didn't have to repeat Joyce (if that were even possible) but could use aspects of his achievement.

MCCAFFERY: One of your most evident abilities is your gift at mimicking a wide range of styles, jargons, lingoes. Where do these voices come from?

BARTHELME: I listen to people talk, and I read. I doubt that there has ever been more jargon and professional cant—cant of various professions and semi-professions—than there is today. I remember being amazed when I was in basic training, which was back in the early '50s, that people could make sentences in which the word "fucking" was used three times or even five times.

MCCAFFERY: How did your relationship with *The New Yorker* begin?

BARTHELME: I sent them something in the mail and they accepted it. Agented by probably a nine-cent stamp.

MCCAFFERY: It wasn't long before *The New Yorker* began publishing a story of yours almost every month. You didn't develop a specific understanding with them about regularly accepting your work?

BARTHELME: I had moved to New York to work with Tom and Harold doing *Location,* and since I was only working half-time on the magazine, I had more time to write fiction. I had and have what they call a first-reading agreement.

MCCAFFERY: Have you had a specific editor working with you at *The New Yorker*?

BARTHELME: Yes; Roger Angell.

MCCAFFERY: Do your stories usually require much in the way of editing?

BARTHELME: Roger makes very few changes. If he and the magazine don't like a piece that I've written, they'll turn it down. The magazine sometimes turns down a piece I don't think should be turned down—but what else can I think? Roger is a wonderful editor, and if he objects to something in a story he's probably right. He's very sensitive about the editing process, makes it a pleasure.

MCCAFFERY: Do you see yourself working out of some kind of *New Yorker* tradition?

BARTHELME: The magazine in recent years has been very catholic. Anybody who publishes Singer, Merwin, Lem, Updike, Borges, and Márquez has got to be said to be various in terms of taste. Plus Grace Paley and Susan Sontag and Ann Beattie and who knows who else.

MCCAFFERY: I've noticed that in your last few books you seem to have dropped the interest in typographical or graphic play that was so evident in *City Life* and *Guilty Pleasures.* What got you interested in this sort of thing in the first place?

BARTHELME: I think I was trying to be a painter, in some small way. Probably a yearning for something not properly the domain of writers.

MCCAFFERY: Surely this opinion doesn't derive from a belief in the need to keep aesthetic categories separate . . .

BARTHELME: Maybe I was distracted by the things that painters can do. Look here and over there [pointing at an Ingres poster and a Richard Lindner poster on his living room walls]—an ambition toward something that maybe fiction can't do, an immediate impact—a beautifully realized whole that can be taken in at a glance and yet still be studied for a long time. There's a Flannery O'Connor quote where she says, very sourly, very wittily, that she doesn't like anything that looks funny on the page. I know what she's talking about, but on the other hand, I'm intrigued by things that look funny on the page. But then there was the flood of concrete poetry which devalued looking funny on the page.

MCCAFFERY: I recall a comment of yours that you not only enjoyed doing layout work but that you could cheerfully become a typographer. Did you do all your own visual work?

BARTHELME: They're mostly very simple collages, Ernst rather than Schwitters.

MCCAFFERY: Have you tried your own hand at drawing?

BARTHELME: Can't draw a lick.

MCCAFFERY: At the end of the title story of *City Life,* Ramona comments about "life's invitations down many muddy roads": "I accepted. What was the alternative." I find a similar passivity in many of your characters—an inability to change their lot. Does this tendency spring from a personal sense of resignation about things, or are you trying to suggest something more fundamental about modern man's relationship to the world?

BARTHELME: The quotation you mention possibly has more to do with the great world than with me. In writing about the two girls in *City Life* who come to the city, I noticed that their choices—which seem to be infinite—are not so open ended. I don't think this spirit of "resignation," as you call it, has to do with any personal passivity; it's more a sociological observation. One attempts to write about the way contemporary life is lived by most people. In a more reportorial fiction one would, of necessity, seek out more "active" protagonists—the mode requires it, to make the book or story work. In a mixed mode, some reportage and some part play (which also makes its own observations), you might be relieved of this restriction. Contemporary life engenders, even enforces passivity, as with television. Have you ever tried to reason with a Convenience Card money machine? Asked for napkin rings in an Amtrak snack-bar car? Of course you don't. Still, the horizon of memory enters in. You attempt to register change, the color of this moment as opposed to the past or what you know of it.

MCCAFFERY: Is it because you're dealing with this common kind of modern life that your characters so often seem concerned with coping with boredom?

BARTHELME: I don't notice that so much. I think they're knitting lively lives—perhaps in subdued tones. Are you asking for T. E. Lawrence?

MCCAFFERY: Hmmm. Maybe I should call this aspect of modern life "the cocoon of habituation that covers everything, if you let it," as your narrator in "Daumier" says.

BARTHELME: Recently I've come to believe that, as one of the people in *Great Days* says, "Life becomes more and more exciting as there is less and less time." True, I think.

MCCAFFERY: Related to what we're talking about is a criticism I've heard directed at your fiction. It's been claimed that your fiction isn't "relevant" enough—to use that ugly word—to be really significant. That is, it has been said that rather than dealing with the "big issues" in a direct way—the Vietnam war, political scandals, minority rights, violence, the Holocaust, and so on—your fiction has tended to deal with what one critic has called a "range of minor, banal dissatisfactions . . . no anomie or accidie or dread but a muted series of irritations, frustrations, and bafflements." How do you respond to such criticisms which, as you know, are regularly leveled at Barth, Gass, Nabokov, and other postmodernists?

BARTHELME: I'd argue that this was a misreading. I would not attempt the Holocaust, but aside from that I think a careful reading of what I've written would disclose that all the things you mention are touched upon, in one way or another—not confronted directly, but there. The Vietnam war colored a lot of pieces. It's found in "The Indian Uprising" and very much in "Report," where the narrator endeavors to persuade a group of engineers to abandon their work in exotic military technology; also in other odd places.

MCCAFFERY: Do you recall the germinating idea for *The Dead Father*?

BARTHELME: A matter of having a father and being a father.

MCCAFFERY: In some basic sense the book deals with the notion that we're all dragging around behind us the corpses of our fathers, as well as the past in general.

BARTHELME: Worse: dragging these *ahead* of us. I have several younger brothers, among them by brother Frederick, who is also a writer. After *The Dead Father* came out, he telephoned and said, "I'm working on a new novel." I said, "What's it called?" and he said, "*The Dead Brother*." You have to admire the generational wit there.

MCCAFFERY: Was "A Manual for Sons" originally conceived as being part of the novel? It seems like a marvelous set piece.

BARTHELME: Originally it was distributed throughout the book as a kind of seasoning, but in time it became clear that it should be one long section. My German publisher, Siegried Unseld, said rather sternly to me one evening, "Isn't this a digression?" I said, "Yes, it is." He was absolutely right, in technical terms.

MCCAFFERY: In *The Dead Father*—and even more obviously in the recent series of structurally related stories in *Great Days*—you strip the narrative almost completely of the old-fashioned means of story development. In fact, by the time we get to the stories in *Great Days* what we find are simply voices interacting with one another. I recall in "The Explanation" one of your characters speaks of the "many valuable omissions" certain narrative formats allow. What advantages do you find in pursuing this type of narrative strategy?

BARTHELME: In *The Dead Father* there are four or five passages in which the two principal women talk to each other, or talk *against* each other, or over each other's heads, or between each other's legs—passages which were possible because there is a fairly strong narrative line surrounding them. It's a question as to whether such things can be made to fly without the support of a controlling narrative. As, for example, in the final story in *Great Days* which is, I think, more or less successful.

MCCAFFERY: Do you worry about losing your hard-won audience in moving in this direction?

BARTHELME: There's always the tension between losing an audience and doing the odd things you might want to try. The effort is always to make what you write nourishing or useful to readers. You do cut out some readers by idiosyncrasies of form. I regret this.

MCCAFFERY: Was Beckett an influence in this recent form of experimentation your fiction has been working with?

BARTHELME: Beckett has been a great influence, which I think is clear. But the effort is to not write like Beckett. You can't do Beckett all over again, any more than you can do Joyce again. That would waste everyone's time.

MCCAFFERY: Have you ever tried writing poetry, as such?

BARTHELME: No. Too difficult. I can't do it. A very tough discipline, to be attempted by saints or Villons.

MCCAFFERY: Are you alarmed by reports of the death of the novel?

BARTHELME: A form of this strength and capacity can't expire—it may emphasize new aspects of itself.

MCCAFFERY: We've talked about the influence of painting on your work. What about the cinema?

BARTHELME: I was bombarded with film from, let us say, my sixth year right up to yesterday, when I saw Wiseman's *Basic Training*. There's got to have been an effect, including the effect of teaching me what waste is—as with painting, film has shown us what not to pursue. The movies provide a whole set of stock situations, emotions, responses that can be played against. They infect contemporary language. One uses this.

MCCAFFERY: I noticed that you were writing movie reviews for *The New Yorker.* Is this likely to develop into a habit?

BARTHELME: This was just a short stint to fill in—six weeks. They had several of us lend a hand when Pauline Kael left for a sabbatical. I enjoyed it, wouldn't want to make a habit of it.

MCCAFFERY: Your fiction has often drawn materials from the realm of pop culture—Snow White, Batman, the Phantom of the Opera, King Kong, and so forth. What do you find useful in this kind of material?

BARTHELME: Relatively few of my stories have to do with pop culture, a very small percentage really. What's attractive about this kind of thing is the given—you have to do very little establishing, can get right to the variations.

MCCAFFERY: What initially intrigued you about using the Snow White mythology in your novel?

BARTHELME: Again, the usefulness of the Snow White story is that everybody knows it and it can be played against. The presence of the seven men made possible a "we" narration that offered some tactical opportunities—there's a sort of generalized narrator, a group spokesman who could be any one of the seven. Every small change in the story is momentous when everybody knows the story backward; possibly I wasn't as bold in making these changes as I should have been.

MCCAFFERY: It's very obvious in *Snow White*—and in nearly all your fiction—that you distrust the impulse to "go beneath the surface" of your characters and events.

BARTHELME: If you mean doing psychological studies of some kind, no. I'm not so interested. "Going beneath the surface" has all sorts of positive-sounding associations, as if you were a Cousteau of the heart. I'm not sure there's not just as much to be seen if you remain a student of the surfaces.

MCCAFFERY: Let me ask you about a specific feature of your work that I've always admired—your lists, which rank with those of William Gass and Stanley Elkin as the best around. What function would you say these serve?

BARTHELME: Litanies, incantations, have a certain richness per se. They also provide stability in what is often a volatile environment, something to tie to, like an almanac or a telephone book. And discoveries—a list of meter maids in any given city will give you a Glory Hercules.

MCCAFFERY: Who are some of the contemporary writers you find most interesting?

BARTHELME: Along with the South Americans, who everyone agrees are doing very well, I think the Germans: Peter Handke, Max Frisch, certainly Grass, Thomas Bernhard, who did *Correction*. I think the Americans are doing very well. The French perhaps less so.

MCCAFFERY: Who are some of the American writers you admire?

BARTHELME: Gass, Percy, Jack Hawkes, Grace Paley, Ralph Ellison, Barth, Bellow and Updike, Vonnegut and John Sayles, Susan Sontag, Peter Taylor, Pynchon. Barry Hannah and Ann Beattie—the spectrum is quite large, as you can see. A dozen people I can't think of at the moment. There seems to be considerable energy in American writing at the moment; it seems a fruitful time.

MCCAFFERY: Do you read much poetry?

BARTHELME: Not as much as I should. I read Ashbery and Koch and Schuyler with great pleasure, Merwin with great pleasure, and there are others.

MCCAFFERY: Raymond Federman recently made a comment to me that I found very relevant to what's been happening in fiction during the past few years. He says that while Samuel Beckett had devised a means of taking the world away from the contemporary writer, Márquez had shown writers a way to reconnect themselves with the world.

BARTHELME: I don't agree with Ray that that's what Beckett has done; the Márquez portion of the comment seems more appropriate. I think they've both opened things up, in different ways. Márquez provided an answer to the question of what was possible after Beckett—not the only answer, but a large and significant one. Robert Coover, among American writers, seems to be doing something parallel, to good effect.

MCCAFFERY: What are you working on right now?

BARTHELME: I'm working on three things: the story I mentioned earlier, a novel, and a filmscript someone's asked me to do.

MCCAFFERY: Have you worked on filmscripts before?

BARTHELME: Richard Lester asked me once to write one years ago. I was unable to do it, so I had to give him his money back. Painful but necessary.

MCCAFFERY: Do you feel that New York City has helped shape your sensibility over the years?

BARTHELME: I think my sensibility was pretty well put together before I came here. Although I've now lived here close to twenty years, I've also lived in other places in the meantime—Copenhagen for a year, Paris, Tokyo. I like cities. But this is a tiny corner of New York, very like a real *village*-village. Once I was walking down Seventh Avenue with Hans Magnus Enzensberger. We'd just finished lunch, and we bumped into my daughter, who was then about eight, and I introduced them and she went home and told her mother she'd just met Hans Christian Andersen. And, in a way, she had.

MCCAFFERY: Do you see any changes having taken place in your approach to writing over the past twenty years?

BARTHELME: Certainly fewer jokes. Perhaps fewer words.

INTERVIEW WITH J. D. O'HARA, 1981

J. D. O'HARA: You're often linked with Barth, Pynchon, Vonnegut, and others of that ilk. Does this seem to you inhuman bondage or is there reason in it?

DONALD BARTHELME: They're all people I admire. I wouldn't say we were alike as parking tickets. Some years ago the *Times* was fond of dividing writers into teams; there was an implication that the *Times* wanted to see gladiatorial combat, or at least a soccer game. I was always pleased with the team I was assigned to.

O'HARA: Who are the people with whom you have close personal links?

BARTHELME: Well, Grace Paley, who lives across the street, and Kirk and Faith Sale, who live in this building—we have a little block association. Roger Angell, who's my editor at *The New Yorker,* Harrison Starr, who's a film producer, and my family. In the last few years several close friends have died.

O'HARA: How do you feel about literary biography? Do you think your own biography would clarify the stories and novels?

BARTHELME: Not a great deal. There's not a strong autobiographical strain in my fiction. A few bits of fact here and there. The passage in the story "See the Moon?" where the narrator compares the advent of a new baby to somebody giving him a battleship to wash and care for was written the night beforc my daughter was born, a biographical fact which illuminates not very much. My grandmother and grandfather make an appearance in a piece I did not long ago. He was a lumber dealer in Galveston and also had a ranch on the Guadalupe River not too far from San Antonio, a wonderful place to ride and hunt, talk to the catfish and try to make the windmill run backward. There are a few minnows from the Guadalupe in that story, which mostly accompanies the title character through a rather depressing New York day. But when it appeared I immediately began getting calls from friends, some of whom I hadn't heard from in some time and all of whom were offering Tylenol and bandages. The assumption was that identification of the author with the character was not only permissible but invited. This astonished me. One uses one's depressions as one uses everything else, but what I was doing was writing a story. Merrily merrily merrily merrily.

Overall, very *little* autobiography, I think.

O'HARA: Was your childhood shaped in any particular way?

BARTHELME: I think it was colored to some extent by the fact that my father was an architect of a particular kind—we were enveloped in Modernism. The house we lived in, which he'd designed, was Modern and the furniture was Modern and the pictures were Modern and the books were Modern. He gave me, when I was fourteen or fifteen, a copy of Marcel Raymond's *From Baudelaire to Surrealism,* I think he'd come across it in the Wittenborn catalogue. The introduction is by Harold Rosenberg, whom I met and worked with sixteen or seventeen years later, when we did the magazine *Location* here in New York.

My mother studied English and drama at the University of Pennsylvania, where my father studied architecture. She was a great influence in all sorts of ways, a wicked wit.

O'HARA: Music is one of the few areas of human activity that escapes distortion in your writing. An odd comparison: music is for you what animals were for Céline.

BARTHELME: There were a lot of classical records in the house. Outside, what the radio yielded when I was growing up was mostly Bob Wills and his Texas Playboys; I heard him so much that I failed to appreciate him, failed to appreciate country music in general. Now I'm very fond of it. I was interested in jazz and we used to go to black clubs to hear people like Erskine Hawkins who were touring—us poor little pale little white boys were offered a generous sufferance, tucked away in a small space behind the bandstand with an enormous black cop posted at the door. In other places you could hear people like the pianist Peck Kelly, a truly legendary figure, or Lionel Hampton, or once in a great while Louis Armstrong or Woody Herman. I was sort of drenched in all this. After a time a sort of crazed scholarship overtakes you and you can recite band rosters for 1935 as others can list baseball teams for the same year.

O'HARA: What did you learn from this, if anything?

BARTHELME: Maybe something about making a statement, about placing emphases within a statement or introducing variations. You'd hear some of these guys take a tired old tune like "Who's Sorry Now?" and do the most incredible things with it, make it beautiful, literally make it new. The interest and the drama were in the formal manipulation of the rather slight material. And they were heroic figures, you know, very romantic. Hokie Mokie in "The King of Jazz" comes out of all that.

O'HARA: Are there writers to whose work you look forward?

BARTHELME: Many. Gass, Hawkes, Barth, Ashbery, Calvino, Ann Beattie—too many to remember. I liked Walker Percy's new book *The Second Coming* enormously. The weight of knowledge is extraordinary, ranging from things like how the shocks on a Mercedes are constituted to how a nineteenth-century wood-burning stove is put together. When the hero's doctors diagnosed *wahnsinnige Sehnsucht* or "inappropriate longings" as what was wrong with him I like to fell off my chair. That's too beautiful to be real but with Percy it might be. Let's see . . . Handke, Thomas Bernhard, Max Frisch, Márquez.

O'HARA: Even *Autumn of the Patriarch*?

BARTHELME: After *One Hundred Years of Solitude* it was hard to imagine that he could do another book on that scale, but he did it. There were technical maneuvers in *Autumn of the Patriarch*—the business of the point of view changing within a given sentence, for instance—that I thought very effective, almost 100 percent effective. It was his genius to stress the sorrows of the dictator, the angst of the monster. The challenge was his own previous book and I think he met it admirably.

It's amazing the way previous work can animate new work, amazing and reassuring. Tom Hess used to say that the only adequate criticism of a work of art is another work of art. It may also be the case that any genuine work of art generates new work. I suspect the Márquez's starting point was *The Tin Drum*, somehow, that Günter Grass gave him a point of departure . . . that the starting point for the essential Beckett was *Bouvard and Pecuchet* and that Bellow's *Henderson the Rain King* is a fantasia on the theme of Hemingway in Africa. This is not the anxiety but the pleasure of influence.

O'HARA: You don't, then, believe in entropy?

BARTHELME: Entropy belongs to Pynchon. I read recently that somebody had come forward with evidence that the process is not irreversible. There is abroad a distinct feeling that everything's getting worse; Christopher Lasch speaks of it, and so do many other people. I don't think we have the sociological index that would allow us to measure this in any meaningful way, but the feeling is there as a cultural fact. I *feel* entropy—Kraus on backache is a favorite text around here.

O'HARA: Do you see anything getting better—art, for instance?

BARTHELME: I don't think you can talk about progress in art—movement, but not progress. You can speak of a point on a line for the purpose of locating things, but it's a horizontal line, not a vertical one. Similarly the notion of an avant-garde is a bit off. The function of the advance guard in military terms is exactly that of the rear guard, to protect the main body, which translates as the status quo.

You can speak of political progress, social progress, of course—you may not *see* much of it, but it can be talked about.

O'HARA: Well, you've established yourself as an old fogey.

BARTHELME: So be it.

O'HARA: Your own influences—whom would you like to cite as your spiritual ancestors?

BARTHELME: They come in assorted pairs. Perelman and Hemingway. Kierkegaard and Sabatini. Kafka and Kleist. Kleist was clearly one of Kafka's fathers. Rabelais and Zane Grey. The Dostoevsky of *Notes from the Underground.* A dozen Englishmen. The Surrealists, both painters and poets. A great many film people, Buñuel in particular. It's always a stew, isn't it? Errol Flynn ought to be in there somewhere, and so should Big Sid Catlett, the drummer.

O'HARA: Why Errol Flynn?

BARTHELME: Because he's part of my memory of Sabatini, Sabatini fleshed out. He was in the film version of *Captain Blood,* and *The Sea Hawk.* He should have done *Scaramouche* but Stewart Granger did it instead, as I recall.

O'HARA: You have a story called "Captain Blood."

BARTHELME: A pastiche of Sabatini, not particularly of that book but all of Sabatini. You are reminded, I hope, of the pleasure Sabatini gives you or has given you. The piece is in no sense a parody, rather it's very much an *hommage.* An attempt to present, or recall, the essence of Sabatini. Also it hopes to be an *itself.*

O'HARA: What about the more awkward question of writers standing in your way?

BARTHELME: I think deep admirations force you *away* from the work admired, as well as having the generating influence we've mentioned. Joyce may have done this for Beckett, Márquez may do this for young Latin American writers—force them to do something that is not Márquez.

O'HARA: But hasn't everything been done?

BARTHELME: One can't believe that because it's not profitable. The situation of painting is instructive. Painters, especially American painters since the Second World War, have been much more troubled, beset by formal perplexity, than American writers. They've been a laboratory for everybody. Some new attitudes have emerged. What seems clear is that if you exacerbate a problem, make it worse, new solutions are generated. Ad Reinhardt is an example. Barnett Newman, proceeding by subtraction, or Frank Stella rushing in the other direction.

O'HARA: Why this constant invocation of the word "new"?

BARTHELME: It equates with being able to feel something rather than with novelty per se, it's a kind of shorthand for discovery. Probably a bad choice of words. Rosenberg's *The Tradition of the New* deals precisely with the anomalies involved.

O'HARA: Has this anything to do with your continuing attempt to reexamine or complicate your style or procedures?

BARTHELME: You isolate aspects of the process, look at them separately, worry about this and then worry about that. It's like a sculptor suddenly deciding to use rust. Rust was not appreciated at its full value until rather recently. Roger Angell once asked me why I'd single-spaced a story I'd offered him and I told him that I was trying to keep myself interested.

O'HARA: You have said that you enjoyed teaching because the young writers talk about their concerns, about what's happening to them, that you learn from them.

BARTHELME: And they learn from each other. I've just read an article that strongly implies that teaching writing is a dismal racket, an impoverishing fraud, and maybe it is as practiced in some venues, but I'd hate this to be taken as generally true. At City College, where I teach a graduate workshop, the writing students are fully the equals in seriousness and accomplishment of the other graduate students. Maybe writing can't be taught, but editing *can* be taught—prayer, fasting and self-mutilation. Notions of the lousy can be taught. Ethics.

All of this is new in universities, didn't exist when I was in school, but it's hardly a racket.

O'HARA: Your feelings about the new are ambivalent. . . .

BARTHELME: I'm ever-hopeful, but remember that I was exposed early to an almost religious crusade, the Modern movement in architecture, which, putting it as kindly as possible, has not turned out quite as expected. The Bauhaus, Mies van der Rohe and his followers, Frank Lloyd Wright and his followers, Le Corbusier, all envisioned not just great buildings but an architecture that would engender a radical improvement in human existence. The buildings were to act on society, change it in positive ways. None of this happened and in fact a not insignificant totalitarian bent manifested itself. There's a brand-new state university campus not far from here that the students call, with perfect justice, Alphaville. The architects somehow managed eeriness. Now we find phrases like "good design," or "planning," quite loaded, quite strange.

There is an ambivalence. Reynolds Price in the *Times* said of my story "The New Music" that it was about as new as the toothache. He apparently didn't get the joke, which is that there is always a new music—the new music shows up about every ten minutes. Not like the toothache. More like hiccups.

O'HARA: Which reminds me: some of your detractors say that you're merely fashionable.

BARTHELME: Well, the mere has always been a useful category.

O'HARA: That you're a jackdaw, and your principle of selection is whatever glitters most.

BARTHELME: I weep and tear my hair. And disagree.

O'HARA: Let's look at a specific jackdaw's nest, the barricade in "The Indian Uprising."

BARTHELME: I don't see anything particularly fashionable. The table made from a hollow-core door may be a 1960s reference but aren't people still making them?

O'HARA: But your barricade is not intended as straightforward realism; these things are artifacts of a certain culture.

BARTHELME: An archeological slice. Not much glitter.

O'HARA: Won't it require scholarly annotation in the future?

BARTHELME: I'd say no. If you read *The Swiss Family Robinson* and you're reading about what they unpack from the pinnace as they shuttle from ship to shore you don't need any footnotes, even though there may be 400 pounds of tallow in the cargo. You have a vague recollection that it's used to make candles.

Actually I think the jackdaw business is a function of appearing in *The New Yorker* with some frequency. People read the fiction with after-images of Rolls Royces and Rolexes still sizzling in their eyes. Rare is the reviewer who can resist mentioning the magazine's ads when talking about the fiction. One is gilded by association.

O'HARA: Suppose we turn things around. Suppose I say that when I read that story I'm not at all concerned about whether people made tables from hollow-core doors in the 1960s. Rather, I'm interested in the speaker, who in the metaphorical context of the story is besieged by Comanches.

BARTHELME: Is besieged by very much more than Comanches, but also by Comanches. He's not meant to be a walking-around person so much as a target, a butt. The arrows of the Comanches but also sensory insult, political insult, there are references to the war there, to race, to torture, jingoism. . . . But none of the references in the story were picked at random, and none are used simply as decor. If they seem random it's probably because the range of reference is rather wide for a short piece—you have Patton and Frank Wedekind and the Seventh Cavalry coexisting on the same plane—but the crowding is part of the design, *is* the design.

O'HARA: What starts your stories off?

BARTHELME: It's various. For instance, I've just done a piece about a Chinese emperor, the so-called First Emperor, Ch'in Shih Huang Ti. This came directly from my wife's research for a piece she was doing on medical politics in Chinatown—she had accumulated all sorts of material on Chinese culture, Chinese history, and I began picking through it, jackdaw-like. This was the emperor who surrounded his tomb with that vast army of almost full-scale terra-cotta soldiers the Chinese discovered just a few years ago. The tomb, as far as I know, has yet to be fully excavated, but the scale of the discovery gives you some clear hints as to the size of the man's imagination, his ambition. As I learned more about him—"learned" in quotation marks, much of what I was reading was dubious history—I got a sense of the emperor hurrying from palace to palace, I gave him two hundred some-odd palaces, scampering, almost, tending to his projects, intrigues, machinations. He's horribly, horribly *pressed for time*, both actually and in the sense that many of his efforts are strategies against mortality. The tomb itself is a strategy, as is the imposition of design on the lives of his people, his specifications as to how wide hats shall be, how wide carriages shall be, and so forth.

"The Emperor" might be considered as another version of the story I did about Cortés and Montezuma, and both as footnotes to *The Dead Father*, another emperor.

O'HARA: You do your homework, in other words.

BARTHELME: Everybody does, I think. Research yields things that you can react to, either accept or disagree with. My Montezuma and Cortés are both possibly nobler figures than responsible historians would allow, but I hope not implausible. There are conflicting versions as to how Montezuma died. I have him killed by a stone flying through the air, presumably from the hand of one of his subjects. The alternative is that the Spaniards killed him. I prefer to believe the former.

O'HARA: You take the Cortés-Montezuma friendship to have been a reality, not just a matter of political manipulation?

BARTHELME: There seems to be little question that Cortés was a master manipulator. Still, he seems to have been genuinely impressed by Montezuma. Bernal, as you read his account of the Conquest, enlarges in a very respectful way on Montezuma's qualities, as priest-king at the center of an elaborate religious/political establishment, about which Cortés was wonderfully obtuse. It's as if you marched into present-day Salt Lake City at the head of your brave little group, listened politely and with interest to a concert by the Mormon Tabernacle Choir, sitting in the front row, and then whipped out your sword and claimed the state of Utah for Scientology.

O'HARA: Suppose a reader took the story's limousines and detectives to mean that you're being comic about it?

BARTHELME: The limousines are only a way of making you see chariots or palanquins.

O'HARA: What about the woman's golden buttocks?

BARTHELME: A way of allowing you to see buttocks. If I didn't have roaches big as ironing boards in the story I couldn't show Cortés and Montezuma holding hands, it would be merely sentimental. You look around for offsetting material, things that tell the reader that although X is happening, X is to be regarded in the light of Y.

O'HARA: Aldous Huxley argued that Ophelia could not appear on stage naked. He opposed the necessary conditions of tragedy to those of comedy, instancing the scene in *Tom Jones* in which Sophia Western falls off her horse, baring her comely buttocks to the admiring lookers-on.

BARTHELME: I can imagine a tragic nakedness, even on the stage. A little hop past the pathetic.

O'HARA: Why don't you write tragedy?

BARTHELME: I'm fated to deal in mixtures, slumgullions, which preclude tragedy, which requires a pure line. It's a habit of mind, a perversity. Tom Hess used to tell a story, maybe from Lewis Carroll, I don't remember, about an enraged mob storming the palace shouting "More taxes! Less bread!" As soon as I hear a proposition I immediately consider its opposite. A double-minded man—makes for mixtures.

O'HARA: Apparently the Yiddish theater, to which Kafka was very addicted, includes as a typical bit of comedy two clowns, more or less identical, who appear even in sad scenes—the parting of two lovers, for instance—and behave comically as the audience is weeping. This shows up especially in *The Castle.*

BARTHELME: The assistants.

O'HARA: And the audience doesn't know what to do.

BARTHELME: The confusing signals, the impurity of the signal, gives you verisimilitude. As when you attend a funeral and notice, against your will, that it's being *poorly done.*

O'HARA: Once you've written a story, is there anyone to whom you show it?

BARTHELME: First to my wife; if she has a bad reaction, then I go back and wonder what I did wrong. Occasionally, I'll show something to Grace Paley. The scene in *The Dead Father* where Tom and Julie make love I showed to Grace because I'd never written a sexual set piece before. She said she thought it was okay.

O'HARA: Why do writers have such a hard time writing about sex?

BARTHELME: Faint equivalents can sometimes be found. In the passage mentioned I relied on verbal extravagance, but a cold extravagance. Or it can be rendered obliquely—an adolescent's mental image of his or her parents making love, which must be something on the order of crocodiles mating.

O'HARA: When you've finished a story you send it to Roger Angell at *The New Yorker.*

BARTHELME: Yes. He often makes very acute suggestions, usually criticism of particular lines.

O'HARA: Do they ever turn anything down?

BARTHELME: Of course. Sometimes a piece has not been thought through by its author, sometimes they're just wrong. I'll look at a piece that they've turned down very suspiciously, though.

O'HARA: On occasion you have arranged and rearranged stories in a collection up till the last possible moment, and you also make considerable changes in individual stories—notably in "The New Music," to cite a recent instance. On what bases?

BARTHELME: The order of pieces in a given book is mostly a matter of trying to make sure they don't get in each other's way. Much like hanging pictures for a show. Some pictures fight other pictures, not because either is a bad picture, but because the scale fights or the color fights. "The New Music" was originally two stories with the same characters. For the book version I added about six pages of new material, there was more to be said, and combined them. A matter of not getting it right the first time or even the second time.

O'HARA: This is one of the ten or more dialogue stories you've done recently. Why dialogues?

BARTHELME: The opportunities are those of poetry without the stern responsibilities. Dialogues are rather easy to write but there are some fine points. The sentence rhythms are rather starkly exposed, have to be weirdly musical or you send the reader off to Slumberland posthaste.

O'HARA: They're Beckett-y. Are they Beckett-y?

BARTHELME: Certainly they couldn't exist without the example of Beckett's plays. But I have other fish to fry. The dialogues in *Great Days* are less abstract than those between the two women in *The Dead Father,* which aren't particularly reminiscent of Beckett and preceded them. There's an urge toward abstraction that's very seductive—

O'HARA: Art about art?

BARTHELME: No, I mean the sort of thing you find in Gertrude Stein and hardly anywhere else. Phillipe Sollers, the *Tel Quel* man, approaches it in his book *Paradis,* of which I've read some excerpts in translation. I'm talking about a pointillist technique, where what you get is not adjacent dots of yellow and blue which optically merge to give you green but merged meanings, whether from words placed side by side in a seemingly arbitrary way or phrases similarly arrayed, bushels of them . . .

O'HARA: An example?

BARTHELME: "Petronius mothballs." Of course you can do this all day long and the results will be fully as poor as the specimen furnished. Still it's a North Sea to be explored.

O'HARA: A computer could make that sort of combination.

BARTHELME: But the lovable computer doesn't know when it's made a joke. The worm in the Apple. The only time I've ever tried this kind of thing at any length was in a piece called "Bone Bubbles" which consisted of blocks of phrases which rubbing together had a kind of irritating life. I wouldn't claim that it was a great success; Henry Robbins, my book editor at the time, wanted me to leave it out of *City Life,* but it was included, as a sort of lab report.

Computer people have a phrase, "garbage in, garbage out," which reflects the kind of thinking necessary to their work; artists on the other hand occasionally refer to the "happy accident"—a different style of thinking.

O'HARA: But this is not problem-solving thinking.

BARTHELME: No, it's not. But the task is not so much to solve problems as to propose questions. To quote Karl Kraus, "a writer is someone who can make a riddle out of an answer." There's also an element of reportage, the description of new situations or conditions, but that's pretty much a matter of identifying them rather than talking about solutions. Baudelaire noticing that the boulevards of Paris were no longer a means of getting from here to there but had become more like theater lobbies, places to be, and writing about that. The search is for a question that will generate light and heat.

All this has to do with a possible extension of means. Abstraction is a little heaven I can't quite get to. How do you achieve, for example, "messy"? De Kooning can do "messy" by making a charcoal stroke over paint and then smudging same with his talented thumb—in prose the same gesture tends to look like simple ineptitude. De Kooning has a whole vocabulary of bad behavior which enables him to set up the most fruitful kinds of contradictions. It frees him. I have trouble rendering breaking glass.

O'HARA: What about the moral responsibility of the artist? I take it that you are a responsible artist (as opposed, say, to X, Y, and Z), but all is irony, comic distortion, foreign voices, fragmentation. Where in all this evasion of the straightforward does responsibility display itself?

BARTHELME: It's not the straightforward that's being evaded but the too-true. I might fix your eye firmly and announce "Thou shalt not mess around with thy neighbor's wife." You might then nod and say to yourself, quite so. We might then lunch at the local chili parlor and say scurrilous things about X, Y, and Z. But it will not have escaped your notice that my statement has hardly enlarged your cosmos, that I've been, in the largest sense, responsible to neither art, life, nor adultery.

I believe that my every sentence trembles with morality in that each attempts to engage the problematic rather than to present a proposition to which all reasonable men must agree. The engagement might be very small, a word modifying another word, the substitution of "mess around" for "covet," which undresses adultery a bit. I think the paraphrasable content in art is rather slight—"tiny," as de Kooning puts it. The *way* things are done is crucial, as the inflection of a voice is crucial. The change of emphasis from the what to the how seems to me to be the major impulse in art since Flaubert, and it's not merely formalism, it's not at all superficial, it's an attempt to reach truth, and a very rigorous one. You don't get, following this path, a moral universe set out in ten propositions, but we already have that. And the attempt is sufficiently skeptical about itself. In this century there's been much stress placed not upon what we know but on knowing that our methods are themselves questionable—our Song of Songs is the Uncertainty Principle.

Also, it's entirely possible to fail to understand or actively misunderstand what an artist is doing. I remember going through a very large Barnett Newman show years ago with Tom Hess and Harold Rosenberg, we used to go to shows after long lunches, those wicked lunches which are no more, and I walked through the show like a certifiable idiot, couldn't understand their enthusiasm. I admired the boldness, the color and so on, but inwardly I was muttering "wallpaper, wallpaper, very fine wallpaper but wallpaper." I was wrong, didn't get the core of Newman's enterprise, what Tom called Newman's effort toward the sublime. Later I began to understand. One doesn't take in Proust or Canada on the basis of a single visit.

To return to your question: if I looked you straight in the eye and said, "The beauty of women makes of adultery a serious and painful duty," then we'd have the beginning of a useful statement.

O'HARA: Can you point out a specific too-true evaded in a specific story?

BARTHELME: Perhaps in "The Death of Edward Lear." Charming into ferocious, Edward Lear into King Lear.

O'HARA: Wordsworth spoke of growing up "Fostered alike by beauty and by fear," and he put fearful experiences first; but he also said that his primary subject was "the mind of Man." Don't you write more about the mind than about the external world?

BARTHELME: In a commonsense way, you write about the impingement of one upon the other—my subjectivity bumping into other subjectivities, or into the Prime Rate. You exist for me in my perception of you (and in some rough, Raggedy Andy way, for yourself, of course). That's what's curious when people say, of writers, this one's a realist, this one's a surrealist, this one's a super-realist, and so forth. In fact, everybody's a realist offering true accounts of the activity of mind. There are only realists.

O'HARA: Have you ever been mugged?

BARTHELME: Not even in print. (*Considers*) Once in print, by Gore Vidal. He likes to straighten out us uppity young people.

O'HARA: In *The Dead Father* you edge into Kafka country and suggest that God has shown himself to be a bad father. But you seem not to believe in God, whereas Kafka did.

BARTHELME: Well, actually the Holy Ghost is my main man, as we say. I don't think I've ever had much to say about God except as a locus of complaint, a convention, someone to rail against. *The Dead Father* suggests that the process of becoming has bound up in it the experience of many other consciousnesses, the most important of which are in a law-giving relation to the self. The characters complain about this in what I hope is an interesting fashion. Cursing what is is a splendid ground for a writer—witness Céline.

O'HARA: Beckett's pronouncements on art imply something curious: that artists who in the past assumed and sought to convey ultimate truths (as Dante did) were quite right, but that in our own time these truths don't exist and therefore the artist must proceed differently. Do you share that sense?

BARTHELME: In the dialogues with Duthuit, Beckett, as you know, rejects what can be accomplished "on the plane of the feasible"—he seems to be asking for an art adequate to the intuition of Nothingness. I don't want to oversimplify his esthetics, about which I know nothing firsthand, but the problem appears to be not one of announcing truths, or that truths do or do not exist, but of hewing to the intuition, which seems central, and yet getting some work done. Beckett's work is an embarrassment to the Void. I think of the line from the German writer Heimito von Doderer: "At first you break windows. Then you become a window yourself."

O'HARA: Why do you live in New York?

BARTHELME: Because in American terms, it's an old city. I think writers like old cities and are made very nervous by new cities. I lived in Copenhagen for a bit more than a year and was very happy there. At moments, in New York, I like all the filth on the streets, it reminds me of Kurt Schwitters. Schwitters used to hang around printing plants and fish things out of waste barrels, stuff that had been overprinted or used during make-ready, and he'd employ this rich accidental material in his collages. I saw a very large Schwitters show some years ago and almost everything in it reminded me of New York. Garbage in, art out.

O'HARA: Do you eavesdrop?

BARTHELME: More than is decent. Out of context you frequently get instant Dada. I once overheard a woman in a restaurant on Fifty-fifth saying earnestly to her companion, "But Henry, I've never *taught* in the daytime before." *The Teacher From the Black Lagoon.*

O'HARA: You said that you're working on a novel.

BARTHELME: Perpetually.

O'HARA: What's the attraction of the form?

BARTHELME: The sustained involvement with a single project. I don't find them particularly easy to write. *Snow White* is strictly speaking a novella, and *The Dead Father* isn't terribly long. The new one—the working title is *Ghosts*—will be longer, I think. I've made a lot of false starts, souvenirs of which are sometimes published. "The Emerald," which is about a witch who is impregnated by the man in the moon and gives birth to a 7,335-carat emerald, was going to be a novel. But I couldn't sustain it, and it finally appeared as a long story.

O'HARA: What's your greatest weakness as a writer?

BARTHELME: That I don't offer enough emotion. That's one of the things people come to fiction for, and they're not wrong. I mean emotion of the better class, hard to come by. Also, I can't resist making jokes, although that's much more under control than it used to be. And of course these weaknesses have to do with each other—jokes short-circuit emotion. I particularly prize, but can't often produce, a kind of low-key emotional touch that speaks volumes. At the end of Ann Beattie's *Falling in Place,* for example, Jonathan's made a wish and Cynthia asks Spangle what he wished for and the reply is "The usual, I guess." That's beautiful.

O'HARA: Is there any subject you'd like to entertain, but haven't yet?

BARTHELME: We spoke earlier about fear, a tricky terrain. There are things to be said about it. If you go through the psychological literature there's not much that's very good—lots of stuff on anxiety, very little on fear. There are aphorisms. Nietzsche said that civilization makes all good things available even to cowards, sound enough but also contemptuous. It's a difficult subject, but of our moment. Little Redcap once set out with her basket for grandmother's house in perfect confidence; nowadays we'd send her in a Brink's truck. This is a strange time. I was in a cab not long ago and the cabbie cut a corner too close and a well-dressed man with an attaché case standing on the corner banged the rear fender with his hand—a very New York gesture. So the cabbie jumps out of the cab ready to fight and the man with the attaché case opens his coat with one hand like a flasher and he's wearing a .38 in a shoulder holster. This is on Park Avenue!

O'HARA: What did the cabbie do?

BARTHELME: Backed off, quite sensibly. Anyhow, there's all sorts of fear around and I haven't even mentioned the contributions of governments. Something to be done there but I haven't figured out what.

O'HARA: You keep up in philosophy and psychology, do you not?

BARTHELME: Not really. I have a very mercantile approach, I read whatever I think might be useful, might start something. I read other writers to discover what they do well; that helps me, reminds me why I got into this peculiar business in the first place. It's most unsystematic.

O'HARA: One of your depressed admirers contends that Hogo, in *Snow White,* told the truth about male-female relationships.

BARTHELME: Maybe *a* truth. Hogo's a thoroughly vile creature, or critter, and can be counted upon to take the vilest possible view of things.

O'HARA: He corrupts the seven men.

BARTHELME: He's taken into partnership; that they're corrupted is not clear. He's efficient, a comment on efficiency.

O'HARA: *Snow White* at once anticipated and superseded much feminist writing. Would you like to say something about its feminist themes? About the replacement of the wicked stepmother with a coeval of Snow White?

BARTHELME: Changing the stepmother-figure was a way of placing the emphasis on Snow White's network of relationships with the seven cohabitors. Her chief plaint is that the seven of them only add up, for her, to possibly two real men—this arithmetic is the center of the novel, gives rise to the question of what *real men* are, what the attitudes of the male characters mean. The situation of the horsewife can then be examined in regard to this, the situation of the potential world-redeeming hero examined.

I think that in this book the prose is far too worked, wrought, banged upon, too many jokes—a nervousness on my part that shouldn't be there. I don't regret having published it or anything of that sort, but it could have been better.

O'HARA: Let's look at another passage, this one from "The Rise of Capitalism." "As a flower moves toward the florist, women toward men who are not good for them. Self-actualization is not to be achieved in terms of another person, but you don't know that, when you begin."

BARTHELME: Not a particularly tender passage. My mental image of the voice while writing that piece was that of a loudspeaker rigged to a pole in some sort of re-education camp. Incessant sloganizing, a metallic drone, personal messages mixed with political messages, propaganda, left propaganda, in this case. "Cultural underdevelopment of the worker, as a technique of domination, is found everywhere under late capitalism." If I may quote.

O'HARA: But it's not expressed sincerely.

BARTHELME: It is and it isn't. Everything in the story is true enough, but is undercut by the loudspeaker-like tone. What this means—forgive me for telling you what this means in so many words—is that we all know these propositions are true (I'm referring now to the political propositions) but that nothing, nothing, will be done about them. I think sincerity is betokened by the viciousness of expression; it's an angry piece.

The lines you quoted are of a different kind—a different kind of proposition not unlike the first kind but having to do with the personal rather than the social. And these sentences work differently. The effect of the first, if any, is generated by its majestic certainty. In the second, "self-actualization" is at once a lump of jargon and one of those puffy ideas that nevertheless have some trace of value. Combine these various tidbits with the other elements of the story and you have—When I was in the army we had these odd platoons called Loudspeaker and Leaflet Units. I never ran into one in the flesh but I conceive of this piece as a Loudspeaker and Leaflet Unit in action. Bravely broadcasting and lustily leafleteering.

O'HARA: You've spoken harshly of *Snow White*'s rococo style and of your admiration for an improverished kind of writing, but a woman who is impregnated by the moon and produces an emerald-child would not be most people's example of a stripped-away style.

BARTHELME: Of course that's the plot, which is quite solidly rooted in anthropology, nothing in it unknown to anthropology. The style is another matter. If you look at it you'll see that the actual writing is rather bare-bones. Glittering with poverty.

O'HARA: I've always thought of the moon as female.

BARTHELME: The emerald raises the same objection. The mother correctly states that in some cultures it's been seen as female, in some cultures as male. Moll is a poor witch, a witch in reduced circumstances. She says of one of her spells that it can't even put a shine on a pair of shoes. She speaks of the scrabble for existence. Magic has been devalued, hardly exists. The reliquary that's at issue in the piece, which contains the Foot of Mary Magdalene, has barely enough efficacy as a magical object to resolve the plot, in the end. And this general paucity is reflected, I think, in the language.

O'HARA: When you wrote "A Shower of Gold" did you intend to satirize the new values as presented by all these philosophy-prone people?

BARTHELME: Not philosophy-prone but jargon-prone. Around the time that was written, a debased Sartrean language was on every lip. This was a long time ago, almost two decades ago. Peterson's barber in the story has written four books called *The Decision To Be* and the television people are all babbling madly about authenticity. There was a huge amount of this kind of thing collecting in the air conditioning vents, the elephants were throwing it in the air and taking baths in it. . . . The piece was not about values but about language. You could do the same story today and substitute the current vocabulary and very little of the structure of the story would have to be changed. Call it "The Lacanthrope."

O'HARA: Aside from furnishing you with curiosities of jargon, has any type of criticism or any individual critic ever warned you away from a fault or aided your work?

BARTHELME: Yes. Diane Johnson, in the course of an extremely kind review of *Great Days,* said that the book had this, that, and *no pictures.* I had done a number of pieces combining text with collages, Max Ernst collages, really, and I hadn't realized that the combination had worn out its welcome so completely. I therefore went back into the closet with the collages. Although sometime I'd like to do an entire collage-novel, as Ernst did, just for the exercise. A Closet Edition.

And many people have pointed out that there are too many jokes, and many people have pointed out that everything is too short. I've been called a miniaturist, a comment I have difficulty enjoying. I read less criticism now, criticism in general, than in days of yore. Gass's essays are invariably stimulating, as are Susan Sontag's. Richard Howard's criticism is very fine, very acute—he knows how things are done, and even more important, what might be done, with good luck.

O'HARA: Asked what aspect of his work had been sadly neglected, Albert Camus answered "humor." What would be your answer?

BARTHELME: I don't think anything's been neglected. There was for a long time a dismaying identification with the pop artists which still crops up now and then—made me extremely uncomfortable. That seems to have faded.

There's a degree of confusion among critics about how to deal with "postmodernist" fiction, how to slap a saddle on this rough beast. It's not unprecedented in the history of criticism. I imagine this will continue for a while.

O'HARA: What's it like to be interested in politics and be a writer, in a time when poets make nothing happen? How do you feel about your connection with P.E.N. for instance?

BARTHELME: It's worth the effort, I think. Internationally, P.E.N. attempts to get writers out of jail in cases where they've been put away by the government for political or literary activity, as happens all too often with insecure or insane governments. I remember that when Richard Howard was president of the American center he got two Philippine writers out of jail during his trip to Manila—Madame Marcos handed them over with great ceremony during some kind of bizarre state banquet, drew a curtain and there they were. It's a kind of chipping away at the bad behavior of governments, the same kind of thing Amnesty International does—a consistent effort, year in and year out.

O'HARA: What do you think of publishing? Does *Publishers Weekly* raise your pulse rate? Or hackles? What about book reviews? If you wrote reviews, about whom would you like to write?

BARTHELME: Speaking as a member of the raw material, I've been published well, I think, consistently. There's no question but that much of what is published in this country is cotton candy and that this cluttering-up of the bookstores damages writers. To say nothing of what such a diet does to the brain's stomach, if you're a reader. But you can't complain about this too much; it's a pluralism that allows R. Crumb and Walter Benjamin and William Gaddis and Julia Child all to live in paperback heaven together. But I'm making a publisher's argument, which is ridiculous. More shame would be salutary.

As to reviewing, I would have liked, had I had the time, to have written appreciations of Thomas Bernhard's *Correction* or Max Frisch's *Man in the Holocene* or one of Ashbery's books—I would have learned something in the process.

O'HARA: In Academe the conventional thing is to point to Ashbery's attention from the media and the awards he has won and to treat this as evidence that poetry has fallen on evil days, that criticism has no standards, and that nobody knows what's happening.

BARTHELME: Ashbery would be damned difficult to get hold of, if you were a critic. The awards and so on are a sign that people understand that he's doing something important, even if they don't understand precisely what. The first time I read "The Waste Land," when I was a pup, I hadn't the faintest idea of what I had in front of me but still said "Zounds!" or whatever. I think Eliot himself wrote about being overtaken by something before you understood it. Also, there's a peculiar negative reaction to the celebrated that's ordinary as beans, to be expected.

O'HARA: Presumably a scholar gives the same care to a scholarly article about you that you give to a piece, because that's his metier.

BARTHELME: Peter Yates, the music critic, said that the proper work of the critic is praise, and that that which cannot be praised should be surrounded with a tasteful, well-thought-out silence. I like that.

INTERVIEW WITH JO BRANS: "EMBRACING THE WORLD," 1981

JOE BRANS: You have said that your father's example, as an innovator, as a modern architect, was important in your career somehow.

DONALD BARTHELME: Oh yes, it was very important.

BRANS: Could you elaborate on that?

BARTHELME: It was an attitude toward his work. First, he was very much involved in the early modernism. He went to architecture school—his degree is from the University of Pennsylvania, which is why I was born in Philadelphia. He met my mother there—she was also a Penn graduate. He was trained in architecture entirely in the Beaux Arts tradition. No whiff of modernism was allowed to penetrate the Penn architecture school at that time. And he got out of school and suddenly the whole world changed for him. But he is, for example, a marvelous draftsman, because that's one of the things the Beaux Arts system stressed, those meticulous wash drawings and so on. It was very fine training, but it had nothing to do with what was really going on in architecture. So he went through a complete reversal—his world turned upside down, in a way. Remember, at that time—we're talking about the late twenties and early thirties—the architecture of the country didn't look like it does today. The modern building was quite, quite rare. To get hold of Le Corbusier's books was a task. You had to write to France for them, or find some wonderful shop that had already written to France for them. So, his task was to do an entirely new thing, which was contrary to his training in important ways. And he did it with great enthusiasm, with great zest, and he did it very, very well. It was the whole atmosphere of the home, because, when he built our house, it was a terrible anomaly amidst all the houses around it. It looked weird, although it was a very beautiful house, somewhat similar to Miës's Tugendhat house. And then, inside the house, the furniture was all Aalvar Aalto stuff. It was not like real furniture, in a way. I mean we all know what real furniture is, and this stuff was weird-looking. Now, this has been assimilated all over the country. You've got Aalto-derived furniture in airport waiting rooms, for example. But it was unusual then, and it had to have been, both visually and spiritually, important.

BRANS: Were you ever tempted by architecture, yourself? You've got a very strong visual sense.

BARTHELME: No, I always wanted to be a writer, even when I was small. . . . A couple of my brothers tried it—Rick started off in architecture at Tulane, and my brother Pete started off in architecture at Cornell, but both of them went into other things.

BRANS: Was there a time in which you felt you had to throw off your father's influence? I can't help but think about you and *The Dead Father* in connection with your own family situation, because a strong father is not an easy person to live with.

BARTHELME: Well, we had, when I was an adolescent, a series of, let us say, temperamental clashes, and I think that was the process of getting away, for me.

BRANS: Carl Killian has been quoted as saying that he was impressed with your family—because it was like a family of giants. I think he meant physically—he had the impression that all of you were big people. Then he also went on to say that all kinds of things were going on. That you actually talked to each other—genuine discussions—it was a very volatile atmosphere.

BARTHELME: Kidding father was an activity that took about seven of us to do, and there were only six of us. Putting father down was the main family sport.

BRANS: Is there any particular reason for the number of fathers in your work who are being done away with in one form or another? I'm thinking of *The Dead Father.* Using a father and beating him—is there anything autobiographical . . . ?

BARTHELME: Well, not directly. The relation is the universal problem. You remember, I think in Gertrude Stein there's a story about the guy who seizes his father by the hair and drags him out of the house into the orchard, and at a certain point the father who is being dragged says, "Stop, stop. In my time I did not drag my father beyond this tree."

BRANS: I had the idea that *The Dead Father* was a lot like Faulkner's *As I Lay Dying,* except with you it's the father that has to be buried, in Faulkner it's the mother.

BARTHELME: Someone also pointed out to me that in Kafka's letter to his father, the image of a giant father presents itself. And I haven't gone back to reread it to see how Kafka handled it.

BRANS: Lots of tension, lots of father tension there, of course.

BARTHELME: Yes, sure. But in Kafka the father obliterates the son.

BRANS: In *The Dead Father* it's quite clearly the son's victory. Of course you do kind of wonder what the father's going to do even after he's buried. He may be buried, but he's not dead. He's still sending up lustful feelings. Speaking of the father made me want to ask you something about the relationship between the sexes in your work. I was just thinking of Hogo's remark in *Snow White,* that it's not enough that we have all these problems with women; now we have to acknowledge that *they* have thoughts and feelings too.

BARTHELME: The book has been read as sort of anticipating the great feminist activity of the sixties and seventies. And male resentment is a theme that's there.

BRANS: I don't necessarily think of that as male resentment, but just that men seem to want something simple in women—that there's a more direct mind, let's say, in Hogo about the place of women.

BARTHELME: Well, he speaks also of the replaceability of women. They are as multitudinous as plants.

BRANS: And "durability is not what we want." Jane is durable, but durability is not necessarily what we are—we'll go for a twenty-two-year-old.

BARTHELME: But, remember, Hogo's a bad guy.

BRANS: But he's a very realistic and—he's a very pragmatic guy too. He's obviously inherited the leadership after Bill has been hanged. I know you're leery of this, but is Hogo representative of . . .

BARTHELME: The triumph of evil?

BRANS: Or the triumph of the expedient.

BARTHELME: No. Somebody else has raised that point, and I think that the reader can imagine that the seven guys, who are now six, will in some sense change Hogo.

BRANS: Well now, I didn't get that at all.

BARTHELME: Maybe it's not in there sufficiently clearly.

BRANS: They say, we had Hogo to show us how to hang Bill, and thank God we have Hogo. And they depart at the end in search of a new principle.

BARTHELME: That's true. But the Snow White principle now is no longer available to them.

BRANS: She's been revirginated. Risen into the sky. So they're going to go off in search of a new principle.

BARTHELME: I hope it's implied that that will also mean a new object of their devotion, a new Snow White, in a way.

BRANS: Sure, I think that is implied. I just thought they wouldn't have an effect on Hogo.

BARTHELME: Well, I think there's a sense in which they very likely will change him rather than having him change them.

BRANS: It's a more optimistic book, I suppose, than I had thought of it as being, if you regard being changed by the dwarfs as . . .

BARTHELME: They're not dwarfs. I know, it's hard to say.

BRANS: Not dwarfs? I didn't realize that they weren't dwarfs, so this really changes my whole view of the book.

BARTHELME: They are consistently spoken of as men. Of course that could be read as little men, but . . .

BRANS: I'll have to go off in search of new principles, to read *Snow White.*

BARTHELME: It's not my favorite book, by the way.

BRANS: I chose it to read with students because I thought it would be fun for them. Undergraduates all love the sixties. They have aggrandized the sixties—the sixties are sort of what the Roaring Twenties used to be.

BARTHELME: I've noticed that, yes.

BRANS: So I thought it would work for them, and I think it did. What is the new book about? What is *Ghosts* about?

BARTHELME: Oh, I'm not clear on that yet.

BRANS: I thought it was coming out very soon.

BARTHELME: Well, in theory, it's coming out next year. I'm inured to worrying about that book. It doesn't really matter whether it comes out next year or the year after, because there are no deadlines.

BRANS: Are you bouncing off of Ibsen in any way?

BARTHELME: No, I'm trying to avoid it. Indeed, that's a working title, and I'm not really clear whether I'll use it. It's just the way I identify it to myself. It may be that it seems presumptuous. On the other hand maybe it won't have any effect at all. I don't know. There's also an Ed McBain mystery I discovered called *Ghosts* published in 1979. It just happened—which I don't like. It's not that I don't like Ed McBain; I guess since it's in another genre, it would have no effect.

BRANS: Do you think that there are social forces that you would hold responsible for our loss of purity of language? The kind of garbage language that you're always making fun of? *Kinds*, I should say, because there are just multitudinous parodies.

BARTHELME: Well, I think there are two devices that have clearly had an enormous impact on language. One is television. I don't wish to blame television for all the faults of the world, but it has had a vulgarizing effect. The other is the telephone, because we don't write letters anymore. I don't write letters—I don't even write business letters. I call up on the telephone. When people don't write letters, language deteriorates.

BRANS: Do you keep a journal?

BARTHELME: I keep a workbook with stray pieces of paper with things written on them. A kind of mulch pile.

BRANS: One of the students called my attention to another statement of Hogo's, and he wanted me to ask you about this. Hogo says, "Our becoming is done." And the student offered the explanation that the society has become static and isn't changing.

BARTHELME: That was not the intention. It was rather a reference to the aging process. Both Hogo and Jane are older than the other people. Hogo is realizing that, or stating it.

BRANS: You're not attempting to write about an essentially static society?

BARTHELME: No.

BRANS: I'm relieved, because I don't think this society is static.

BARTHELME: No, I don't either.

BRANS: I disagree with the basic premise. I'm glad to have you on my side. You told the class that you don't expect to effect any social changes. I wondered about that, because I didn't quite believe it.

BARTHELME: It is not a declaration of intent so much as a declaration of powerlessness. The effect that any individual writer is going to have in this time seems to me to be very, very minimal.

BRANS: You'd like to be able to do it, but you don't think . . .

BARTHELME: If I could clean up the world by writing about it, if I thought it could be done, I would do it, and I'd have everything tidied up within one generation, but I don't think I have that power. I mean it is really a declaration of powerlessness. Some small effect, possibly—nothing on the scale of what Tolstoy thought he was going to do, and in some measure did. I can't do a Tolstoy.

BRANS: Of course, the difference between a writer and a social reformer—one difference among many—is that a writer, I think, doesn't have a sense of his own power because he doesn't get an instant response.

BARTHELME: If I were a Marxist, say, I'd have a system which I believed would effect social change, and I would be morally bound to think that way and write that way, but I'm not a Marxist.

BRANS: But you have affected our perception of the world with your use of form. Was there a dramatic moment in which the form of a Barthelme short story emerged?

BARTHELME: Yes, but it was a ten-year moment.

BRANS: What were you trying to do those ten years? Were you trying to find some way . . .

BARTHELME: I was trying to write fiction that I myself thought was worth publishing—and I wrote a lot of garbage.

BRANS: But you've also said that you really admire the traditional form of fiction. John Cheever, for instance.

BARTHELME: Of course I do. I'd be a fool not to.

BRANS: You were just trying to do what? To find your voice?

BARTHELME: I was trying to do something different. Well, I was trying to make art, and I didn't want to do it as Cheever does it, although I admire very much what Cheever does—but that's what Cheever does. I was trying to do something else. I suppose I was trying—in the crudest statement—I was trying to make fiction that was like certain kinds of modern painting. You know, tending toward the abstract. But it's really very dicey in fiction, because if you get too abstract it just looks like fog, for example.

BRANS: Words, after all, have referents. They mean something—colors don't.

BARTHELME: Not in the same way. So, the project is next to impossible, which is what makes it interesting. There's nothing so beautiful as having a very difficult problem. It gives purpose to life. And to work. I'm still worrying with it.

BRANS: Trying to create new forms. And essentially the first thing you have to do is get rid of the older forms.

BARTHELME: Well, not get rid of them. I don't think I've gotten rid of anything. People seem to regard it as a process of destruction in some sense, but I don't see why the two things can't coexist.

BRANS: But you are—in a story you do get rid of our traditional expectations in plot and characterization.

BARTHELME: I don't get rid of them in the sense that they're gone once and for all. I don't abolish anything.

BRANS: You're not wiping out anything already in the language.

BARTHELME: Just choosing to do different things. I believe that the way that's perceived has much to do with the tradition of—as each new movement of art comes along, the people involved traditionally issue manifestoes, claiming that everything has been overturned, and a whole new order is extant. And what they are talking about, of course, is "Our Gang." Like the Futurists—they produced more manifestoes than art, probably. But I have issued no manifestoes. Just doing my number. The sort of revolutionary rhetoric associated with art movements makes people assume that everybody is issuing manifestoes. Or that the work itself is a manifesto.

BRANS: Right, sort of a gauntlet thrown down. Another problem in writing your fiction must be that you're dealing with a reader who has certain expectations about what fiction ought to do. So short of creating a whole new generation of readers, and we don't seem to be doing that. . . .

BARTHELME: I am glad to see you've got Joseph Campbell there—*The Hero with a Thousand Faces.* It's a book I give to my writing students—it's wonderful.

BRANS: Oh, I went through a period of passion about that book, and then I began to feel that I was getting to be too formulaic in my use of it, so I put it up there and I haven't looked at it in about five years.

BARTHELME: Have you read *The Masks of God*? That has some wonderful things in it too. And there's much of Jung that is useful to writers. Not in terms of psychoanalytic theory, but in terms of his interest in myth. Anyhow, what were we talking about?

BRANS: Eudora Welty has said that in a short story there should be a kind of tension that runs all the way through. And she said that ideally one should write a short story in one sitting, but she wants that thread, that tautness that goes through it. I wonder if you would comment on what she said.

BARTHELME: I don't agree. I agree with her about the tension. But I disagree that it should be written in one sitting, because as a practical matter I don't think that that necessarily would produce the tension she's looking for, and I doubt very much that . . .

BRANS: No, she said she couldn't do that. She said there was a time when she always tried to get it down in one sitting.

BARTHELME: Well, Hemingway described writing two of his best stories the same day, and it probably happened. I forget which two stories he refers to. But I remember he says he got in bed with a bottle of brandy and began it after finishing the first one, and then he wrote the second one. They're very short, of course.

BRANS: Did you learn much from Hemingway?

BARTHELME: Oh, sure. Hemingway taught us all. First, wonderful things about rhythm, his sentence rhythms, and wonderful things about precision, and wonderful things about being concise. His example is very, very strong.

BRANS: I belong to that generation that rebelled against him. Thought he was just so much dreck until I started teaching him, and then I began to see how marvelously those books are crafted. Now, I teach *The Sun Also Rises* over and over.

BARTHELME: His best novel by far. Although I also like *A Farewell to Arms* and the stories—just beautiful. I certainly can't be said to write like Hemingway, but he certainly is an influence. There are a lot of influences that are not very apparent. Sabatini. And S. J. Perelman.

BRANS: You mentioned John Gardner earlier. Where do you stand in the Gass-Gardner controversy regarding morality in fiction?

BARTHELME: With Gass. I think Gass is right.

BRANS: But don't you think Gass takes it too far?

BARTHELME: I don't think it's been taken far enough. At what point is it taken too far? Anyway, going too far is something I'm in favor of.

BRANS: Obviously, that's true. I guess I want something moral and beautiful to come out of fiction. Except I don't want it to be overt and programmatic. Maybe I'm just a fence-sitter.

BARTHELME: I do believe that my every sentence trembles with morality—it's full of morality. But it's the morality of an attempt. It's not the morality of giving you precepts. To decide as Gardner would that my enterprise is immoral because it doesn't preach to you or elevate you in some dubious way—.

BRANS: Then send you off with a cake of soap and a towel. That's what I was judging, too, in Gardner: the idea that certain writers were just going to be sent to the gas chamber because they didn't conform to his conceptions of what moral fiction was. Of course I don't think he's a very good writer.

BARTHELME: That book was clearly an attempt at a Saint Valentine's Day Massacre. That's what's so funny about it. It's so overt.

BRANS: I'll tell you why I think Gass goes too far. Because he makes all these statements about how fiction shouldn't have any morality in it, and yet I think I find a contradiction to what he says theoretically in his own fiction. I think *Omensetter's Luck* is an enormously moral book.

BARTHELME: Sure it is.

BRANS: But he apparently wants to make the point so clear that he will reject the plain evidence in his own fiction.

BARTHELME: No, I don't think he's overstating it simply to make a point. I think he believes what he says, and I also believe what he says. I think he's right. His position is the correct one.

BRANS: Even though he's writing moral fiction.

BARTHELME: Yes, but it's not moral so much in the way that Gardner conceives fiction as moral. It's the morality of art. And you're not going to persuade me that making art is not a highly moral act in itself. It's certainly difficult enough to qualify as a moral act.

BRANS: Do you know Gass?

BARTHELME: Yes, we're friends. I don't know him very well. He's a nice fellow.

BRANS: And you know Grace Paley?

BARTHELME: Oh yes, she lives across the street. She's one of my best friends.

BRANS: She is a delight. She was wonderful when she came here. She had about twelve students following her around at all times.

BARTHELME: I believe it.

BRANS: What qualities do you admire in other writers? What do you look for?

BARTHELME: That's a general question. Many different things. I always look at another writer to see what he or she does well, because it's reassuring, refreshing, gives me something to admire. It imposes goals. For example, when Updike wrote *The Coup*—I haven't read the new one yet, although I have it—I was impressed with him all over again because of the richness of imagination and conception. Just being able to renew himself to that extent is wonderfully impressive.

BRANS: That is a fantastic book. I was so pleased that he could do it.

BARTHELME: I've never really told him how much I liked the book. I guess I should.

BRANS: It's so totally unlike anything else he'd done.

BARTHELME: That's right, it was a departure.

BRANS: I have to say that the Rabbit books have gone up in my estimation tremendously since I read the third. I always thought *Rabbit, Run* was fine, but I had my doubts about the second one. But I was reading V. S. Pritchett the other day on the subject of *Rabbit Is Rich* and he said that he thought the best of them was *Rabbit Redux*. It really made me think I had to go back and read that again.

BARTHELME: Well, I've only read excerpts from the new one, and I'm much impressed, again.

BRANS: Rabbit comes of age, his whole being comes of age at this point. It enriches the whole attempt. I don't think we have anything else like it.

BARTHELME: Nothing springs to mind.

BRANS: I'd like to go back to that anathematization line from *Snow White.*

BARTHELME: It's a jaw-breaker, isn't it?

BRANS: "Anathematization of the world is not an adequate response to the world." You said that you wrote that because you began to feel some discontent with what you had done in the book. Do you think that in the later book, *The Dead Father,* and the stories that you have written, and the book that you're working on, do you think you've gone beyond cursing?

BARTHELME: I hope.

BRANS: Can you say how?

BARTHELME: It's hard to say precisely what you have done, because at some level you don't quite understand what you have done.

BRANS: You're not as angry?

BARTHELME: Yes, I guess that's probably it. Gass objected in *Fiction and the Figures of Life* to some lines in one of my earlier stories. The male character asks the female character, "Do you think this is a good life?" and she says, "No." And I think that got Bill upset at me, a bit, because he felt it wrong to think that. And I wouldn't write those lines now, so I suspect he was right in being mad at me, to the extent he was mad.

BRANS: What has happened to make you think this is a good life?

BARTHELME: Well, as you're in the process of leaving it you begin to cherish it more. That's true.

BRANS: Don't say you're in the process of leaving it. I know when you were born.

BARTHELME: When you get to be fifty, you begin counting forward—you begin doing arithmetic.

BRANS: No, I don't like to think that approaching fifty equips me with wings or whatever is necessary to leave. I think I've begun to live. But maybe that's another way of saying the same thing.

BARTHELME: Yes—in one of the stories in *Great Days,* there is a quite clear statement to the effect that things become more exciting as there's less and less time. I think that's true.

BRANS: Well, I felt I perceived a lot of anger in some of your earlier work.

BARTHELME: Probably true.

BRANS: I mentioned this to students, and they said, "Oh, he's not angry. How can anybody so funny be angry? You're mistaken in seeing anger."

BARTHELME: Joking very often conceals a lot of anger.

BRANS: Jokes are a kind of defense mechanism.

BARTHELME: That's true. Gregory Bateson has a great line in which he says, "Humor is the great alternative to psychosis." It's true.

BRANS: And what my mind immediately goes to is John Berryman's Henry poems, because there's so much dark humor in them. I sometimes attempt to teach some of his poems, and the students always think, This is not funny. But maybe again, age is required to see it.

BARTHELME: Certainly true of some things. I mean, I like being this age. I don't want to be twenty again. . . . It's not that I'm uncomfortable being this age, I'm enjoying it very much.

BRANS: Just that the days are dwindling down to a precious few?

BARTHELME: Yes, well, we're getting there.

BRANS: What do you think the proper response to the world is, then?

BARTHELME: Embracing it.

BRANS: Embracing the world. In fiction?

BARTHELME: In fiction and out of fiction, sure.

BRANS: How can you embrace the world in fiction when you write the sort of fiction that you're writing, which is not realistic fiction?

BARTHELME: But I take the position I am writing realistic fiction. Everybody's a realist. Every writer is offering a true account of the activities of the mind.

BRANS: Of mind, yes—but of body, no. You're not recording the minutiae of everyday life.

BARTHELME: Yes, I am. At the end of one of the stories in *Great Days* the two men are talking about the passage of time, and so on, and they begin reciting a list of beautiful things, and one guy says, "Like when you see a woman with red hair, I mean really red hair." And there's a list—and each detail is a real thing—an accurate report. But I think the distinction between who's a realist and who's a surrealist and who's a superrealist is slightly specious. By definition, one can only offer the activity of the individual mind, however it's notated. It's all realism.

BRANS: It's your brand of realism.

BARTHELME: Yes.

BRANS: Realistically, are you hopeful about human life in the 1980s?

BARTHELME: Worried. Worried.

BRANS: What really scares me is the idea that people are talking about a safe bomb. Of course they've *been* talking about a safe bomb.

BARTHELME: That's madness. The doomsday clock has been set up a few notches, I gather. The way our present government is talking is absolutely mad.

BRANS: You said present government, but you've been railing at the government as long as I've been reading you.

BARTHELME: Well, I haven't seen a government I liked yet.

BRANS: I remember that you got off the plane for the Texas Institute of Letters banquet in 1979, and the first thing you said to us was, "What happened to the hydrogen bomb?" It was the weekend of Three Mile Island and you were apocalyptic. And I wondered if you had changed your . . .

BARTHELME: No, no, no. I think we are governed by some very strange people. What can you say to this century with the two great wars and all the other wars and the concentration camps? Sorry century.

BRANS: Do you think we might really destroy ourselves?

BARTHELME: Accidentally, sure. There's the ability.

BRANS: Then you were talking about writing. You said writing lasts.

BARTHELME: I said that I believe that writing will last as long as human beings last.

BRANS: Oh boy, the wind-chill factor is high at this point! You've faulted yourself for the lack of emotion in your fiction. Do you think you're becoming more able to express emotion?

BARTHELME: Yes, I think it's coming out now.

BRANS: Is the emotion that you want to express love?

BARTHELME: It's various—it's various. Not restricted to love or any particular emotion.

BRANS: Do you think that the vicissitudes of your personal life have anything to do with your ability to express—I mean—I don't know anything about your personal life, but I'm just wondering if lowering of those defenses in your personal life makes you more willing to take chances.

BARTHELME: No, I think it's got more to do with being my present age.

BRANS: Are you trying something specifically different in your recent fiction?

BARTHELME: Well, I've written a number of dialogues—stories.

BRANS: I've read the ones at the end of *Sixty Stories*.

BARTHELME: I may have written too many of them. I have more that I'm not satisfied with.

BRANS: What is interesting to you specifically about dialogue?

BARTHELME: It's stripped, allows essentials to be dealt with in a rather pure way.

BRANS: Essentials being . . . ?

BARTHELME: I don't have to get people in and out of doors. I don't have to describe them. I don't have to put them in a landscape. I just deal with their voices.

BRANS: So the essentials—are their relationship?

BARTHELME: Yes. The dialogues really came from trying the dialogues in *The Dead Father* between the two women. That was the impulse. The dialogues in *The Dead Father* are really collections of non sequiturs, intended to give the novel another kind of voice, to provide a kind of counter-narration to the main narration. Then I got interested in doing them for their own sake, with a little more narrative introduced.

BRANS: Are you going to go from the dialogue to the monologue?

BARTHELME: I've done a monologue or two.

BRANS: Well, the monologues of the dead father.

BARTHELME: Yes, and also the story in the new book called "Aria," which is a woman's monologue.

BRANS: And "How I Write My Songs."

BARTHELME: A monologue of a kind. So, I don't know what I'm going to do next. We'll see. I gave a student an assignment a couple of weeks ago. She was having problems because she was writing a certain kind of thing, and it was too tentative—it was too jokey—too whimsical. So I tried to deprive her of her humor. The assignment was to write something on the highest possible level of abstraction—say four pages—to see what she got. And I gave her a couple of things to read: Ashbery's *Three Poems,* Robert Wilson's *Letter to Queen Victoria,* and I forget the third. Not so that she would do a pastiche of these, but so that she would get some feeling for what direction the assignment was going in. She produced the most marvelous four pages—just marvelously inventive. It reminded me a little bit of Stein—at the top of her form. She was going along, reading it to the class—and at one point she reached down and tinkled a little bell.

BRANS: You seem to be caught up in teaching. Is there any connection between your writing and your teaching?

BARTHELME: When you've spent all these years sitting by yourself in a room, you like to get out in society once in a while—that's the original impulse. And I'm very fond of the students.

BRANS: Does your writing ever benefit from these exchanges with students, or is that such a private—?

BARTHELME: In the sense that you meet new people and see what their concerns are, you see what they're worried about, you see what they're enthusiastic about—it's just like any social situation where you can get rather close to people over time—get to know them to some extent. It's refreshing, in other words, as opposed to staying home and sitting in my room spoiling paper.

BRANS: Do you write on an Olivetti typewriter?

BARTHELME: No—an old IBM Selectric.

BRANS: The Olivetti typewriter kept coming up in book after book, and I decided that either you had that kind of typewriter or it represented something to you.

BARTHELME: In New York, once, someone had permanently mounted in front of a store one of these flat Olivettis, on a stand, and it was there even at night when the store was closed. And they put a long piece of paper in it, and people used to type messages—and so you'd go to see what crazy things people had written on the Olivetti today.

BRANS: Oh, wonderful.

BARTHELME: And that's in one of the stories. It's quoted in "The Shower of Gold." One of the Olivetti messages.

BRANS: Do you talk about your own work to your students?

BARTHELME: Well, I talk sometimes about my own practices.

BRANS: Do you take one of your stories and show them how you did it?

BARTHELME: No. Occasionally I'll read something that has some pedagogic value. For example, there's a story called "Nothing," which I also use as an assignment. When somebody is stuck, I'll say, well, do me a piece that describes "nothing." Sometimes if I give that to a whole class, when they're finished reading theirs, I'll read mine just to show how I dealt with it.

BRANS: Well, that's an interesting assignment. It really has to come out of your innards somehow.

BARTHELME: Another story I did came from an assignment that I had given a class, which was to do a version of Mozart's *Abduction from the Seraglio*. I had set it up in such a way that they had to make certain changes in the situation, so I got interested in these, and I did it myself. So there is some back and forth effect of teaching. And then students indirectly help with the problem of allusion, because you have to stop if you make an allusion to something and say, Will people remember this—or will they get it? I had to ask my younger brother the other day, I had Chill Wills in the story, will everybody know who Chill Wills is? He assured me that they would. So, I try to use more allusions than perhaps every reader will get, so that there will be things that if he doesn't remember *this,* he will get *that.*

BRANS: Are the allusions connected?

BARTHELME: To each other?

BRANS: Yes.

BARTHELME: Yes, in the framework of the story. I like to pack it as closely as possible.

BRANS: You know, students always ask teachers of literature—I don't know if they ask teachers of writing this—after you've finished doing the job on the story, they'll say, now, how much of that did he really put in there? And I have finally, over eleven years of teaching, developed an answer, which is, Everything. Because I'm tired of implying that the critic is smarter than the writer, and so I just say, Give him the benefit of the doubt, he knew what he was doing.

BARTHELME: Yes, it's true that a good piece will take on added presences that were perhaps not specifically built into it.

BRANS: I try not to let them ever go off on a tangent that is somehow contradictory, or is contrary to the spirit of the piece, but that's just common sense.

BARTHELME: But because of the new criticism, that intensely close reading, I think people did tend to read into pieces very often things that were not—and should not be—attributable to them.

BRANS: Sometimes I think writers today are very skittish about this in ways that maybe are detrimental to a proper appreciation of their writing. For example, Welty read a story called "Livvy," and in it there's an old black man, a very tightly curled character, everything is controlled by the clock. He's married to this young girl whose name is Livvy, a young black girl who just simply escapes with a young man. The students asked her about things it seemed to me—the young man was wearing a green suit, for example—and the old man has a black umbrella, which you know—is . . .

BARTHELME: Does the umbrella symbolize death, and the green symbolize hope? No, it's just a green suit.

BRANS: That's what she said. She said it's a green suit, it's a black umbrella. And I thought, you know, lady, you're not really dealing with this quite straight. I can see why she did it, but at the same time it bothered me that she would take those precautions.

BARTHELME: Well, the way to protect yourself from that is not to make the suit green in the first place.

BRANS: Right. But the fun of reading it is in seeing that it really is all put together that way, and that it's not just telling a story but much more, and I think students ought to be given this sense of the excitement of the find—even if they find things that aren't there. Do you have an ideal reader, any particular person in mind when you write?

BARTHELME: Just ordinary folks like us.

INTERVIEW WITH BILLIE FITZPATRICK, 1987

BILLIE FITZPATRICK: Robert Coover has said that creative writing programs "have been something of a disaster" in their leveling force on American writing and that "literature itself is being closed down by way of a narrow, pathetically conservative vision." Do you think programs are the problem (or at least part of the problem) as Coover sees it?

DONALD BARTHELME: No, I think that most of the people who go through programs do not publish.

FITZPATRICK: You mean while they're in the programs?

BARTHELME: Or subsequently. If they do not publish, they can hardly be a negative influence on American literature. My impression is that most of the writing programs produce better teachers, certainly better readers, but not necessarily greater numbers of writers. I don't understand how he can argue that they have had a negative or repressing effect on literature.

FITZPATRICK: I think he was alluding to a certain leveling-off, a mediocrity, perhaps a sameness, found in the writing coming out of programs.

BARTHELME: That may be his experience; it's not my experience. I've taught at four universities, and the students were notable for diversity rather than sameness. I mean you've seen work here [University of Houston]: if there's anything that marks it, it is a rather spectacular difference.

FITZPATRICK: As programs become a more prevalent force in American literature, can you foresee any adverse effects, especially for the writer who does not wish to participate in the institution? Do you think it will become more and more difficult for the writer struggling outside the program?

BARTHELME: What writing programs do is save people time. I think the person who works on his or her own takes about three times as long to get to where he's publishing than someone who is in a program. There is no feedback, no criticism, no shocks to the system. Being enrolled in a writing program, however may raise expectations in the individual which the program can't satisfy. Not everyone who goes through a program will publish.

FITZPATRICK: In a recent discussion on the same subject, you said that "you can teach the notion of what's dead or alive; you can teach them how to be critics of their own work." What's "dead" in contemporary writing?

BARTHELME: I don't want to name fourteen of my colleagues and say that they're dead, though publishing, writers. If that's what you're asking.

FITZPATRICK: No, I'm not asking you to name names as much as identify styles, imitative styles, that you've seen crop up again and again, that you've seen before and for some reason don't work any longer.

BARTHELME: Some of the work being published in imitation of the post-modernists is pretty dead. As is some of the work being published in imitation of Ray Carver, Ann Beattie, Mary and Jim Robison, my brother Frederick—that group of people has produced a third generation.

The easiest way to talk about this is to talk about painters. There were the Abstract Expressionists, then there was another group of painters classified as second-generation Abstract Expressionists, which indeed went on to form a third generation of Abstract Expressionists. The impulse had become attenuated in, at least, the third generation, and some of the second generation.

FITZPATRICK: Who would be some of the third generation?

BARTHELME: The third generation has become so attenuated, I can't even remember any names.

FITZPATRICK: Like a Jean-Paul Basquiet?

BARTHELME: No. He's another tendency entirely. Michael Goldberg, for example, is a very good painter and is usually spoken of as part of the second generation. In Goldberg, the impulse is strong enough still to be useful.

FITZPATRICK: My next question centers more specifically on the imitation of your style, as you may see it in your students. That is, in the workshop where the desire to please and desire to be accepted is often formidable, have you confronted too-close-for-comfort imitations of your style and how have you handled it?

BARTHELME: Once in a long while, I run into somebody who is doing something either that I've already done or dangerously close. And I just say, look, this is too close to—and I point out what it is too close to. And the person immediately recognizes it.

FITZPATRICK: It's usually unintentional, in other words.

BARTHELME: It may be subliminal. I don't think the desire to please has that much to do with it. Obviously I'm going to discourage it wherever I see it. It doesn't come up that often.

FITZPATRICK: Today's writers currently in the limelight, the so-called "Brat-Pack" writers, have been labeled minimalists; they are said to write fiction which lacks passion and a hope for change and to depict characters who won't commit themselves to an emotion. Do you think that "minimalist fiction" is so wholly vacuous?

BARTHELME: I assume you're talking about people like Bret Easton Ellis and Jay McInerney and Tama Janowitz.

FITZPATRICK: Yes, I was thinking of Ellis and McInerney as the third generation coming after, or out of—

BARTHELME: —The Beattie-Carver-Robison tradition. All these classifications are very rough. I don't want to be in the position of saying the newest guys are terrible.

FITZPATRICK: But that's what everyone keeps saying, making these blanket statements.

BARTHELME: It's entirely possible that they're writing something I can't appreciate; in other words, I just can't get it, I can't hear it. I may be tone deaf to what they're trying to say. Tama Janowitz is often funny and she gets into some nice conceits. Jay McInerney is quite clever and also sometimes funny. Ellis . . . I think I wrote a parody of him in *The New Yorker* that was published as "More Zero."

In the opening scene this guy is trying to do a line of coke off the rearview mirror of a moving car. That, I think is—

FITZPATRICK: Your comment—

BARTHELME: Yes. Anyhow, in principle I don't want to knock these guys. I don't admire them as much as I do the Beattie-Carver-Robison generation. They're doing something radically different.

FITZPATRICK: One generation of writers has been generalized to promote some kind of nihilism, not committing to either a political stance or a belief in anything for that matter. This seems to be such a general criticism. Do you find that to be part of a trend?

BARTHELME: Everything goes in waves. When I was in my late

twenties and thirties, the big philosophical effort was after Sartre, after *Being and Nothingness.* The phenomenologists—Sartre, Husserl, and Heidegger—were at the core of one kind of philosophical thinking, what is called Continental philosophy, as opposed to British philosophy or language analysis. Then ten years later, structuralism—Lévi-Strauss and that group of people—was being talked about in Paris, in the fifties or early sixties. Sartrian philosophy had completely washed away. The new wave is deconstruction—Derrida and people like that. But as my philosophy teacher, Maurice Natanson, said, "It is a mistake to regard philosophy as a graveyard of dead systems." While there is movement, it's a kind of cyclical washing: the tide comes up onto the shore and brings in different things each time. None of them makes the previous rage invalid. It's just looking at things from a different point of view. I feel the same way about tendencies in writing. People are astonished to discover that I hold John Updike in high regard, which I do, or Saul Bellow.

FITZPATRICK: The realists—

BARTHELME: Yes. All these guys—Bellow, Cheever, Updike, Malamud—I hold in the highest regard. It's just a different kind of thing.

FITZPATRICK: Rosellen Brown, in an August 1986 article in the *Boston Review,* comments that the younger contemporary writers suffer from a lack of political scope, that their fiction centers on the insular, the intimate, the familial. She sees this smallness of vision as an unwillingness to take a risk. Do you think the writer has a responsibility to actively engage the world's problems and thereby offer the possibility of change?

BARTHELME: Yes. The "engager" political writing—what Sartre called for in his book *What Is Literature?*—is not much practiced by younger writers nowadays. There are some exceptions—John Sayles, for example. It's a reflection of American politics. If you grow up in the age of Reagan, it's hard to decide that politics are not meaningless to the individual. Remember at the time of the Vietnam War, writers were all very active politically. I even wrote some overtly political pieces.

FITZPATRICK: So, it depends more on the current conditions?

BARTHELME: The stuff we're doing in Central America is clearly wrong. For one thing, the efforts seem to be failing. But it's certainly not on the scale of the Vietnam war.

FITZPATRICK: It seemed to be then that the sides were clear, and that now with the United States involved in so many countries, the political situation is much hazier.

BARTHELME: I think our government is still doing lousy things, but they're not the kind of lousy things that send people out in the streets. And a lot of it is undercover, as with the Oliver North stuff. We find out about it two years after it happens. You can't get mad about something you don't know is going on. Getting mad in retrospect is not that satisfying.

FITZPATRICK: Do you think this apolitical stance is particular to America?

BARTHELME: American writers have always been less political than European writers. In one sense, it's very good for European writers because (like with Kundera) it gives everything they write a very important dimension. Here, you can attack the government as violently as you want and no one is going to throw you in jail. The government doesn't even notice. Over there, writers are given much more value.

The United States is so big—bigger than all of Europe—that local ways of looking at things become American ways of looking at things; they're atomized in a certain way, just by geography. The tragic history of the twentieth century has been really enacted so far in Europe. We've been very protected. Consequently, our political involvement is watered down.

FITZPATRICK: As a member of P.E.N. America and the former Program Chairman of the International P.E.N. Conference in 1986, you've had the opportunity to spend time with writers outside of the United States. And although your stories often resound with colloquial language and Americana, your perspective is universal. Has your international exposure shaped your own vision?

BARTHELME: The P.E.N. Congress was very educational. We had to come up with a theme for the conference and Richard Howard and I fixed on the imagination of the writer and the imagination of the state, balancing these two things. We found that a lot of the European writers did not want to admit that the state had an imagination. So we had the spectacle of very good writers getting up at public meetings and saying that the state has no imagination. The faculty of the imagination was so precious to them that they did not want to take the sociological view of the state as a creation of many individuals acting together; somebody is thinking up those concentration camps, somebody is putting people in jail.

FITZPATRICK: Did their reaction surprise you?

BARTHELME: I was surprised. Not everybody reacted this way. Norman Mailer said afterwards (Norman had been very enthusiastic about the theme before the congress) that maybe it was a theme for sociologists or philosophers, not for writers. Maybe he's right.

I've learned a lot from people like Max Frisch, who is a Swiss writer and a friend of mine. And Kundera, who although I don't know him, I watch him very closely. Grass, whom I have met. And Peter Handke. I pay attention to what these people are doing.

FITZPATRICK: Despite the danger and inaccuracy of classifications, your work has often been described as metafictional; the critic Alan Wilde distinguished between meta- and midfiction, asserting that your work is more midfiction in that it presents a "contemporary humanism" that lifts it away from the skepticism and unrelenting fatalism of metafictionists such as Robert Coover, William Gass, and Ted Mooney. Most recently, *Paradise* and your newer stories in the collection *Forty Stories* reveal a much stronger narrative line, which some critics cite as evidence of a "creeping realism." Is this a result of a movement away from something in your work?

BARTHELME: I don't think there's anything that can accurately be called metafiction because that would be fiction about fiction. And I don't think that anybody wants to do that. What gave rise to that term was that in the work of some so-called postmodernists, devices of fiction were called attention to.

I think everybody is a realist. I do not think that we have a choice. The nature of consciousness is such that we are always doing realism. Consciousness is always consciousness of something. We are always writing about the world.

I have a formulation for this idea: art is the true account of the activity of the mind. This definition excludes a lot of things, but it is also pretty accurate. It solves a lot of philosophical problems—the truth problem, for one. It also points out that realism is a kind of sloppy category.

FITZPATRICK: In the last year, you have participated in a couple of collaborations, one with the artist Seymore Chwast and another with Jim Love. Why and how do artistic collaborations feed your own writing?

BARTHELME: You're dealing with another mind; you surrender your autonomy to another artist. It changes your normal way of proceeding, which is a big plus. I can do something in a slightly different way or in a considerably different way. It's stimulating. Collaboration is a very healthy thing.

FITZPATRICK: Do you see collaborations as part of an interdisciplinary approach that might help art evolve?

BARTHELME: I just think it's another thing artists do. It's been going on for centuries, collaborations. I don't think it will solve all artistic problems, but it will give you a fresh set of problems. There's nothing more rewarding than a fresh set of problems.

INTERVIEW WITH BOBBIE ROE, 1988

BARBARA ROE: What does this word *innovative* really mean, or does it mean anything in regard to fiction?

DONALD BARTHELME: I take it to be congratulatory, if imprecise. I doubt that there's much beyond new combinations of quite well-known maneuvers. "Make it new" as a battle cry seems naive today, a rather mechanical exhortation. If a piece of writing is of this time, of a particular time, that seems quite enough to ask of it.

ROE: But there's something exciting about the new. . . .

BARTHELME: Very much so, there's a frisson there, but perhaps nothing lasting. I think it has to do with seeing something done well. Above all, we like to see something done well, and in writing, when it's done really well, there's always an element of freshness which is probably an aspect of craft but may appear to be an aspect of time, may appear to be "the new."

ROE: Or a response to new cultural or historical situations—

BARTHELME: That happens. These usually take a long while to understand or get an intuition about, but sometimes one has something to say immediately—as in response to a war one finds morally reprehensible. The Vietnam War shook up American writers, including those like myself too old to soldier. One suddenly finds oneself in a new relation to the government.

ROE: At Brown University last spring [1988], you, along with William Gass, John Hawkes, and Stanley Elkin, took part in a symposium on postmodernism organized by Robert Coover. What issues were discussed?

BARTHELME: Some very tired ones, including "What is postmodernism?" The term is, after all, only one of a half-dozen equally unsatisfactory formulations, probably the one that has come closest to sticking. The chief misconception is that this kind of writing is metafiction, fiction about fiction. It's not. It is a way of dealing with reality, an attempt to think about aspects of reality that have not, perhaps, been treated of heretofore. I say it's realism, bearing in mind Harold Rosenberg's wicked remark that realism is one of the fifty-seven varieties of decoration.

ROE: What about the term *experimental,* which is often applied to your work?

BARTHELME: It's not quite a hostile remark, but it does contain within it the notion of the failed experiment. Something like "Bone Bubbles" was, yes, an experiment and although I wouldn't suggest it was wholly successful, I thought it worth publishing. It's something I do along with a number of other things.

ROE: In his 1968 article "Dance of Death," John Aldridge criticized one of your collections for failing to dramatize the significant forces behind the everyday "dreck," for failing to reconcile the "apocalyptic" and the "doggy world."

BARTHELME: The sentiment here is that I'm using dreck—playing with it, essentially—rather than condemning it in good right-minded fashion or analyzing the dynamics of its production in good leftminded fashion. I'd argue that I was probably doing something of both and that he didn't notice. Fiction is not academic argument.

ROE: During the 1960s, you defended the status of the art object *as object,* but in your recent "Not-Knowing," you seem to recant somewhat. What caused the change?

BARTHELME: Both positions are defensible. The first idea, that the artwork is an object in the world in much the same way a dog biscuit or a mountain is an object in the world, is an effort to deny that the artwork is a rendering or a copy of the world. The second position attempts to be a little clearer about the relation between art and world, and I ended by saying that art is a meditation about the world rather than a reproduction of some aspect of the world. The two ideas are not directly contradictory. The relevant line is "Art is a true account of the activity of mind." I don't mean to suggest that that's all art is, merely that this is a place to begin. The statement does take into account the controversy about the truth value of art, does a bit of work there.

ROE: Do you expect readers to recognize the cohesive elements in your stories?

BARTHELME: Feel rather than recognize. If the story is written well enough, there's enough built into it to make it cohere. Every reader will not get every reference, perhaps, or be hooked by every little hook. But if the thing is successful, there will be enough of that to bind the reader to the piece.

ROE: A few years ago, you seemed worried that perhaps a lack of emotion was a weakness in your stories.

BARTHELME: A constant worry. I'm still worried. I tell my students that one of the things readers want, and deserve, is a certain amount of blood on the floor. I don't always produce it. Probably a function of being more interested in other parts of the process.

ROE: You use all sorts of language levels.

BARTHELME: I mix levels which is really not kosher but allows certain useful effects, like mixed media in painting. It's zone-crossing, sociologically speaking.

ROE: As a reader, I'm very aware that certain sentences or parts of sentences repeat, much as I notice a painting's repetitive line, form, or color.

BARTHELME: Rhythm is important, and it's one of the things you notice about student work. Very often students don't, in the beginning, understand that their sentences are supposed to have certain rhythms and that the rhythms are part of the texture of the story. It's hard to teach, something that's more a knack than directly teachable. But it's central, it's a factor in every sentence, and you have to insist on it, remember to insist on it.

ROE: In "Not-Knowing," you said that art, ideally, should have a meliorative aspect, should change the world.

BARTHELME: But I didn't say in what degree. The ambition, or necessity, if you will, is present, but the change might be very small. I like very much and have often quoted what de Kooning said about content in painting—"It's very tiny, content, something like a flash." This was in an interview with David Sylvester, I believe. And the degree to which any given piece of writing might be said to alter the world might also be tiny. But I don't want to lose sight of the impulse.

ROE: You've said that the problems of the contemporary writer arise from the contamination of language by all sorts of things—politics, commerce, philosophical cant. What are the problems of the ordinary American?

BARTHELME: Americans have political problems which they don't recognize as political. The impoverishment of the country by the arms race is a good example. Money spent on arms is, among other things, useless money in terms of the economy because it's stored. It's in nerve gas, aircraft carriers, the Stealth bomber. I gave a reading at the University of Alabama a couple of years ago, and on the way to the campus, we passed an airfield packed with military aircraft, trillions of dollars worth of planes stacked up there, National Guard stuff, not even first-line stuff. The cost, the weight of this, is not understood by most Americans. They don't know where their money's going. They know they're pressed for money and that their school systems are being eighty-sixed by national accrediting organizations, but they don't connect this to that National Guard elephant graveyard. Black people think they're poor because they're black and the white folks control the money. This is true, but black folks are damaged more by lousy economic policy than by racism.

ROE: You write about these social inequities?

BARTHELME: I do. There is a consistent social concern in my stories from the 1960s to the present. Tends to be slipped in while your attention is directed toward something else. It's not Lincoln Steffens, and it's not Mike Harrington, but it's there. I'm not talking about the direct political satire in *Guilty Pleasures,* but rather an obligato, always present in everything—also, the worse the political situation, the more stimulating it is for the writer. Most of the pieces in *Guilty Pleasures* were written during the Nixon administration, when things were so egregiously wrong that we were on a continual ladder of amazement and outrage. The Reagan administration probably did as much damage to the country but in ways more difficult to identify. A great advantage Central European writers have is the absolutely miserable political conditions in their home countries. It's what gives Kundera his bite, his ability to be radical, go to the root. Outrages have been done him and his countrymen of a dimension we can barely intuit. He derives an insight into the dark side of human possibility from this, it informs his work every step of the way.

ROE: To what extent do you discuss writing with other writers or artists?

BARTHELME: With someone like Grace Paley, who is a dear friend and who lives across the street from us in New York, there are always lots of things to talk about besides art because first we have the life of our street to worry about. Grace is very concerned with our street, and we have really significant conversations having to do with our street. For a long time we talked about the war because Grace was very much an antiwar activist. At a certain point she was arrested along with some colleagues for holding a protest on the White House lawn, a misdemeanor case, and we had to combat that and that took a lot of conversation. I did a *New York Times* op-ed piece about it in which I quoted Grace as saying that the protesters had walked on the lawn, wonderful line, "Very softly and carefully." And we had school conversations because both of us were teaching and P.E.N. conversations and children conversations and some purely literary conversations. Grace does not have other than strong opinions except about lunch. She usually shows up at lunchtime and eats what is put before her with appropriate appreciative comment. So literature would be maybe 15 percent of the conversation. Grace is a Russian writer—Chekhov should do as well—we're different kinds of writers and that's interesting.

ROE: You and Raymond Carver seem mutually appreciative of each other's work. He mentioned in *Alive and Writing* that you have had a tremendous impact on creative writing classes. You've been called one of the most imitated writers in America. Do you see this?

BARTHELME: No, because I don't think the imitations, if they're there, get published. Carver would probably be the most imitated writer in America at the moment. I like his work and liked him, although I knew him very slightly.

ROE: Is the new generation of writers more concerned than their predecessors with politics, economics, and social class?

BARTHELME: I think there are lowered expectations, not aesthetic expectations for the work, but lowered expectations in terms of life. My generation, perhaps foolishly, expected, even demanded, that life be wonderful and magical and then tried to make it so by writing in a rather complex way. It seems now quite an eccentric demand.

NOTES

ON WRITING

AFTER JOYCE

Previously uncollected. It appeared in *Location* 1, 2 (Summer 1964), edited by Harold Rosenberg and Thomas B. Hess. Barthelme was the managing editor of the magazine. He left Houston for New York in 1962 to work on *Location*, which saw only two issues, one in 1963 and the other in 1964.

In "The Stockade Syndrome," Harold Rosenberg's editorial introduction to the first issue, he argued that *Location* was intended to fill what he perceived as a "vacancy" in American letters. The magazine would combine "art and literature on a fairly equal basis," and follow the lead of publications like *The Dial, transition,* and *View,* as well as a number of European journals that featured collaborations between writers and painters. No journal in the United States had followed such a course, claimed Rosenberg, because art and literature had become segregated in an age of specialization, they had "simply gone the way of the other intellectual professions in America. As a reward they are now included among the academic 'disciplines'—which means that their jargons and systems of clichés are officially recognized by university administrations. . . . The point of departure of *Location* was therefore a literary magazine without poems, short stories, or essays. This unattainable objective was then compromised piece by piece in favor of writers who had not solved the problem of form by shoving it aside."

Rosenberg was interested that *Location* provide critical "continuity" for artists and writers by furnishing them with a forum for critical discussion and debate. Thomas B. Hess, in his editorial introduction, "Ideas in Search of Words," reiterates Rosenberg's emphasis: "The magazine will be a place where an artist's talk will have continuity. . . . We have invited painters and sculptors to write about their work and to widen the discussion to include politics, ethics—even literature. We hope that writers will come forward who are sufficiently informed about art to treat it with relevance and accuracy. And we hope to make explicit some of the intellectual forces that continue to make the American art world the most important place in postwar international culture."

"After Joyce" and a short story, "For I'm the Boy," were the only appearances by Barthelme in *Location,* but the magazine as a whole clearly bore the stamp of his interests. In its two issues, *Location* published an essay by Saul Bellow and a section from his yet-unpublished *Herzog,* as well as pieces by John Ashbery, William H. Gass, David Hare, Kenneth Burke, Robert Rauschenberg, Marshall McLuhan, and a section from Kenneth Koch's then-uncompleted *The Red Robins,* illustrated by Larry Rivers.

"After Joyce" is Barthelme's earliest extended aesthetic statement. Together with "Not-Knowing," published some twenty-two years later, "After Joyce" supports and informs much of what he wrote, and is indispensable for our understanding of Barthelme's work.

NOT-KNOWING

Barthelme wrote the basis of this often reprinted essay for a talk he delivered for New York University's Writer at Work lecture series at the Bobst Library on February 16, 1982. *The New York Times* reported it on February 18 in an article headlined "Barthelme Takes On Task of Almost Deciphering His Fiction." He delivered a fuller version in 1983 at the 10th Alabama Symposium on English and American Literature, "The Autonomous Voice: Encounters With Style in Contemporary Fiction," the proceedings of which were published in *Voicelust,* edited by Allen Wier and Don Hendrie, Jr. (Lincoln, Nebraska: University of Nebraska Press, 1985). The essay was published in altered form in *The Georgia Review* 39 (Fall 1985). The text reprinted here is that which appeared in the *Georgia Review,* and subsequently in *The Best American Essays 1986,* edited by Elizabeth Hardwick (New York: Ticknor & Fields, 1986).

The letter from Alphonse to Gaston first appeared in *The New Yorker* ("Notes and Comment," August 11, 1975), was used in his Writer at Work speech in 1982, and again in *Here in the Village.* The "Not-Knowing" version shows some differences from the earlier versions. Readers may compare these two published versions by turning to "Letter to a literary critic . . ." in *Here in the Village.*

HERE IN THE VILLAGE

Published as a limited edition of 325 copies by Lord John Press, Northridge, California, in 1978. All of the pieces in *Here in the Village,* with the exception of the "Introduction," had been previously published, all but one in *The New Yorker.* The texts reprinted here are those that appeared in *Here in the Village.* First publication of individual pieces is as follows:

"Walking around the Village . . ." was first published as an untitled, unsigned "Notes and Comment" piece in *The New Yorker,* June 23, 1975. *The New Yorker* version begins "Well, things were pretty interesting last week down here in the West Village . . ." It is otherwise the same as the version published in *Here in the Village.*

"I have lately noticed . . ." was first published as an untitled, unsigned "Notes and Comment" piece in *The New Yorker,* October 24, 1977.

"A fable . . ." was first published as an untitled, unsigned "Notes and Comment" piece in *The New Yorker,* September 29, 1975.

"After spending an exciting eight or nine days . . ." first appeared as an unsigned, untitled "Notes and Comment" piece in *The New Yorker,* November 11, 1974.

"I like to think of myself . . ." was first published as an unsigned, untitled "Notes and Comment" piece in *The New Yorker,* August 28, 1978.

"I went last week . . ." first appeared as an untitled, unsigned "Notes and Comment" piece in *The New Yorker,* October 11, 1976.

"In the morning post . . ." first appeared as an unsigned, untitled "Notes and Comment" piece beginning "I have just received . . ." in *The New Yorker,* June 26, 1978. Barthelme actually did receive a letter in 1978 from Editor John Brady of *Writer's Digest,* asking him to answer a questionnaire for use in their cover story for October, the projected title of which was "Writers Who Drink/Drinkers Who Write." He was informed that the magazine wished to include him in a sidebar that was being developed for the issue. The questions quoted in "In the morning post . . ." are, in fact, taken verbatim from the *Writer's Digest* questionnaire. The article in question appeared in *Writer's Digest* for October, titled "Booze & the Writer," and Kate Millett, Malcolm Cowley, Erica Jong, Ross Macdonald, Norman Mailer, Irving Wallace, and John Hawkes, among others, were featured in the sidebar. Barthelme's response, apparently, came only in the form of *The New Yorker* piece. There are some minor textual differences between the version in *The New Yorker* and that printed in *Here in the Village.*

"There is something . . ." was first published as an unsigned, untitled "Notes and Comment" piece in *The New Yorker,* November 24, 1975.

"Letter to a literary critic . . ." was first published as an unsigned, untitled "Notes and Comment" piece in *The New Yorker,* August 11, 1975. There are no significant differences between the original *New Yorker* publication and that in *Here in the Village.* Attentive readers will notice that it was later used, somewhat altered, as the Alphonse–Gaston letter in "Not-Knowing."

"Worrying about women . . ." first appeared in 1970 as an untitled, introductory preface to the catalog for *she,* an exhibition held at the Cordier & Ekstrom Gallery, New York, from December 3, 1970–January 16, 1971.

"Because the government isn't very good . . ." first appeared as an unsigned, untitled "Notes and Comment" piece in *The New Yorker,* October 20, 1975.

"Spring in the Village! . . ." was first published as an untitled, unsigned "Notes and Comment" piece in *The New Yorker,* June 14, 1976.

REVIEWS, COMMENTS, AND OBSERVATIONS

ACCEPTANCE SPEECH: NATIONAL BOOK AWARD FOR CHILDREN'S LITERATURE

The National Book Award Ceremony was held in New York at Alice Tully Hall at Lincoln Center on April 13, 1972. Barthelme won the award for *The Slightly Irregular Fire Engine; or, The Hithering Thithering Djinn,* which he illustrated himself. The text of Barthelme's acceptance speech was unpublished until 1990, when it appeared in *Gulf Coast* 4, 1, a Barthelme Memorial issue.

ON "PARAGUAY"

Previously uncollected. It first appeared in *Writer's Choice,* edited by Rust Hills (New York: David McKay, 1974).

A SYMPOSIUM ON FICTION

The "Symposium on Contemporary Fiction" took place in October 1975 at Washington & Lee University in Lexington, Virginia. The text printed here, which first appeared in *Shenandoah* XXVII, 2 (Winter 1976), is an abbreviated version of an informal, day-long discussion that took place at the conference.

MR. HUNT'S WOOLY UTOPIA

A review of *Alpaca* by H. L. Hunt. It appeared in *The Reporter* 22 (April 14, 1960). This was Barthelme's first regularly published book review.

THE TIRED TERROR OF GRAHAM GREENE

A review of *The Comedians* by Graham Greene. It was published in *Holiday* 39 (April 1966).

THE ELEGANCE IS UNDER CONTROL

A review of *The Triumph* by John Kenneth Galbraith. It appeared in *The New York Times Book Review,* April 21, 1968.

AMPHIGOREY ALSO: A REVIEW

A review of *Amphigorey Also* (N.Y.: Congdon & Weed, 1983), a book of illustrated stories by Edward Gorey. It first appeared in *New York,* November 28, 1983.

THE MOST WONDERFUL TRICK

First published in *The New York Times Book Review,* November 25, 1984. John Hawkes had just published *Humors of Blood and Skin: A John Hawkes Reader* (New York: New Directions, 1984).

A NOTE ON ELIA KAZAN

Previously uncollected. It first appeared in the University of Houston *Forum* 1 (September 1956).

THE EARTH AS AN OVERTURNED BOWL

Previously uncollected. It appeared in *The New Yorker,* September 10, 1979, the first week of the six he served as one of the magazine's film reviewers in the absence of Pauline Kael. Here Barthelme reviews Werner Herzog's *Woyzeck,* and the review's title refers to a line from the film, which was based on the play by Georg Büchner.

Though "The Earth as an Overturned Bowl" was his first film review for *The New Yorker,* it was by no means his first published film review. Barthelme reviewed films for the Houston *Post* between July 1951, when as a twenty-year-old university student he reviewed *Best of the Badmen* with Robert Ryan, and September 1955, when he signed off from reviewing films for the *Post* with his discussion of Jennifer Jones and William Holden in *Love Is a Many-Splendored Thing.* He reviewed 100 films for the newspaper between July 1951 and February 1953, when he left Houston for military service, and another twenty-five between January and September 1955.

PARACHUTES IN THE TREES

Previously uncollected. It first appeared in *The New Yorker,* September 17, 1979. It reviews *Soldier of Orange,* directed by Paul Verhoeven, and *Run After Me Until I Catch You,* directed by Robert Pouret.

SPECIAL DEVOTIONS

Previously uncollected. It first appeared in *The New Yorker,* September 24, 1979. Barthelme reviews *The Green Room,* directed by François Truffaut, and *Love and Bullets,* directed by Stuart Rosenberg and starring Rod Steiger and Charles Bronson.

DEAD MEN COMIN' THROUGH

Previously uncollected. It appeared in *The New Yorker,* October 1, 1979. It reviews *The Onion Field,* directed by Harold Becker and written by Joseph Wambaugh; *Yanks,* directed by John Schlesinger; and *Nest of Vipers,* directed by Tonino Cervi. The review's title comes from a line from *The Onion Field.*

THREE FESTIVALS

Previously uncollected. It appeared in *The New Yorker,* October 8, 1979. Here Barthelme reviews Bernardo Bertolucci's *Luna* (from the 17th New York Film Festival); Richard Pearce's *Heartland* (from the "American Independents" subfestival of the New York festival); and Rebecca Horn's *Der Eintanzer* and Lawrence Weitner's *Altered to Suit* (from the Whitney Museum's 10th New American Filmmakers Series).

PECULIAR INFLUENCES

Previously uncollected. It appeared in *The New Yorker,* October 15, 1979. Barthelme reviews *The Europeans,* directed by James Ivory (and, like Truffaut's *The Green Room,* based on a work by Henry James), and *Nosferatu, the Vampyre,* directed by Werner Herzog.

EARTH ANGEL

Previously uncollected. It first appeared in *The Movies,* August 1983, and reviews, in its way, Richard Lester's *Superman III. Earth Angel* was Barthelme's final film review.

CULTURE, ETC.

Previously uncollected. It first appeared in the *Texas Observer* 51 (March 25, 1960).

THE CASE OF THE VANISHING PRODUCT

Previously uncollected. It appeared in *Harper's* 223 (October 1961). The occasion of Barthelme's remarks was the *39th Annual of Advertising and Editorial Art and Design*, but this piece seems not so much a book review as a cluster of observations about advertising *circa* 1961, which his reading of the *Annual* had confirmed.

SYNERGY

Previously unpublished in this form. Barthelme delivered "Synergy" on September 30, 1987, for the Houston Forum for the Humanities at the University of Houston. An essay based on the text for the speech, entitled "A Little Synergy," was published in the *Texas Architect*, March–April 1988, and again in the Houston *Post* on March 20, 1988, as "On Houston and making a difference." The text printed here is the text of the Houston Forum speech. It is somewhat longer than the two published versions which, for instance, do not include the sweetly speaking architects who begin the piece.

PRESIDENT NIXON'S ANNOUNCEMENT . . .

Previously uncollected. It appeared as an untitled, unsigned, "Notes and Comment" piece in *The New Yorker*, January 29, 1972.

MY TEN-YEAR-OLD DAUGHTER . . .

Previously uncollected. It first appeared as an untitled, unsigned, "Notes and Comment" piece in *The New Yorker*, July 12, 1976.

AS GRACE PALEY FACES JAIL WITH THREE OTHER WRITERS

Previously uncollected. It first appeared in *The New York Times* (Op-Ed page), February 2, 1979. As Barthelme's article notes, Grace Paley and ten others were arrested on September 4, 1978, when they broke away from a White House tour group and raised a banner on the lawn to protest nuclear arms and nuclear power. Paley, a close friend and neighbor of Barthelme's, and her co-defendants were convicted of unlawful entry in December. The "White House Lawn 11," as they were briefly called, faced the possibility of six months in jail when they appeared in Washington, D.C., for sentencing on February 12, 1979. They were instead fined $100 apiece, and given a 180-day suspended sentence and unsupervised probation of two years or three years.

The case was the subject of considerable comment and discussion at the time. A rally was held in New York on February 11, with speeches in support of Paley and the others by Dave McReynolds, Bella Abzug, and Rep. Theodore Weiss, after which the eleven and several busloads of supporters left for Washington, D.C. An hour after the sentencing, twenty-three more people were charged with disorderly conduct for sitting down in front of the northwest gate of the White House. P.E.N., for which Paley and Barthelme acted as vice presidents, issued a statement: "We are glad Grace Paley and the other defendants are not in jail this afternoon, but if she had to step softly on a few blades of grass to make her point, that expression should be allowed in a free country."

NOT LONG AGO . . .

Previously uncollected. It first appeared as an untitled, unsigned, "Notes and Comment" piece in *The New Yorker,* March 22, 1982.

THERE'S ALLEGED . . .

Previously uncollected. It first appeared as an untitled, unsigned, "Notes and Comment" piece in *The New Yorker,* February 23, 1987.

ROME DIARY

This unfinished piece was found on a computer disk in 1990. Barthelme worked on the piece in 1989 while he was in Rome, staying with his wife Marion at the American Academy. This is very possibly the last piece Barthelme worked on before his death. Previously unpublished.

ON ART

ARCHITECTURAL GRAPHICS: AN INTRODUCTION

This essay was written as an Introduction for the catalog of the Architectural Graphics exhibition held at The Museum of Fine Arts in Houston (April 8–March 7, 1960), and sponsored by the Contemporary Arts Association. It was Barthelme's first publication for the Association, which sponsored most of the exhibitions at the Houston Contemporary Arts Museum—as well as this one at the Museum of Fine Arts—from its inception in 1948 through the middle 1960s. The Association was a nonprofit, essentially volunteer, organization that promoted and sponsored contemporary arts programs of all kinds at a time when there was no other forum for contemporary art in Houston. Barthelme's complete essay is reprinted here, with the exception of its last sentence, which refers the reader to the catalog's illustrations. Previously uncollected.

THE EMERGING FIGURE

Previously uncollected. The piece first appeared as the catalog text for the Houston Contemporary Arts Museum's exhibition, "The Emerging Figure" (May–June 1961). It was reprinted in the University of Houston *Forum* (Summer 1961).

ROBERT MORRIS: AN INTRODUCTION

Previously uncollected. It first appeared as a catalog introduction for the Robert Morris exhibition at the Washburn Gallery in New York, February 10–March 6, 1976.

JIM LOVE UP TO NOW: AN INTRODUCTION

Written as an Introduction for the catalog of the *Jim Love Up to Now* exhibition, held at the Institute for the Arts, Rice University, Houston, in 1980. Love, who worked as exhibition preparator at the Houston Contemporary Arts Museum from 1956–1959, was a friend of Barthelme's. Previously uncollected.

NUDES: AN INTRODUCTION TO *EXQUISITE CREATURES*

This essay, previously uncollected, was first published, untitled, as an Introduction to *Exquisite Creatures*, edited by Jim Clyne (New York: Morrow, 1985). The book features photographs, mostly of nudes, by Gilles Larrain, Robert Mapplethorpe, Deborah Turbeville, and Roy Volkmann. The title *Nudes* did not appear in the book. It has been adopted from a projected table of contents for a book Barthelme was considering putting together in 1989. The projected book, *Pleasantries: A Compendium*, was to include the *Exquisite Creatures* introduction, as well as twelve other essays reprinted in *Not-Knowing* and four that appeared in *The Teachings of Don B.*

BEING BAD

First published in 1985 as an introductory catalog "Appreciation" for *Robert Rauschenberg: Work from Four Series,* an exhibition of Rauschenberg's work held at Houston's Contemporary Arts Museum from December 21, 1985, to March 16, 1986. The catalog was reprinted in 1991, but "Being Bad" has never been collected.

REIFICATIONS

Written as an introductory essay for the catalog of an exhibition of work by Elaine Lustig Cohen, October 17–November 23, 1985, at the Exit Art Gallery in New York City. Previously uncollected.

ON THE LEVEL OF DESIRE

Written as an introductory essay for the catalog of an exhibition of the work of Sherrie Levine, held September 12–October 10, 1987, at the Mary Boone/Michael Werner Gallery in New York City. Previously uncollected.

INTERVIEWS WITH DONALD BARTHELME

Barthelme was interviewed reasonably often, and he almost always had the chance to read over and edit his remarks before actual publication. There were a number of interviews published before 1974, but they always took the form of feature articles. For *Not-Knowing,* we have retained only those in traditional interview format, without interpretative narration from the interviewer. Readers interested in the interview-based articles on Barthelme published before 1974 should consult Richard Schickel's rather Barthelmean "Freaked Out on Barthelme," *New York Times Magazine,* August 16, 1970, pp. 14–15, 42; and Leslie Cross, "Down in the Village With Donald Barthelme," *Milwaukee Journal,* February 14, 1973, p. 4, Editorial Section. Also see John F. Baker, "*PW* Interviews Donald Barthelme," *Publishers Weekly* 206 (November 11, 1974): 6–7. The interviews that follow are arranged in the order in which they were conducted; publication often came significantly later.

INTERVIEW WITH JEROME KLINKOWITZ

First published as "Donald Barthelme" in *The New Fiction: Interviews with Innovative Writers,* edited by Joe David Bellamy (Urbana, Ill.: University of Illinois Press, 1974). The questions were sent to Barthelme in New

York in fall 1971 and summer 1972. The final question, according to the interview's introduction, was posed by Barthelme himself.

INTERVIEW WITH CHARLES RUAS AND JUDITH SHERMAN

This is an edited transcription of an interview that Barthelme did for Pacifica Radio in New York in 1975 and broadcast in four separate programs on radio station WBAI during January 1976. It was one of a series of programs on contemporary writers, particularly those seen to be experimental, to be broadcast on WBAI during these years. The interview was originally interspersed with Barthelme's extended readings from a number of works, including pieces from *City Life; Unspeakable Practices, Unnatural Acts; Sadness; Guilty Pleasures;* and *Come Back, Dr. Caligari;* excerpts from *Snow White* and *The Dead Father;* and some then unpublished stories. The Pacifica Radio interview is the longest and most comprehensive ever conducted with Barthelme, but unlike most of the published interviews, he did not edit his own remarks for the interview's final version. The interview as it appears here has been edited by Kim Herzinger and Derek Bridges. The editors have attempted to retain the conversational flavor of the broadcast interview and have eliminated as little as possible from it. What deletions there are mainly include repetitions, hesitations, false starts, unfinished sentences, and brief interjections by both Barthelme and the interviewers. The transcription of the broadcast interview and raw tapes is by Derek Bridges.

INTERVIEW WITH LARRY McCAFFERY

First published as "An Interview with Donald Barthelme" in *Partisan Review* 49, 2 (1982) and reprinted in altered form in *Anything Can Happen: Interviews with Contemporary American Novelists,* edited by Tom LeClair and Larry McCaffery (Urbana, Ill.: University of Illinois Press, 1983). McCaffery began the interview on April 4, 1980, at Barthelme's apartment in New York City. The text reprinted here is that which appeared in *Anything Can Happen,* which differs in format from that published in *Partisan Review.*

INTERVIEW WITH J. D. O'HARA

First published as "Donald Barthelme: The Art of Fiction LXVI" in *Paris Review* 80 (Summer 1981). According to the introduction to the interview, it began at dinner in Barthelme's apartment in New York City, where Ann Beattie was among the guests, continued for two days in his living room, and ended at a dinner prepared by Marion Knox Barthelme. The transcribed interview was sent to Barthelme and "after much brooding and revision the following dialogue emerged, cleansed of mere actuality and posing its figures in no landscape. The Platonic Idea of an interview."

INTERVIEW WITH JO BRANS: "EMBRACING THE WORLD"

First published in *Southwest Review* 67, 2 (Spring 1982) under this title. Brans interviewed Barthelme in November 1981 in Dallas, where he had come to speak at S.M.U.'s Seventh Annual Literary Festival.

INTERVIEW WITH BILLIE FITZPATRICK

Fitzpatrick, then a Creative Writing student at the University of Houston and co-editor of *Gulf Coast,* the student journal of the Houston Creative Writing Program, interviewed Barthelme in March 1987 in Houston. The interview was undertaken for *Frank,* a journal of literature and the arts edited by David Applefield and published in Paris. As usual, Barthelme asked to edit the final version, but became ill before he could do so. The version that appears here was edited for publication by Frederick Barthelme and first appeared in the Donald Barthelme Memorial issue of *Gulf Coast* 4, 1, published late in 1990.

INTERVIEW WITH BOBBIE ROE

Bobbie Roe, the author of *Donald Barthelme: A Study of the Short Fiction* (N.Y.: Twayne/Macmillan, 1992), interviewed Barthelme at his home in Houston in August 1988. She sent a transcription of the interview to Barthelme for his approval in November 1988, and he returned it to her, much edited and shortened, in March 1989. The interview which appears here was that authorized by Barthelme. The full text is previously unpublished, although sections of it—as well as some other material from the interview which Barthelme gave Roe permission to use—were printed in her book on Barthelme's short fiction. This was, apparently, the last formal interview conducted with Barthelme.